Risk Pricing

Using Quantum Electrodynamics for Higher Order Risks

Dr Dimitris N. Chorafas

HARRIMAN HOUSE LTD

3A Penns Road
Petersfield
Hampshire
GU32 2EW
GREAT BRITAIN

Tel: +44 (0)1730 233870
Fax: +44 (0)1730 233880
Email: enquiries@harriman-house.com
Website: www.harriman-house.com

First published in Great Britain in 2010

Copyright © Harriman House Ltd

The right of Dimitris N. Chorafas to be identified as the author has been asserted
in accordance with the Copyright, Design and Patents Act 1988.

ISBN: 978-1-906659-37-0

British Library Cataloguing in Publication Data
A CIP catalogue record for this book can be obtained from the British Library.

Printed and bound in the UK by CPI Antony Rowe

Contents

Figures   vii

Acknowledgements   ix

Introduction   1

Prologue: Physics, Quantum Theory, QED, QCD and Risk   7

    1. Theories in physics   9

    2. The forces of nature   11

    3. Quantum electrodynamics   14

    4. Space-time   17

    5. Entropy   19

Part One: Risks of the 21st Century   23

Chapter 1: Risk in Finance   25

    1. Risk defined   25

    2. Effects of volatility   28

    3. The risk's long tail   33

    4. Risk and quantum logic   37

    5. The complexity of modern risks   43

    6. Risk appetite   49

    7. Black swans   54

    Appendix: VIX, the measurement of volatility   58

Chapter 2: Virtual Economy and Risk Management   63

    1. Real and virtual economy   63

    2. Market liquidity and funding liquidity   67

    3. CDOs, CDSs and systemic risk   72

    4. Structured finance is different to classical banking   77

5. Advanced statistical methods and tolerances in the virtual economy   81

6. A bird's-eye view of charts for quality assurance and risk control   85

7. Know yourself and your institution   93

Appendix: derivative financial instruments   96

Chapter 3: Product Pricing in the Virtual Economy   103

1. Why the old pricing theory does not apply   103

2. Price discovery through credit spreads   107

3. Discounted cash flow and intrinsic value   113

4. Price discovery through auctions   117

5. PPIP: example of an imperfect auction   122

6. From marking to market, to marking to myth   127

7. Conflicts of interest in opposing marking to market   131

Part Two: Using Quantum Electrodynamics for Risk Control   137

Chapter 4: Not Everything that Counts Gets Counted   139

1. Basel Committee's proposed revision of the 1996 Market Risk Amendment   139

2. Underrating risk is bad management   143

3. Lessons from the credit and banking crisis can help in risk control   147

4. Incremental risk charge and stress tests   151

5. The contribution of scenarios to realistic estimates of exposure   156

6. The scenarios' flexibility   160

7. The Delphi method   164

8. Refining judgmental opinions through Delphi   167

Appendix: why the value at risk model is irrelevant   172

Chapter 5: Applying Feynman Diagrams in Risk Management   177

1. The probability of an event   177

2. Feynman diagrams   181

3. A broad field of QED implementation   185

4. Are we planning for failure?   189

5. Promoting contrarian opinion   192

6. Quantum electrodynamics and compound events   195

7. A space-time graph   200

8. The risk control structure beyond QED   205

9. Risk fever blues   210

Appendix: vectors, linear vector spaces and polygons   213

Part Three: Three Themes for Quantum Chromodynamics   **221**

Chapter 6: Legal Risk and Ponzi Risk   223

1. Using quantum electrodynamics for legal risk   223

2. Legal risk is a disruptive force   227

3. Shareholder lawsuits at Bank of America   230

4. The twilight between legal and illegal practices   233

5. Transborder legal risk   237

6. Creative accounting distorts risk pricing   239

7. Legal risk, political risk and fraudulent conveyance   244

Chapter 7: Overleveraging Risk   251

1. Leverage defined   251

2. The aftermath of gearing is entropy   254

3. Leveraging with financial instruments   258

4. The fate of leveraged persons, companies and states   261

5. Exercising due diligence in leverage   266

6. Leverage, solvency, liquidity and transparency   270

7. Cash flow management   275

8. Deleveraging   279

Appendix: the basic notion of entropy   283

Chapter 8: Risk of Poor Supervision   287

1. The hypotheses regulators have to make   287

2. Capital inadequacy is condoned by regulators   291

3. Basel II should undergo a major overhaul   296

4. Stress tests of default risks   299

5. The 2009 stress tests mandated by the US Treasury   304

6. Bad banks, bad assets and the experience of China's
AMCs   310

7. Assessment of toxic after-effects in central banks' vaults   314

8. Thinking out of the box, when confronted with insolvent
banks   318

Conclusion   325

Bibliography   339

Figures

Figure 1.1: S&P 500 annualised daily volatility January 1950
to 31 December 2008.   29

Figure 1.2: The theoretical and practical distribution of risk
events don't match at their tails.   33

Figure 1.3: Three-and-a half years of global market
capitalisation of the banking industry.   44

Figure 1.4: Risk appetite at the long leg of the distribution.   53

Figure 2.1: Strategic inflection points and their impact.   64

Figure 2.2: The interminable motion money machine of
toxic waste.   74

Figure 2.3: Notional principal amount outstanding in the
global credit default swaps market over the 2002 to 2008
time frame.   76

Figure 2.4: A sequential sampling plan permits avoidance of
inflexible yes/no answers to a request for loans, taking a
reinsurance for higher credit risk.   87

Figure 2.5: Operating characteristics curves for sampling plans.   88

Figure 2.6: Control charts by variables for mean of means and
mean of ranges.   90

Figure 2.7: Three standard deviations usually fit between
quality control targets and customer specifications. But this
is not always enough.   92

Figure 2.8: Annual increase in notional amounts of
derivative instruments, at a major bank.   99

Figure 3.1: Spike in Dubai's credit default swaps (2006-2009).   108

Figure 3.2: CDS spreads: United States versus Russia over a
9-month time horizon (1 May 2008 to 1 February 2009).   110

Figure 3.3: Credit default swaps for three integrated oil firms.   111

Figure 3.4: Spread between corporates and government bonds in the 2007 to early 2009 time frame.   129

Figure 4.1: Ranges and impact of risk factors in the body and tail of a risk distribution.   162

Figure 4.2: Voting by experts on the correlation of two instruments by using Delphi, an established methodology.   170

Figure 5.1: Partial reflection of light by two surfaces.   181

Figure 5.2: Vectorial representation of the probability of events.   183

Figure 5.3: A lognormal distribution for option pricing reflecting volatility and maturity.   197

Figure 5.4: A space-time diagram maps the stage on which all actions in the universe take place.   201

Figure 5.5: A space-time diagram for risk exposure with extreme events.   202

Figure 5.6: Using a statistical quality control chart to track daily exposure.   209

Figure 5.7: Cartesian coordinates and the mapping of points and lines.   215

Figure 5.8: Examples of a polygon of vectors in a linear space.   219

Figure 7.1: Leveraging makes a difference in return on equity (ROE) but it also magnifies risk.   257

Figure 7.2: Omega Bank; a member of the club of super-leveraged financial institutions.   259

Acknowledgements

I am indebted to a long list of knowledgeable people and organisations for their contribution to the research which made this book feasible, as well as to several senior executives and experts for important suggestions and constructive criticism during the preparation of the manuscript. Dr Heinrich Steinmann and Dr Nelson Mohler have been among the most valuable contributors.

Let me take this opportunity to thank Myles Hunt for suggesting this project, to Suzanne Anderson for seeing it all the way to publication. To Eva-Maria Binder goes the credit for compiling the research results, typing the text, making the index and suggesting valuable insights.

Dimitris N. Chorafas

November 2009

Valmer and Vitznau

Introduction

Every industry experiences strategic inflection points which offer promises as well as threats. It is at such times of fundamental change that the cliché 'adapt or die' takes on its true meaning. The crisis of 2007-2009 was a strategic inflection for the Western economy and its banking industry, with a significant part of the danger coming from the fact that risk pricing, transparency and corrective action left much to be desired.

"Sunshine is the best disinfectant," Louis Dembitz Brandeis (1856-1941), the former US Supreme Court Justice, once said. There is now a consensus among governments, regulators and some of the leaders of the financial community that new tools and methods are required to regulate banking and prevent such crises in the future. Following on Brandeis' dictum, this book:

- Challenges the current risk pricing concepts and solutions which have proved to be ineffectual, and
- Introduces a high level approach based on the physicists' top methodology: quantum electrodynamics (QED).

QED is a simple, comprehensible and powerful method whose adaptation to finance will help to do away with the various incomplete and misleading approaches to risk pricing. The goal is not to eliminate risk, because risk in the system is what actually makes it work. What we need is a comprehensive, accurate and dependable method to measure, price, and manage risk.

A high level risk control plan is necessary because, in many banks and other financial institutions, even CEOs and senior managers have often lacked the timely and detailed information they require to rein in their own traders, and watch over exposures building up in warehoused positions. Regulators, too, have struggled to do any better.

There is no time to lose in implementing a better method, because the new major global economic crisis has already been programmed. The programmers are Western governments, particularly those of the United States and Britain, and their inadvertent method of destroying the Western (read: capitalist) economy is the combination of:

- Unstoppable huge fiscal deficits, and
- King-sized expansion of the monetary base, through quantitative easing and bloating of the central banks' balance sheets.

In an article in the *Financial Times*, published 27 May 2009, John Taylor, professor of economics at Stanford University, wrote that the American government "is now the most serious source of systemic risk." Moreover, the national mood is for public leveraging and against budget balancing – as evidenced by the fact that in recent referendums in California voters rejected all budget balancing proposals. "History is full of the errors of states and princes," wrote Benjamin Franklin (1706-1790) in his autobiography. "Look round the habitable world; how few know their own good, or knowing it, pursue."

* * *

Written for the trade market as well as for academics and professionals, the text of this book is divided into a prologue and three parts. The prologue's objective is firstly to familiarise the reader with the physical sciences and briefly explain the ongoing research on gravity, electromagnetism, and strong and weak nuclear forces (and their terminology). It will also clarify Feynman's space-time diagrams; and entropy – which measures the degree of disorganisation in companies and in nature.

These are the main interdisciplinary concepts underpinning the new methods and tools of an evolving 'rocket science': the financial industry's advanced analytical tools, which are implemented through the skills and experience of engineers, physicists and mathematicians.

The higher order risks confronted by the banking industry in the 21st century are detailed in Part One. Chapter 1 brings to the reader's attention the effects of volatility and complexity on modern finance. It also highlights the effects of exposures found in the long tail of the risk distribution, of risk appetite and of plausible but rare events known as black swans. Chapter 2 introduces the reader to derivative financial instruments, including collateralised debt obligations (CDOs) and credit default swaps (CDSs). It then concentrates on the discipline of risk management from the virtual economy's perspective.

Products, evidently including sophisticated financial instruments, have to be priced right. If not, then sooner rather than later the company selling them will be on its way to oblivion. Chapter 3 presses home this point of right pricing, and underlines the need for subsequent price testing in conjunction to market volatility, marking to market (which was repealed in the US, but is still valid in Europe), capital adequacy, solvency, and liquidity.

Part Two questions whether current approaches to risk measurement and management are able to ensure that whatever counts is really counted. Through case studies, Chapter 4 documents how the use of scenarios and of the Delphi method improve present-day performance in risk awareness by upgrading the organisation's communications channels. It also demonstrates that we now have much more powerful models and methods available than the obsolete value at risk (VaR).

Chapter 5 provides the reader with the fundamentals of quantum logic. It introduces for the first time the use of Feynman diagrams for risk control, and outlines the way they can be used in finance. Space-time graphs can be converted to price-time, leading to an interdisciplinary approach to the control of exposure by focusing on incremental change in each risk factor – not only in the aggregate.

The message Part Three offers the reader is that some formerly independent variables have become an integral part of a bank's exposure. These include legal risk (Chapter 6), overleveraging (Chapter 7), and the risk of poor supervision (Chapter 8). The proposed methodology for all three is quantum chromodynamics (QCD). "Modern physicists consider quantum chromodynamics an almost ideally simple theory," said Nobel prize winner Frank Wilczek. We will see this borne out with careful application.

Legal risk is not new. What is novel is its intensity and its integration with other exposures. As Chapter 6 demonstrates, legal risk is rampant in the virtual economy, where its cost is steadily rising; therefore it should in no way be left out of the pricing equation. The number of lawsuits by shareholders and other investors is booming, and their causes range from excesses in management bonuses to misinformation and outright fraud by CEOs. The case of Madoff is taken as an example.

Like the old saying that "one train may hide another", super-leveraging can conceal fraud, and vice versa. Gearing is the banking industry's entropy which, theoretically, has been regulated through capital requirements. Practically, however, innovation in banking as well as the size of accounts kept off the balance sheet have made small game of regulatory capital. They have also promoted the banks' uncanny ability to have impact beyond their reach; Chapter 7 explains why this leads to boom and bust.

Chapter 8 makes the point that bank supervision must be dynamic, steadily adapted to the evolving conditions of the banking industry. New methods such as QED and QCD are needed to enable regulators to be in charge of the capital structure and liquidity of institutions they supervise. QED and QCD can also help regulators to be better – and to appreciate how novel financial instruments can morph into unfamiliar forms, taking us well beyond the already known factors of exposure.

There is plenty to consider, and good solutions (particularly global ones) will not come easily. But the job is doable. The Prussian military theorist and historian Carl von Clausewitz (1780-1831) once observed that it is the mark of inadequate commanders to fail to seize the initiative because they overestimate the strength of their opponents or the size of the problem they are confronted with. The Clausewitz dictum applies hand-in-glove to the CEOs of financial institutions and their regulators.

The challenge is to effectively use QED's and QCD's methods and tools to establish a universal model for risk pricing, the results of which cannot be cooked to hide the facts. This model should be transparent, market-sensitive, comprehensive and able to account for quantitative and qualitative risk factors – treating them individually and as an aggregate.

It is not the aim of this book to present the details of a QED-based methodology for risk pricing ready to be implemented. Rather, the aim of this text is to explain what the risk pricing problem *really* is, and to reach an understanding of its complexities; as well as to document how the tools we currently have for risk measurement and management are substandard and need to be urgently upgraded. QED is presented as the best method for doing so.

Why are risks hard to value? It is because, as has been recently pointed out by many well-known economists, the rapid innovation in financial instruments has made them opaque. Minor adjustments in current tools and methods of risk pricing, including those promoted by Basel II, will change nothing. New departures are urgently needed.

A new departure in risk pricing must be coordinated with the change in regulatory rules and regulations in the banking industry. Mid-October 2009, Mervyn King, the governor of the Bank of England, suggested that banks be forced to separate their social utility functions, such as deposits, savings, loans and payments, from their riskier activities in trading and investment banking.

Paul Volcker, the respected former Federal Reserve chairman, has made a similar argument about "banks too big to fail"; as has Sheila Bair, chair of the Federal Deposit Insurance Corporation (FDIC). Bair stated that banks should face a "credible threat of failure". Forecasting the day the bubble of "the mother of all carry trades" will bust, on November 2 2009, Nouriel Roubini, the economist, also pleaded for separating commercial banking from investment banking.

At the heart of all these arguments lies the belief that no amount of regulation will be sufficient to prevent another meltdown. Sooner rather than later, the rules of the financial system will again be gamed. The only way to keep banks from being too big too fail is to separate assets that need protection from a crisis – the deposits base – from those which are the subject of highly leveraged exposure.

Accurate and globally appreciated risk pricing is therefore important at both sides of the line dividing an exposure's lower impact from higher impact in a systemic sense. Without a dependable, well-understood and controllable way of monitoring and measuring risk, banks will continue applying the so-called waterbed principle: the regulators try to flatten it in one place and its excesses simply pop up somewhere else.

The implementation of QED for risk management in the financial industry, in all its details, is a major project to be undertaken by regulators at the Bank for International Settlements (more precisely by the Basel Committee and Financial Stability Board), as well as by national regulatory authorities of the G-20 with coordination by the BIS.

As the Conclusion of this book brings to the reader's attention, it is time that regulatory authorities establish and endow first class risk management laboratories able to measure and manage the short, medium and long term exposure from all financial instruments; and in particular the most novel ones. Short of that, the reckless behaviour of some financial parties will continue, a new crisis will be forthcoming and the regulators will never be ahead of the curve in prudential supervision.

When done well, risk measurement, pricing and management safeguards the value of capital, rewarding people and companies who are ahead of the competition. As Mayer Anselm Rothschild (1743-1812) said: "Permit me to issue and control the money of a nation, and I care not who makes its laws."

Prologue

Physics, Quantum Theory, QED, QCD and Risk

1. Theories in physics

Like all physical theories, as well as all applications in engineering and other sciences, *quantum mechanics* consists of two main parts. One is mathematical, and the other operational. In the area of their overlapping lies experimentation, which is the wheel of science, as well as the vast domain of the use of intellect for the discovery of new concepts, rules and theories.

Equations, from probabilities to calculus, logic and analytics, are the muscles of the mathematical side of science; the tools necessary to observe and describe the long series of physical events. The skeleton of the mathematical side is provided by rules and theories formulated and implemented in connection to specific problems. These two parts sustain and give value to one another. *When scientists develop an intuitive argument, they support it with calculations.*

But as opposed to the rules of a mathematical system itself, which we unconsciously use every day, the rules of science are not set in stone. Raised by the operational side of science, this issue to a considerable degree reflects the fact that the deep structure of the world around us is quite different from the superficial image we make of it. We tend to concentrate on the surface; as we dig deeper, scientific laws are challenged and tend to change.

Our flexibility to explore the unknown and develop new rules is based on the hypotheses we make. Hypotheses are tentative statements which have to be tested and proven. When a tentative statement is confirmed it becomes a stepping stone to the next hypothesis, all the way to morphing into a scientific law. Scientific laws, however, are themselves tentative and they can be demolished by a nasty new fact – whether the genius that made them was Isaac Newton, Albert Einstein, some other famous scientist, or a lesser mortal.

This is necessary and welcome, because science evolves through the creative destruction of its laws and theories. Typically, we are more sure when we reject a hypothesis than when we accept it. We reject it because we have found evidence that it does not hold. By contrast, acceptance means that there is no evidence we should reject a hypothesis or theory. However, lack of evidence about something is not evidence of its non-existence and all we can say is that we don't know the negative side. Hence, for the time being, the hypothesis and intuition behind it might hold.

Classical mechanics, for example, has been largely based on intuition. This comfortable state was upset with the *quantisation of energy* – which is a characteristic feature of quantum mechanics based on the physicist Werner Heisenberg's uncertainty principle. (As the reader will see in Chapter 1, in 1900 Max Planck suggested that light, X-rays and other waves could be emitted not in an arbitrary rate but in packets, which he called *quanta*. One of the best definitions of *risk*, incidentally, also comes from Max Planck, as we will see in the same chapter).

One of the scientific theories demolished in the 1960s was based on the belief that protons and neutrons are *the* elementary particles.[1] In this case, the 'nasty fact' came from experiments with protons colliding with electrons and other protons, which suggested that these were made of still smaller particles. Murray Gell-Mann, the physicist, named them *quarks*.[2]

There are thought to be at least six flavours of quarks: up, down, strange, charmed, bottom and top.[3] Each flavour comes in three colours: red, green, blue – which are labels. Quarks are much smaller than visible light wavelengths, and they do not have 'colour'.

---

[1] The earliest known attempt at a theory of atoms was made in ancient Greece by Democritos (455-370 BC). It is he who suggested that the properties of matter were determined by the properties of atoms, of which they were composed.

[2] While quarks are the building blocks of protons, neutrons, and other 'heavy' components of the atomic nucleus, *leptons* are the light particles like electrons.

[3] A proton contains two up quarks and one down quark. A neutron has one up quark and two down quarks.

Quarks, flavours and colours have been the domain of the very small elements of research in physics and, as the opening paragraphs to this text have suggested, as with everything else in science, they are provisional. This plainly conforms to the thesis advanced by Nancy Cartwright in her book *How the Laws of Physics Lie*.[4] Science, she says, does not describe a profound physical reality. It advances phenomenal models, valid only in a limited space or under certain conditions.

2. The forces of nature

Physicists have also occupied themselves with the very large: with the goal of providing a single theory able to describe all of the forces acting on the universe – and eventually the universe itself, too.[5] It is the mission of science to create new knowledge, not just to interpret the old in an even greater but uncertain detail. The forces of nature are:

- Gravity

- Electricity

- Magnetism

- Weak nuclear force[6]

- Strong nuclear force[7]

---

[4] Nancy Crawford, *How the Laws of Physics Lie*, Oxford University Press, 1983.

[5] Necessarily such a theory must be based on another which deals with laws governing the initial state. The way current beliefs have it, these are grouped under the label 'the big bang' – a theory which has never been, and might never be, proven. The only Big Bang we surely know to have taken place was in the City of London, in the late 1980s under Margaret Thatcher. This was probably the single most important reason for London's rise to the top of global financial centres.

[6] Which is responsible for radioactivity.

[7] Its remit is to hold the quarks together in proton and neutron; and protons and neutrons together in the atom's nucleus.

Physicists today consider four fundamental forces, not five, since electricity and magnetism have been unified. The so-called *strong force* is the stronger of them and features the shortest range. It holds quarks together with protons and neutrons to form atoms. The *weak force* is the second weakest of the four, with very short range, and it affects all matter particles other than those which are force-carrying.

Gravity was the first force to attract human interest in terms of inquiry and application of intelligence. So far, however, it is also the least well understood. Isaac Newton described gravity and advanced a law; but to this day nobody really knows what gravity is. What we know are the effects of gravity. What we don't know is what produces gravity; that is, the fuel.

Yet, there is no lack of theories and explanations about gravity. We know, or think we know, that it acts on a macro-basis (the cosmic) and micro-basis (the sub-atomic level). But we still have no inkling how the macro-field is produced and how it is maintained, even if Newton, Kepler and a score of other physicists worked intensively on that macro-field. We must therefore appreciate that if we cannot explain gravity then we cannot generate it artificially; in fact, nobody has managed that feat.

This poses an intriguing question which goes beyond the fact that all scientific disciplines begin with a kind of stamp collecting – the gathering of data and examples without really knowing what to do with them. Does science involve nothing more than collecting facts and data and then interpreting them? Or does it begin where what one knows is too limited, obscure or incomplete? Or does it begin when one knows what one is looking for, even if one's findings are limited, obscure or incomplete?

The answer lies in the second option – where knowledge is limited, and in that sense scientists had more success in learning about, and combining into an integral theory, electricity and magnetism. The seminal work of Maxwell, Coulomb, Volta and plenty of others is well known and it has led to plenty of evidence about static and dynamic electric fields.

James Clark Maxwell succeeded in unifying the partial theories in 1865. The fact that he was successful in combining electricity and magnetism gave the idea to other physicists to work on combining electromagnetism with weak and strong atomic forces. The policy they followed was that of working outside conventions, and embarking on a voyage uniquely their own.

Werner Heisenberg and Enrico Fermi are two of the great names who worked on the weak atomic field, preceded and followed by a golden horde of physicists who made major contributions to measurements, tests and law-underpinning theories. But not every secret has been cracked. For instance, we cannot produce artificial radioactivity (just like we cannot generate gravity), though we can measure radioactivity and use it for many practical purposes.

This statement needs to be qualified. While in radioactivity we can establish statistics, we can never predict the single photon which is emitted – which has an intriguing similarity to *risk management*. In the world of physics and chemistry, radio isotopes are completely defined and we know their characteristics. More precisely: we know radioactivity emits particles, but we cannot predict exactly when.[8]

In a similar manner, when we establish a system for the control of exposure we know that *expected risks* will come at a given frequency and have a certain impact, but can cannot predict the frequency and impact of *unexpected risk* – except the fact that their frequency will be low, but their impact major.

What happens in physics provides an interesting parallel. We can count the particles, but we cannot master the process of emission – hence we cannot predict the simple event. In finance, this disconnection is a process we thought we had mastered by using engineers, physicists

---

[8] That's why the idea came up to use the emission of isotopes for generation of random numbers.

and mathematicians who know how to develop novel, sophisticated instruments, but have not brought to bear a method robust enough to cope with exposure over the longer term and unprecedented events.[9]

One of the reasons for this is our lack of creative imagination. Another lies in the fact that both the physical and the virtual worlds are made of hundreds and thousands of variables (the same is true of other domains like psychology).[10] Some of these variables interact very strongly while others normally don't; but sometimes they come to life with a major impact. In short, as Dr Heinrich Steinmann points out, this is a multidimensional space, which under present conditions we cannot quite conceive of.

3. Quantum electrodynamics

Within the environment of intellectual effort, research and endeavour, the discipline of *quantum electrodynamics* was born. This occurred when physicists began to think that, under certain conditions, the force of electromagnetism and the weak nuclear field might be manifestations of the same underlying interaction. The hypothesis was that these two forces complement one another through an underlying symmetry, and the symmetry between the weak force and electromagnetic interactions might have been broken by the mass of the intermediate vector bosons[11], the Ws and Zs.

---

[9] Neither are bankers in possession of these skills, as novel instruments have upset earlier established notions.

[10] Indeed, it would be interesting to compare market behaviour to that of an isotope.

[11] Also known as gauge particles or gluons, bosons are force carrying entities which exist for a small fraction of a second. Their presumed mission, in this very short life, is that of maintaining the atomic structure. For a discussion on vectors see the Appendix to Chapter 5.

The concept of particles as small packets of energy follows from Einstein's formula $E=mc^2$. A basic observation by physicists, underpinning the theoretical development of bosons, was that certain particles could behave in the most interesting fashion. For instance: begin with zero mass at high temperature, consume other particles in the field, and emerge with mass as the energy level dropped.

This hypothesis required that the W and Z force-carrying bosons are *extremely massive*. In addition, at high temperature, as might have occurred in the expansion of the universe (another hypothesis) or might be produced in a giga accelerator, the Ws and Zs might not drift along but pick up speed and start to lose their mass. The greater the speed the lesser the mass.

Physicists reckoned that *if* this tentative statement could be proved it would not only document that weak nuclear forces and electromagnetism were one, but also help to answer a puzzling question: 'Why does mass exist at all?' To the mind of physicists, theoretical particles, which appeared to be responsible for the universe, acted like magnets – and those which had the most mass exercised the greatest attraction.

Theoretically at least, a proof of this hypothesis might allow the electroweak interaction to be extended to a higher energy level where the strong nuclear force, and eventually gravity, could integrate into an entire theory. (It has not yet, but there is intensive research in this domain.)

Massive, uninterrupted and virtually unchallenged research, revolving around the unproven big bang's singularity, is aimed at fulfilling the premises of a master plan. But challenging queries lie in the way. The fact that our predictive capability in connection to natural phenomena is limited, has brought to the mind of some scientists a profound thought: is the world like the emitting of protons rather than the orderly result of a big bang?

The thought is challenging, but neither hypothesis – emitting of protons or the big bang – has been proven. It is gravity that determines the evolution of the universe, and our knowledge base today does not include the background of the force of gravity.

However, following the electroweak unification, physicists have been dreaming of a grand unifying theory (GUT). This will bring the strong nuclear force and eventually gravity into the same fold; all subatomic forces will be part of it. The major challenge was to find the underlying symmetry, and determine how it was broken in the short-lived moment of the birth of the cosmos (supposing there was a big bang).

Known as *quantum chromodynamics* (QCD), the theory of the strong nuclear force is much more complex than the weak interaction, but also seems to present similarities to it. The photon, a single particle, is the force carrier of electromagnetism, but there are eight gluons necessary for quantum chromodynamics, as gauge particles of the strong force. Still, it is not the strong nuclear force but gravity that commands the behaviour of matter in space-time.

"If a theory has just a few parameters but applies to a lot of data, it has real power," said Frank Wilczek. "You can use a small subset of the measurements to fix the parameters: then all other measurements are uniquely predicted." Wilczek added that QCD is a powerful theory not only because it does not require many parameters but also because it does not allow many: "Just a mass for each kind of quark and one universal coupling strength."[12]

---

[12] Frank Wilczek, *The Lightness of Being*, Basic Books, New York, 2008.

4. Space-time

Some people say that 'assume nothing' is a good motto in science, as the whole scientific discipline is based on hypotheses, tentative statements and assumptions. One of the basic assumptions in physics is that space and time both affect and are affected by everything that happens in the universe. According to the leading theory, in the symbiotic relationship of the cosmos, space-time is the master and mass is the executor:

- Space-time is four-dimensional and its points are *events*.[13]

- Space-time tells mass how to move, and

- Mass returns the compliment by helping space-time to bend.

This presumably four-dimensional space-time is of course a philosopher's idea, rather than a proven fact. As Heinrich Steinmann suggests, it is the projection of a higher-dimensional world in a way we can comprehend because we are not able to think of it in five, ten or more dimensions.

Stephen Hawking puts it in a different way:

> We see only one time and three space dimensions, in which space-time is fairly flat. On a very small scale (space-time) is ten-dimensional and highly curved, but on a bigger scale you don't see the curvature or the extra dimensions.[14]

---

[13] Each event is specified by its time and place. In diagrams included Chapter 5 space-time has been simplified and presented in two dimensions.

[14] Stephen W. Hawking, *A Brief History of Time*, Bantam Books, New York, 1988.

As for time, an excellent reference regarding its substance was made not by a physicist but by a banker, Sigmund Warburg, who was testing his employees, friends and clients by asking them if they knew the difference between *Kairos* and *Chronos*. (See also Chapter 5.)

Kairos is the short-term time, of which busy people never have enough but lazy people have plenty. It is measured and checked; in the case of time and motion (productivity), it is studied by the stopwatch. The concept of *Chronos*, however, is much more fundamental and it envelops that of *Kairos*.

Chronos is the long-term time. It builds up people and events but then 'eats its children'.[15]

People have an individual measure of time, depending on where they are and how they are moving. An event is what happens at a particular point in space, and at a particular point in time. The time at which events happen is a rather personal concept relative, in a way, to who observes it and who measures it.

In addition, time does not of necessity have to only move forwards. If it had ever taken negative value, the world would have collapsed to zero, but it might also have existed before zero.[16] Every physical system would be affected by the direction of time, said John Boslough.[17] Moreover, waves for particle histories may not be in *real-time*, but take place in *imaginary time* (which is a well-defined mathematical concept).

---

[15] In ancient Greek religious mythology Chronos was the God of Gods who ate up his children.

[16] All this might sound contradictory but it is plausible, even if unlikely judged by the current state of our knowledge. It is, however, a proof of our ignorance.

[17] John Boslough, *Masters of Time*, J.M. Dent, London, 1992.

In the late 17th century Gottfried Wilhelm von Leibniz (1646-1716), Newton's contemporary and competitor (in calculus and physics, but not in finance)[18], advanced a relativistic view of time and space. In the late 20th century, talking of *imaginary time* (calculated by using imaginary numbers rather than real ones) Stephen Hawking said that it has an interesting effect on space-time: in it the distinction between time and space disappears.

It is a thesis of Hawking that if one tries to unify gravity with quantum mechanics, then one has to introduce imaginary time, which is indistinguishable from directions in space: "If one can go forward in imaginary time, one ought to be able to turn around and go backward."

Gravity is a property of both space and time. The hypothesis is that not only does space-time's geometry transport gravitational action from mass to mass, but also that it carries gravitational energy through the void at the speed of light. This is one of the "unknown unknowns" to which future generations might provide an answer.

5. Entropy

This introductory text would be incomplete without reference to *entropy*, the physical quantity which is based on the second law of thermodynamics.[19] Its remit is to measure the degree of disorder in a

---

[18] Newton spent a greater share of his life as warden and then master of the Mint (equivalent to governor of the Bank of England) than as a physicist at Cambridge.

[19] In 1824, Sadi Carnot published the first statement of what would much later become the second law of thermodynamics: "Heat will not spontaneously flow from cold objects to hot ones". This had most significant repercussions in physics and chemistry.

system. To create order out of disorder requires energy (and, in a bank, plenty of effort in an organisational sense). Left to its own devices, disorder, and therefore entropy, tends to increase.

The word entropy was coined by Rudolf Clausius, a medical doctor[20], who wanted to have a term representing the sense of *transformation*. In addition to this, as a label, entropy has acquired the meaning of *uncertainty*, which is closer to its true physical interpretation than that of transformation. What the second law of thermodynamics essentially states in entropy's regard is that:

- In an isolated system entropy always increases, and

- When two systems are combined, their entropy is greater than the arithmetic sum of the entropies of each one of them.[21]

Entropy measures the amount of randomness present in a given construct. In thermodynamics, it represents the amount of energy unavailable for useful work in a system undergoing change. Increase in entropy is interpreted as the passage of a system from state to state. The ratio of actual to maximum entropy is known as *relative entropy*.

In terms of thermal energy, Myron Tribus suggests that it is completely misleading to speak of "heat stored in the body." Only energy can be stored. Heat is energy *in transit* – therefore it is in a process of transition and transformation.

Claude E. Shannon spoke of the *entropy of information*, in analogy to thermodynamic entropy. In information theory, the entropy of a system (or of a source) is maximised when all symbols are equally probable. Uniformity increases the level of entropy. Diversity acts the

---

[20] In his book *Abhandlungen über Mechanische Wärmetheorie*, Brunnswick, 1864.

[21] It is not the objective of this introductory text to deal with the concept of black holes.

opposite way. This is a principle which can, and should be, used very effectively in risk management. Diversification reduces the amount of a portfolio's entropy. By contrast, concentration in names, instruments, countries or other risk factors increases it – as risk, too, increases.

Shannon also underlined that the statistical measure of the content of a message is *negative entropy*, or negentropy. Once they have been developed, information measures can be used to evaluate organisational entropy, including that created by its people – since, fundamentally, organisations are made of people.

In the 21st century, entropy increased tremendously in the global financial system, and most particularly in the American market. All big banks rushed to pool, structure, sell and warehouse the same financial instruments (subprimes). While paying just lip service to diversification, they engaged in massive regulatory arbitrage.[22] This was thought to be magic (for profits and bonuses), but some years down the line it proved to be pure trickery, and ended in an unmitigated disaster.

The notion of entropy can be effectively used in risk control; which has not been done so far, at least not in a systematic way. It can also serve in clarifying our ideas about exposure in a way that allows us to address the most fundamental issues. The first step in the search for answers about the control of exposure is to appreciate what *real risk* is, including how much of it is wanted and beyond which point it becomes harmful.

There is some justification in saying that entropy of information (including information on exposure) and thermodynamic entropy are not merely equivalent but identical. In terms of risk pricing and risk

---

[22] I really wonder not only about what 3400 risk managers were doing at UBS when the bank was dying of entropy, but also (and mainly) how it happens that none of the experts explained to Marcel Ospel, the CEO, that entropy would open his professional grave.

control, what we are interested in is probability density functions which describe a system having the property of maximum randomness.

True enough, current studies in thermodynamics and in communications theory tend to follow statistical patterns characterised by the normal distribution. But as Chapter 1 will explain, we are presently able to focus on what particularly interests us: the long tail of the risk distribution. Integrating the concept of entropy into probability density functions associated with quantum theory, might (superficially) look like a damnable project. But this is true only in terms of conventional thinking – not in the case of thinking, as they say, outside of the box.

From the Pythagorean credo "all things are numbers," we have moved to an age where new concepts leap out of equations to take on a life of their own. Over a century ago, Lord Kelvin, the physicist, noted that when we can measure what we are speaking about, and express it in numbers, we know something about it. But if we cannot express it in numbers, then our knowledge is of a meagre and unsatisfactory kind. It may be the beginning of knowledge, but we have scarcely in our thoughts advanced to the stage of science.

Part One

Risks of the 21st Century

Chapter 1: Risk in Finance

1. Risk defined

Max Planck, the well-known physicist, once said that without occasional venture, or risk, no genuine invention can be accomplished even in the most exact sciences. That the doors of risk and return are adjunct and indistinguishable is also a basic principle in finance – where risk is often expressed in terms of changes in values between two dates. This definition fits well with market risk, and can be extended into credit risk with downgrade and default as triggers.

A major difference between risk in finance and in other domains, like engineering or the military, is that risk is related to variability of the future value of a position due to *volatility* (see section 2), which brings market changes and events of an *uncertain* nature. Risk events are uncertain in the sense that they do not have a well-defined or sure outcome.

Risk must be managed. Of particular importance in the control of exposure are *a priori* estimates of a potential negative change. These may be the consequence of an unexpected or uncontrollable event, or they may be due to errors in pricing and other mistakes when a commitment was made. Risks can be effectively dealt with only insofar as their effect(s) can be measured and controlled. In financial terms, the broader categories are:

1. *Risk of asset loss*. For instance the possibility that mortgages and business loans are given to, as well as bonds are issued by, entities which default. In the general case this is credit risk, an exposure connected to the creditworthiness of the counterparty to a transaction. Asset losses may also be triggered by country risk and other factors.

2. *Loss due to interest rate, currency exchange, equity price and index changes*. These are examples of market risk which, in simple form, are losses resulting from movement in market prices or rates. The

more complex the financial instrument (Chapter 2), the greater tends to be the market risk impact. Practically all commodity prices are volatile. If there is no movement of substance in the price of goods and services, then there will be no concern over market exposure. This is, however, an unrealistic assumption.

3. *Risk of wrong pricing* (Chapter 3). This may be due to a very optimistic estimate of implied volatility (the so-called *volatility smile*),[23] wishful thinking about an instrument's fair value or plain error. There are many types of pricing insufficiency, the majority due to the fact that crucial factors affecting prices now and in the future have not been thoroughly analysed.

Under present policies, risk categories No. 1 and No. 2 are being addressed through incompatible and unrelated methods and models, while category No. 3 has been touched only on the surface. This is clearly incompatible with the ongoing trend of assuming greater and greater amounts of risk.[24]

A unified risk management theory is urgently needed, and for such a purpose this book proposes *quantum electrodynamics* (QED[25], Chapters 4 and 5), which has provided a sophisticated and very successful integrative platform in the physical sciences. In addition, it is necessary to address, also in an aggregate manner, a group of qualitative exposures due to:

---

[23] A volatility smile is an optimistic and undocumented opinion about future volatility, made because of ignorance or, more frequently, as a result of conflict of interest.

[24] D. N. Chorafas, *Financial Boom and Gloom. The Credit and Banking Crisis of 2007-2009 and Beyond*, Palgrave/Macmillan, London, 2009 and D. N. Chorafas, *Capitalism Without Capital*, Palgrave/Macmillan, London, 2009.

[25] Ironically, in Latin QED stands for quod erat demonstrandum, which means 'it remains to be proved'.

4. Legal risk (Chapter 6), overleveraging (Chapter 7), poor supervision (Chapter 8). Other qualitative risks are bad governance, wanting internal control and weak risk management structure – but they are not part of the present text.

This book's proposal is to employ for risk category No. 4 *quantum chromodynamics* (QCD), which is considered by modern physicists an almost ideally simple theory. Each of QCD's eight colour gluons is there for a purpose. Qualitative exposure management can benefit from the concept underlying them.

The reader will note that new departures are necessary if *risk* and *return* are to be meaningfully addressed. The use for that purpose of *quantum logic* (section 4) will not be easy, but it is possible, as we will see in Part Two. One of the main reasons for the breakdown in risk management, which led to the severe economic and banking crisis of 2007-2009, was captured by Aeschylus, the ancient Greek dramatist who said: "God's law is that he who learns must suffer" – and people don't like to suffer. A lot of designers, traders, investment experts, loans officers and senior managers have been negligent in terms of the level of detail and process of aggregation in the calculation of assumed risk.

When banking and the financial services at large were a business largely based on tradition, it was enough to set aside equity capital to cover risks which (to a large extent) were rather well-known and measurable (at least in a statistical sense). Since the 1980s, however, a rapid innovation in banking has made this utterly inadequate.

Looking back on the post-World War II years, the change towards a new and different landscape of financial management started in the 1960s with syndicated loans, accelerated in the 1970s with the repeal of Bretton Woods and flexible currency exchange rates, and really took off in the 1980s as mathematical modelling and computers opened new perspectives for novelty and complexity in financial instruments.[26]

---

[26] D. N. Chorafas, *Chaos Theory in the Financial Markets*, Probus, Chicago, 1994; and D. N. Chorafas 'Rocket Scientists in Banking', Lafferty Publications, London and Dublin, 1995.

The *strategic inflection point* which followed (Chapter 2), led to a shift towards the pre-eminence of financial markets. Markets are made up of individuals, and people's priorities have changed. Back in the 1980s, individuals started to believe that real assets, particularly their homes, may not be their single best investment idea. The notion emerged that financial assets had to provide the bulk of their future well-being – whether to improve their current standard of living, enable them to take vacations in exotic places, send children to university, or finance their retirement plans.

Many economists look at this change in perception from *real assets* to *virtual assets* (Chapter 2), and therefore debt, as a shift in how risk and return are perceived. Little attention has been paid, however, to the fact that caught between rising levels of unpayable debt through overleveraging (Chapter 8) on one side, and economic cycles on the other, the banking system can disintegrate. Contrary to equity that represents ownership, all sorts of debts, including megadebts, have to be repaid. If there is no payment of interest and return of capital then the banking sector is put under severe pressure, as credit institutions can no longer trust the assets recorded in their books.

It follows that the survival of the financial industry requires rethinking of notions underpinning risk measurement and management in a holistic way. The world is now characterised not only by rapid financial innovation, new products and changing markets, but also by growing interdependence between financial institutions, capital markets, and taxpayers' money in the government's vaults.

2. Effects of volatility

Etymologically, *volatility* is the quality of being volatile, changeable, explosive, diffusing, unstable, erratic, mercurial, temperamental, or unpredictable. With stocks and other commodities, volatility is a measure of the variability of an asset's or index's price. Often, it is defined as the annualised standard deviation of the natural log of asset prices, but as we will see in this section and in the Appendix other measures, too, are used. With securities, the price volatility is a statistical measure of the risk of holding assets and, as standard deviation of expected return, the volatility changes with the time period over which it is measured.

Volatility increases in nervous markets and is propelled by unwinding large positions. For instance, in late 2007 and 2008 the liquidation of carry trades increased volatility in the foreign exchange market. In a broader sense, according to a number of analysts, volatility has been a driving force in the development and use of *derivatives* (Chapter 2)[27], at least in regard to the drive of originators and end-users in continuing to develop, refine and utilise new derivative financial instruments to protect against volatility by serving as hedges, or to take advantage of market volatility for speculative purposes.

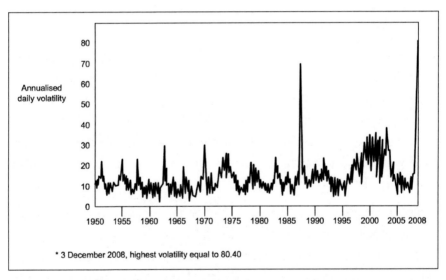

Figure 1.1: S&P 500 annualised daily volatility January 1950 to 31 December 2008.

---

[27] D. N. Chorafas, *An Introduction to Derivative Financial Instruments*, McGraw-Hill, New York, 2008.

In the market at large, volatility can have wide swings, as Figure 1.1 shows, and when this happens it signals a change in leadership. Volatility developments in prices and yields of assets are both stress factors and stress indicators. Volatility also underpins the dynamic evolution or dispersion of asset price movements, which can be seen as patterns under 'normal' conditions or under stress.[28] In volatile markets, the gap between the best performing stocks and the worst performing stocks gets wider.

When dealing with investment themes, financial markets and the economy at large are discounting mechanisms. Assets that used to be leaders tend to under-perform, while some laggards gain the upper ground. This happens even when investors become risk averse (section 6) as market volatility reaches a higher level. Because the increase in volatility affects different assets in unequal ways, its aftermath is both risk and opportunity.

A surging volatility is the nemesis of bankers, traders and investors committing the classic mistake of believing that they can get out of a position as easily as they enter into it. Volatility makes markets prime to nasty surprises, and it particularly penalises investing with borrowed money to play in stocks or other commodities. Also, if a bank or hedge fund was caught out by a sudden sell-off, high volatility can have deep and lasting implications.

It goes without saying that it is important to measure volatility. Today, the most popular volatility index is VIX, established by the Chicago Board Options Exchange (CBOE) and derived from the world of options (see the discussion of VIX in the Appendix to this chapter). VIX is a measure of *implied volatility* (more on this later). Therefore it is forward looking. It is known as the investors' 'fear gauge' and it reflects their best predictions of near-term market volatility, and therefore risk.

---

[28] In this text, 'normal' means within the formation of expectations regarding the future dispersion of prices, whether these relate to equities, debt instruments, currencies or other assets.

Beta is not an index of volatility but a sensitivity measure indicating the volatility of some assets, particularly equities, compared to the benchmark one uses.[29] Sometimes people confuse VIX with *beta*, though the two are very different.

More precisely, beta is a statistic not a driver (like VIX). For instance, it measures a stock's sensitivity to overall movement in the equity market. Its usage has been promoted with the Capital Adequacy Pricing Model (CAPM), as a measure of the strength of the relationship between the market and the price of securities to which it applies.

Based on two statistical measures, the *variance* of the market as a whole and *covariance* of the security price with the market, beta evaluates the extent of a given asset's price fluctuation over a certain period, expressed by means of the standard deviation of changes of logarithmic asset prices.

Contrary to VIX, which is a market index, beta reflects the volatility of a dependent variable. For instance, the sensitivity of a given equity to the market's movement. A beta of 1.2 means that a given equity, whose volatility is measured against the equities index, moves 20% more than the Dow Jones or S&P 500, in either direction (up or down), over the period being measured. Two other notions are important in complementing this discussion:

1. Realised, or historical, volatility.

2. Implied, or future, volatility.

Realised volatility is a statistic constructed by summing squared changes, for instance, of overnight interest rates calculated for each five-minute interval between 9 a.m. and 6 p.m. For technical reasons, this exercise focuses on the logarithm of this measure. The strength and weakness of this metric is that it is based on statistics derived from events which have happened, but these events are in the past.

---

[29] Standard reference against which measurements are made.

Realised volatility is of interest inasmuch as a look back at the past shows that sharp upswings in volatility may occur as an accompanying feature of particular stress situations in the market. Figure 1.1 shows that cyclical swings in realised volatility are typical of equity markets, with spikes frequently associated with economic downturns.

For product pricing, monetary policy, investments and other purposes it is, however, important to account for future volatility. *Implied volatility* is used as a proxy of future volatility, gauging the degree of uncertainty prevailing in markets, and providing information on future volatility expectations. Interesting insights can be gained by examining implied volatility's pattern in options markets as it provides an indication of the price of uncertainty over the period spanned by the maturity of the option. As such, it reflects the market participants' degree of risk aversion.

Implied volatility rose to a high value in the period following the Lehman Brothers collapse, in early September 2008. Thereafter, it declined in a way comparable to previous periods of market panics, but with a tendency to upswings.

A rapid retrenchment in implied volatility indicates that the compensation required for bearing volatility risk has decreased. If implied volatility continues to remain at a high level, then market tension has not subsided. Economists suggest that when this happens the underlying reason may well be the length and depth of an ongoing recession, particularly one synchronised across the globalised economy and characterised by:

- Low returns,
- High uncertainty,
- Need for liquidity,
- Solvency challenges, and
- Risk aversion.

In terms of prognostication, in bond and equity markets implied volatility should tend to rise when a business cycle expansion moves into a mature phase. At that stage, uncertainty begins to increase about the tightening of monetary policy. Also, the onset of rising interest rates typically leads to higher volatility, because of growing uncertainty about future interest rate increases. (There is more on volatility's behaviour in the Appendix).

3. The risk's long tail

Statisticians, mathematicians, physicists, engineers – generally known as 'rocket scientists' when they work in finance – have been trained to understand and use the theoretical, bell-shaped normal distribution.[30] The same is true of economists. To a large measure this is a reflection of the fact that their teachers, too, were trained the same way, because research in the 1920s and 1930s produced some terrific all-weather statistical tables based on the bell-shaped distribution of events.

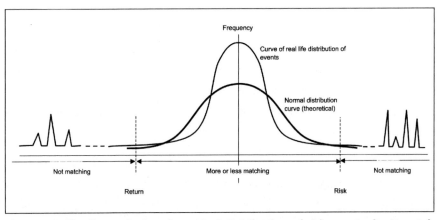

Figure 1.2: The theoretical and practical distribution of risk events don't match at their tails.

---

[30] These 'rocket scientists' are so called because they are scientists; physicists, engineers and mathematicians, who previously worked on nuclear and aerospace projects – hence the name rocket scientists – and brought to finance and banking their analytical skills. The fact that rocket scientists are not bankers and bankers know very little about physics and mathematics has much to do with the growing number of financial models which crack when confronted with reality. Several of these models may be beautiful mathematical constructs but their relevance to financial decisions is limited, at best.

In the last two decades of the 20th century, however, came a rapidly growing body of evidence that neither risk events nor the volatility underpinning them need to be normal.[31] While the bell-shaped distribution closely matches the real world in the middle of the area under the curve, it does not do so at the tails. The pattern shown in Figure 1.2 makes the continuing use of the bell-shaped curve questionable. The tails are the areas where most of the *risks* and *rewards* really lie.

This is true not only in banking and finance but also in the physical sciences and in engineering. Reliability studies, for example, use the Weibull distribution, which is exponential, and in terms of lifecycle quality control the danger zones of an engineering product are at the tails. Respectively these are baby failures and wear-out failures.

It was a deliberate choice in Figure 1.2, designed to identify for the reader the tails of a risk distribution in a financial environment, to use the left side for return and the right side for risk. This alters in no way the fact that in both cases the spikes at the tails matter a great deal. Although in markets (as well as in the sciences) extreme events are not very common, when they happen they have a significant impact. Therefore, following the normal distribution leads to errors in judgment.

Risks events which are found in the right tail of the distribution are those about which analysts, investors, bankers, and regulatory authorities should worry the most. The October 1987 Black Monday was a 14.5 standard deviations event. Two decades later, in 2008, David Vinair, chief financial officer of Goldman Sachs, said in an interview that his bank had seen *25-standard deviation* moves several days in a

---

[31] See, as an example, Figure 1.1.

row.[32] Nervous markets were clearly at the extreme tail of their risk distribution, and normal distribution based models, like value at risk (VaR, Chapter 4), did not even begin to predict that the tails would move so violently, because they were (and are) focused on central values.

This is no critique of modelling as a discipline, but of the way in which models are being designed and used.[33] As long as its artefacts were not developed and employed in the wrong way, the discipline of mathematical modelling produced commendable results. This is not surprising, because the secrets underpinning many arts are akin to mathematics requiring exact weights, proportions and times, as well as a focused, orderly approach. What is surprising is that when using models bankers, regulators and mathematicians pretended to be working in an ideal world. Also, in their appreciation of risk they both entrusted and extensively employed the results of wrong artefacts.

Yet enlightened persons had warned of the danger of model risk. Dr Benoit Mandelbrot, the mathematician turned economist, calculated that if the Dow Jones Industrial Average followed a normal distribution then it should have moved by more than 3.4% on 58 days between 1916 and 2003, while in reality it did so on 1001. It should have moved by more than 4.5% on six days, while it did so on 366. And it should have moved by more than 7% only once in every 300,000 years, while it did so 48 times in these 87 years.

Essentially, what Mandelbrot's statistics indicate is that as far as the financial markets are concerned, working along the normal distribution leads to highly erroneous results (the same is true in science). By

---

[32] *The Economist*, 24 January 2009.

[33] D. N. Chorafas, *Modelling the Survival of Financial and Industrial Enterprises. Advantages, Challenges, and Problems with the Internal Rating-Based (IRB) Method*, Palgrave/Macmillan, London, 2002.

focusing on the normal distribution curve, the mean and ±3 standard deviations either side of the mean, the analyst, economist, banker or regulator cannot observe what happens at the tails, yet that is the most important area for examining risk and return.

Although the body of the bell-shaped distribution is the integral part of a risk-oriented study, because this is where the high frequency events lie, the fact remains that one cannot deduce a significant exposure, or trend towards an exposure, just by looking at high frequency, low impact occurrences. Neither can one appreciate the amplitude and great impact of extreme events from the shape of the curve in the middle.

Both high frequency/low impact (HF/LI) and low frequency/high impact (LF/HI) risk events are important, and although these two risk populations are almost decoupled in a mathematical sense, they interact with one-another.

Failing to estimate the tail of a risk distribution beyond 99% of the probability of occurrence of events leaves out of view some possibly devastating losses. Bankers whose institutions descended into the abyss because of such failures now admit that it is by no means sufficient to predict small day-to-day losses in the heart of the risk distribution. One must take stock of high impact events that are much rarer but not impossible.

Notwithstanding the myriad of regulations and social responsibilities to which the financial industry is subject, a bank is after all a business whose diverse operating units assume exposure through their daily activity. Banks warehouse this exposure, including the impact of outliers, in their trading book and banking book. Therefore, they need to pay attention:

- To the existence of new, potentially extreme risks, and

- Analyse warehoused exposures associated with their assets and liabilities in real-time.

One of the difficulties of addressing both challenges in a knowledgeable way, simultaneously, comes from the fact that mathematicians know too little about finance, while the large majority of financial people know next to nothing about mathematics. As a result, while they talk about gains and losses they usually think about the body of the distribution and maybe also the left side of returns in Figure 1.2. Moreover, they do not appreciate that the two sides (left and right) are asymmetric. This is because risk and return don't balance out in the short term, and winners and losers behave differently in financial markets as psychology changes.

This has important after-effects on market risk and counterparty risk. The outstanding features are never the same from one crisis to the next; what they have in common is their significant impact on frequency and amplitude of events entering the risk distribution. For instance, in an upswing, overconfident bankers, traders or investors take on bets that they later find themselves unable to discharge, thereby altering some outstanding features in regard to frequency and amplitude of exposure. Hence the need for new, more powerful tools and methods in modelling risk – which is the theme of section 4.

4. Risk and quantum logic

On 21 January 2009, in the course of his appearance to the US Senate Committee for confirmation, Timothy Geithner, the treasury secretary of the Obama Administration, said that "innovation in financial instruments got ahead of risk management." He then added he will make it his duty to make sure that in the future the after-effects of financial innovation are not an unknown quantity to bankers and regulators.

Since innovation in the financial industry is practically unstoppable, the only way to implement Geithner's promise is with the use of a powerful universal risk measurement and management model, able to combine the best theory available in physics with a practical methodology for controlling exposure. Based on quantum theory, *quantum logic* is a good candidate for fulfilling that premise, as section 1 brought to the reader's attention.

Underpinning this choice is the fact that only the best scientific methods and tools are good enough to correct a situation which, left unattended, has run out of control. The huge excesses in the financial industry revealed by the 2007-2009 deep economic and banking crisis are by no means chance events. They have taken many years to build up and, as such, they cannot be eradicated by decree. We have to identify them and measure them, then bring them and their perpetrators in line through transparency and corrective action.

The use of quantum analysis and computation, promoted by this book, is an important research field which has opened new horizons to the application of properties of particle physics, including the theories of superposition and entanglement, which are vital to modern finance. Quantum logic, moreover, offers an immense representational space which can help in solving a high number of successive operations, as well as the checks and controls applied to them.

It is not the objective of this book to explain quantum theory, but a few notes can help in understanding what was written in the Prologue. In 1910 Max Planck, the physicist, suggested that light, X-rays and other waves were not emitted at arbitrary rates but in packets he called *quanta*; and that each quantum had a certain amount of energy. Planck's insight fits very well with risk management in the virtual economy.[34]

In the 1920s, Werner Heisenberg, Erwin Schrödinger, and Paul Dirac reformatted the then existing notions of mechanics into a new theory, *quantum mechanics*. The cornerstone to this theory was Heisenberg's *uncertainty principle*, which states that nothing walks in a straight line (which is true not only in physics but also in finance, in management, and in society at large).

---

[34] (Chapter 2).

In fact, not only is the straight line an unreliable representation of real life, but there are also boundaries to values taken by a series of movements. This principle was beautifully exploited by Walter Shewhart, the physicist, who while working at Bell Laboratories (in the 1920s and 1930s) pioneered the use of statistics to assure industrial quality through *statistical quality control* (SQC) charts (Chapter 2).

In addition to the references made in the preceding paragraphs, a competitive advantage of quantum theory is that it provides a set of rules that relate quanta to observations we make. It also accurately describes a large class of observations (which increasingly characterise modern finance), on the basis of a powerful model that contains only a few arbitrary elements. As such, it can serve in making predictions about the results of futures observations.

Quantum mechanics, which has proved to be one of the most successful theories of nature, makes use of the fact that a basic symmetry or regulatory trend might lie beneath all forces, and it employs some useful basic objects called *probability amplitudes*. What particularly interests us in connection to risk pricing is the mathematical part of quantum theory, which:

- Dictates how the amplitudes evolve with time,

- Contains objects known as *observables*, which are linear operators, and

- Integrates most effectively the concept of *Feynman diagrams* (Chapter 5).

In practically all domains of application, the challenge is the mapping of event representations in a way that accounts for state changes and interactions, and also incorporates the statistical nature of quantum phenomena. As we will see in Chapter 5, this is currently done in physics; which is an important reference inasmuch as skills as well as insight are available and can be transferred to practical applications in finance and banking.

The crux of quantum logic is not the number of particles or equations, but the perfection of design they embody. The transition from the physical sciences is helped by the fact that, in banking, risk is expressed quantitatively, as the probability or degree of loss. Such probability is not just mathematical but also a function of:

- *The type of loss that is covered*: Default, interest rate, exchange rate, type of accident (in insurance), and

- *The nature of the counterparty to the transaction*: household, business client, trader, or another financial operator.

Prerequisites to the use of quantum analysis would be no different than those prevailing today in the financial industry, even if their tools and methods stand at lower levels of sophistication. For instance, identifying fundamental risk factors; determining linkages among them; establishing metrics; taking measurements; making forecasts and dynamically correcting them; testing and reaching conclusions.

	Forecast	Actual[35]
1st quarter of 2008	+1.3	+0.9
2nd quarter of 2008	+1.9	+2.8
3rd quarter of 2008	+2.3	-0.5
4th quarter of 2008	+2.6	-6.1

Table 1.1: Failure of Classical Forecasting Approaches in Projecting Changes in US GDP.[36]

---

[35] Notice that the further out the quarter was, the greater is the failure of the forecast.

[36] By Merrill Lynch.

Forecasting the evolution of risks, as well as prognosticating at large, is one of the domains where current tools and methods have been quite unsuccessful. Table 1.1 brings to the reader's attention statistics published in *Blue Chip Consensus*, a January 2009 study by Merrill Lynch. These provide a startling example of failure in projecting change in real gross domestic product (GDP) of the American economy by professional forecasters.

In other cases, particularly in regard to hedging, failures have been due to false concepts or assumptions. An example is the financial market's fairly generalised belief that buying a share and selling a call option[37] on that same share would mean that the bank's or investor's balance sheet has grown but the risk has not. In fact, to the contrary, betting on an equity price going up and selling a call option on that equity will increase assumed risk. If the equity price goes to zero, the loss on that share position will be its full purchase price, mitigated by the small premium received for writing the call.

As this brief example demonstrates, a good way of looking at risk is as a *cost* which is not necessarily balanced by return. More precisely, risk is the cost of yesterday when the commitment was made and of tomorrow at transaction's maturity. Among factors entering the cost equation are:

- Growing speculation as a bubble inflates,
- Volatility driving prices and values further apart,
- Fraudsters peddling fantasies to over-euphoric investors,
- Gathering doubts about a bubble's sustainability,
- Bursting of confidence causing debts that cannot be paid, defaults, and a recession.

---

[37] On options and premiums see Chapter 2.

As the reader will recall, section 1 made reference to QCD, beyond QED, in order to cover qualitative aspects of exposure. Cost factors and their after-effects are magnified by *management risk*: $52,000 is how much cash General Motors was losing every minute as a combined result of the economic meltdown in the US and its own mismanagement. Poor governance has forced the formerly proud global company to go to the US government for handouts, in the (perhaps) vain hope of assuring its survival.

In banking, too, the directives of top management, including prodding, have often led to assuming ill-advised and poorly researched risks. For this reason Part Three and Part Four concentrate on qualitative exposures. Other things being equal, the bigger a credit institution or any other financial organisation is, the less effective the watch of its management. As CEOs built financial conglomerates – and sought to push them hard – legal risks multiplied, super-leveraging increased, regulatory watch was minimised, internal control decreased, the quality of earnings deteriorated, and shareholder value declined, even if bonuses continued unabated.

With no universal system able to reliably identify risk and return, in good times the higher the returns seem to be, the more lavish the salaries, options and bonuses. These "returns" however were often an illusion, most frequently fed by means of creative accounting. At bad times self-gratification continued unabated, even though, at the long leg of the risk distribution, exposure was piled upon exposure until what was left was pure toxic waste.

In conclusion, the purpose of implementing quantum logic is not to correct the aforementioned management ills in a direct way, but to provide a dependable instrument for:

- Quantitative measurement of exposure being assumed,

- Judgment of qualitative issues propelling its potential cost, and

- Promotion of personal accountability.

Risk information that is timely, accurate and dependable will have a benevolent (though indirect) impact on governance, leaving to the board and CEO the task of controlling what John Maynard Keynes called "animal spirits".

5. The complexity of modern risks

"The only law of history worthy of scientific analysis is that there is no law," said Otto Veit, a former president of the Hessen central bank.[38] Or, more precisely, there is no lasting law because what law there might have been in the past has been made obsolete by change, novelty and complexity that goes beyond current skills and tools.

Complexity sees to it not only that the normal distribution of risk events and values is *passé* in terms of its ability to serve as a tool in analytics, but also that modern risks, which have to be studied to remain ahead of the curve, are neither linear nor monotonic. A modern bank trades simultaneously in all sorts of instruments, each characterised by general and specific risks, including:

- Options[39]

- Futures

- Swaps

- Commodities

- Equities

- Credit

- Debt

- Forex

- Interest rates.

---

[38] David Marsh, *The Bundesbank*, William Heinemann, London, 1992.

[39] For definitions see Chapter 2.

Weak methods, limited tools and indecisive management cannot confront this complexity – and a growing amount of leverage does *not* make the bank's holdings safer. Quite to the contrary, it is exchanging everyday smaller risks for the exceptional big risk that causes catastrophic events to happen. Credit insurance, or any other sort of guarantee, does not provide significant protection because even large insurers fail, as AIG did.

Matters are made worse by the fact that while tail risks have grown largely unobserved to an often unexpected dimension, traders and managers look at them as if they are no different to the expected normal distribution risks they were used to confronting in the past.

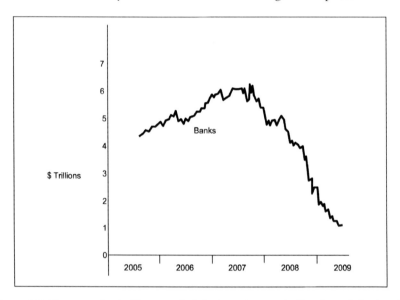

Figure 1.3: Three-and-a half years of global market capitalisation of the banking industry.

Some experts suggest that there is also a conflict of interest in ignoring the existence of outliers, because financial players want to be paid for profit-making and profits are found at high risk levels.

In this way, the long leg of exposure is ignored with risk weights downplayed for two different but complementary reasons:

1. Lack of interest in keeping exposure under lock and key, and

2. The fact that risk management methods and their models have not been updated to reflect the added complexity of financial instruments and sophistication of market players.

The banking industry has paid a heavy price for its lack of interest in keeping exposure under control. The concept of risk as a cost (section 4) can be quantified in terms of capitalisation. As Figure 1.3 shows, in the fourth quarter of 2005, in order of magnitude the global market capitalisation of banks stood at slightly over $4 trillion. This grew to nearly $7 trillion in the fourth quarter of 2007, then shrank to less than $1.5 trillion in the first quarter of 2009. The trillions in difference in capitalisation is the price the banking industry paid for defective risk management. To this should be added many more trillions of taxpayers' money thrown at the problem by governments and central banks to salvage the self-wounded big banks.[40]

Risk models approved by regulators and the Basel Committee (like VaR, Chapter 4), have been of no assistance whatsoever in averting the risk catastrophe. They have failed because, among other weaknesses, they did not and do not take account of falling mortgage underwriting standards. Hence, they do not weight-in the level of confidence associated to credit rating. Post-mortem, after the 2007-2009 disaster, many experts said that the credit rating agencies' models were even less up to the job than those of the issuers.

---

[40] In an interview he gave to Sky News on 30 March 2009 Lord Lamont, a Chancellor of the Exchequer in the Thatcher government, pointed out that Gordon Brown's government is now standing behind all losses of all British banks – whose foreign liabilities are 400% of Britain's GDP. The Royal Bank of Scotland alone has liabilities totalling more than Britain's annual GDP.

Not only the methods, tools and models used by banks have been left behind in terms of addressing the growing risk complexity, but also structural issues have not adapted to the new situation. Responsibility for risk monitoring and control still rests with the centre, while responsibility for maximising return on assumed risks lies with the business units. This discrepancy is made worse by the monthly frequency of reporting and the limited extent of reporting to the centre.

Interestingly enough, such an irrational approach to internal control was adopted because of being relatively simple to implement, with no need for investment in real-time systems. At the same time, it maintains the principle of a decentralised style of management. But it does not allow for close monitoring of assumed risks; and it does not enable the dynamic allocation of risk capital, and liquidity resources.

Moreover, by dismantling the prudent controls put in place by the Roosevelt Administration at national level, US politicians helped the bankers with a big appetite for risk (section 6) to super-leverage the system. Phil Gramm, a senator from Texas, sponsored, and Bill Clinton signed, the repeal of the Glass-Steagall Act, which had separated investment and retail banking since 1933. That was the outcome of intense lobbying, hailed by the pros as "the right step towards modernising a system which had outgrown its past confines." Unfortunately, no attempt was made to modernise the system of supervision at the same time.

Critics had plenty of reasons when they pointed to the risks involved in the repeal of Glass-Steagall, particularly as deregulation continued by leaps and bounds while regulation did not evolve to address the so-called shadow banking system.[41] Also very light in regulation were the new instruments modern banking brought along such as collateralised debt obligations (CDOs) and credit-default swaps (CDSs, Chapter 2).[42]

---

[41] Chorafas, *Financial Boom and Gloom*.

[42] Made by hedge funds, private equity funds, investment banks and other high stakes players.

As an after-effect, not only have the risks taken by the markets significantly increased, but bankers and their supervisors have been caught unaware as exposure assumed with the new instruments is also poorly understood. People paid to watch over the health of the banking system were not particularly bothered by the fact that many of the activities in the shadow banking system were outside the realm of regulations. This is, for instance, the case with hedge funds, private equity funds, and non-bank banks like GE Capital.

At the same time, investment banks and money market funds that are theoretically regulated (albeit in a light way) managed to practically escape all meaningful regulatory controls. Attempts to supervise finance to make it safer have faltered. The end result of paying no attention to all these shortcomings is that a fragile structure open to frequent and dangerous distortions was produced.

People who care about the financial system's survival suggest that plenty of issues have to be brought back to the drawing board. Any new design must account for the likelihood that clever financial people will work around the rules. Most evidently, proactive regulation's goal is not to banish novelty in finance but to create a system that supports economic growth through a mix of:

- State-imposed stability,

- Private initiative, carefully watched to weed-out excesses, and

- The modelling of phenomena that exhibit an alteration of behaviour from normal risk distribution to sudden spikes, then back to normal.

The requirements posed by the third bullet go straight to the heart of the need for using QED, while taken together these three bullets suggest the need for QCD. Quantum logic accounts for the fact that some particles in physics are produced with negative probabilities, and others with probability greater than one. This is important because it also happens with some risk events in finance.

In addition, in both physics and finance, if any of the crucial predictions are wrong there is nowhere to hide. Predictions made on the basis of the old risk management art are frequently wrong, because we live at an infection point in the global economy – which impacts upon research and analysis and the results they are producing. As David Reshef noted in his 2009 thesis at MIT: "Today's data deluge, together with novel statistical tools, makes truly agnostic science a realistic possibility; consequently we must consider a shift in paradigm from hypothesis-driven science to hypothesis-generation science."[43]

* * *

The complexity of modern financial exposures was further increased by the fact that starting in 2008 central banks, too, developed a risk appetite. On the heels of the 27 May 2009 warning by professor John Taylor of Stanford University (to which reference was made in the Introduction) came the alarm bell rung by Angela Merkel, the German chancellor. On 2 June 2009 in a speech about economic policy she formally attacked the central banks – saying that the US Federal Reserve, the Bank of England and the European Central Bank should all retreat on their recent unconventional ways of propping up economies.

Addressing a conference in Berlin, Merkel pointed out that the Fed and the Bank of England were not only adopting loose monetary policies but also constantly expanding their remits. Her words were: "I am very sceptical about the extent of the Fed's powers and the way the Bank of England has its own little line in Europe,"[44] adding that these

---

[43] Hence, deduction. David Reshef, 'VizuaLyzer: An Approach for Rapid Visualization and Analysis of Epidemiological Data', MIT, 2009. Reshef received one of the Chorafas Foundation's best graduate student prizes for 2009.

[44] *Financial Times*, 7 June 2009.

policies "must be reversed," and that the ECB should not be "bowing to international pressure" because of a plan to buy €60 billion ($85 billion) in covered bonds.[45]

Several economists agree with Merkel and Taylor, as they think that the cost of these policies may well prove to be too high and unaffordable. While the tail risk of a new Great Depression seems to have for the moment abated, the risk of a Japan-style 'lost two decades' has not receded. On both sides of the Atlantic, the aggressive central bank response to the post-Lehman crisis is starting to show new dangers, and this is making the implementation of a powerful risk measurement model like QED most urgent.

Even Ben Bernanke, the architect of the disastrous monetary policy of central bank super-leveraging, started to get cold feet. In his early June 2009 deposition to the US Congress he urged the lawmakers to address America's $2 trillion budget deficit, warning that the government could not borrow "indefinitely". The Federal Reserve's chairman said markets were starting to take note of the outlook for America's fiscal position[46] – and, no doubt, of his own disastrous monetary 'policies' as well.

6. Risk appetite

Not long ago James Tobin (1918-2002), a Nobel laureate, also expressed his concern that in the modern financial system there was no balance between risk appetite and risk control:

> I [suspect] we are throwing more and more of our resources
> into financial activities remote from the production of

---

[45] The Bundesbank opposed the covered bond purchase by ECB, but loose canons seem to have prevailed.

[46] *The Economist*, 6 June 2009.

goods and services, into activities that generate high private rewards disproportionate to their social productivity. I suspect that the immense power of the computer is being harnessed to this 'paper economy', not to do the same transactions more economically but to balloon the quantity and variety of exchanges.[47]

This suggests that the risk appetite of the few has been given free reign at the expense of the many. This is bad for the economy because the generally accepted meaning of the term risk appetite is willingness of bankers, traders, speculators and investors to bear a growing amount of financial risk, with the expectation of more and more potential personal profit. They do so by capitalising on:

- Rises and declines in market liquidity and funding liquidity (Chapter 2).

- Changes in asset prices created by leveraged economic events.

- A variety of different risk premiums which, as a rule, prove inadequate to cover the losses.

Risk appetite increases in so-called 'good times' as investor confidence rises, general market sentiment improves, and risk premiums shrink significantly, leading to easy but risky deals which involve a lighter and lighter response to assumed exposure – or no response at all. The opposite of risk appetite is risk aversion.

Risk aversion appears in so-called 'bad times', after one is licking wounds caused by risk appetite. It brings back prudence to the way of dealing, making investors attentive to the subjective attitude of the market towards uncertainty, along with a change in preferences and

---

[47] *The Economist*, 24 January 2008.

weights in terms of risk and return. Risk aversion depends not only on the degree to which investors dislike uncertainty but also on the overall level of uncertainty about fundamental factors which drive asset prices and increase or reduce the availability of credit.

In the background of increasingly optimistic expectations by bankers, traders, investors and other financial agents is found ample liquidity in financial markets; a low interest rate environment; relatively high levels of capitalisation; relaxed and therefore inaccurate pricing practices (Chapter 3); a growing reliance on 'easy profit' business segments, such as proprietary trading; and intensified competition for optimistic announcements on a firm's performance.

When this happens, regulators start being concerned that the financial industry may become more vulnerable to unanticipated future developments. The way to bet with risk appetite on the rise is that there will soon be evidence of aggressive pricing of credit risk in bonds and (especially) in the syndicated loan markets, with observed yields substantially lower than the levels likely to prevail on the basis of their historical relationship with implied volatility and the level of interest rates.

In this environment, speculation is likely to rise. Speculators buy and sell instruments, for instance futures contracts, with the expectation of profiting from changes in the price of the underlying commodity. For this strategy to be profitable, the future price that a speculator pays now will have to match the speculator's expectations. If he is wrong and, say, gold prices do not rise but fall, he will be a loser.[48]

---

[48] Even if the price does not change he will be a loser because of the carrying cost of the futures contract and margin requirements.

While futures and other derivative instruments (Chapter 2) look like an easy, low-cost and leveraged way to make bets on future prices of various commodities, these are by no means sure bets. Another source of greater risk taking is increasing exposure to proprietary trading. Hedge funds are main players in this line of activity, drawing in the banks as lenders and as brokers. Many banks with risk appetite have also invested significant amounts of their own money in the hedge fund industry.

Though the measurement of risk appetite and of risk aversion is by no means an exact science, attempts have been made to put together some meaningful criteria. A rather popular group of risk appetite indicators is that of market-based, but largely theoretical, measures constructed by means of simple statistical approaches which aggregate information extracted from market prices.

Sometimes supplemented by qualitative criteria connected to market sentiment, this rather quantitative group of risk appetite metrics is typically based on implied volatility (section 2) as well as spreads of different asset classes broken down by financial instrument and geographical region. The group of risk appetite and risk aversion metrics typically includes:

- CBOE's volatility index (VIX),

- JP Morgan's risk tolerance indices,

- UBS' FX risk index,

- Westpac's risk appetite index,

- Dresdner Kleinwort's aggregate risk perception index,

- The late Lehman Brothers' market risk sentiment index,

- Merrill Lynch's risk aversion indicator, and

- Bank of America's risk appetite monitor.

Another group of indicators is known under the general label 'model-based measures'. Their particular characteristic is that they employ a financial or economic model applied to a single financial market. Included in this group are:

- The Bank of England index,
- State Street investor confidence index,
- Goldman Sachs risk aversion index,
- Credit Suisse global risk appetite index, and
- Tarashev, Tsatsaronis and Karampatos risk appetite index.

Having been constructed using different approaches and rather heterogeneous criteria, all of these indices measure partly the same and partly different aspects of bankers' and investors' risk appetite. Therefore (apart from an overall trend) their outputs cannot be compared among themselves in a meaningful manner. Moreover, as Figure 1.4 shows, the majority of these indices share a common fault. This is that they measure risk appetite based on expected returns, which may run high at the left leg of the risk distribution, but they take the risks themselves as being normally distributed, which does not correspond at all to the amount of assumed exposure.

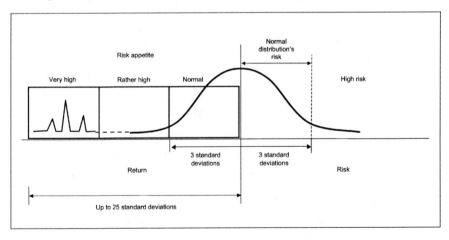

Figure 1.4: Risk appetite at the long leg of the distribution.

On one hand, the existence of more than a dozen risk appetite and risk aversion metrics suggests that this kind of measurement is gaining momentum. But on the other, the devastating results of an asymmetric approach to risk and return have been demonstrated in 2007-2009 as banking and the economy were hit by a horde of problems in a short space of time. Important adjustments are therefore due, to correct the impression that risk appetite indices are weak and spinning.

7. Black swans

Section 1 defined the concept underpinning *risk* in reference to a situation, position, or decision involving possible loss or danger which is apt to be substantial. The reader's attention has been brought to the fact that risk events are uncertain in their nature, in the sense that they *do not* have a well-defined or sure outcome. Quite often, they are also vague in their definition because of involving one or more *unknowns* which may themselves be *known unknowns,* or outright unknown (*unknown unknowns*).

The currency markets, where there are few safe bets, provide an example of the former. Back in January 2008, the US dollar was weak against the euro and clear-eyed analysts offered the opinion that, by all likelihood, the next victim would be sterling, because the British economy was afflicted with even larger financial imbalances than the American. In eastern Europe, high-growth economies had huge current account deficits, and therefore they also looked vulnerable on the currency front; while Asian currencies were strengthening.

Traders and investors who bet on that hypothesis of future trends made profits, as this is precisely what happened to the British pound and east European currencies, including the Russian ruble. By contrast, a year later in January 2009 the yen, Swiss franc and US dollar strengthened versus the euro; and the yen also strengthened, quite significantly, against the dollar. This was a case of betting on known unknowns, essentially an *objective uncertainty* which could be quantified and modelled through QED.

Known unknowns are classically confronted by determination of the amount of capital needed to cover credit risks in the body of the distribution; astute allocation of risk capital to individual risk classes, depending on requirements resulting from business strategy and profit objectives; establishment of overall limits and of limits per risk and by counterparty; as well as targets for return on risk capital and other measures.

Many financial risks, however, involve unknown unknowns. The term stands for *subjective uncertainty* about which one has a mainly qualitative feeling of uneasiness – the QCD stuff. When he was Secretary of Defense, Donald Rumsfeld made this distinction between *known unknowns*, defining them as those things that we know we do not know but try to guess, and *unknown unknowns*. The latter are the things we do not know that we do not know; they are plausible, and often present, but their exact nature, let alone impact and frequency of appearance, escapes us. This distinction aptly expresses the deep differences which exist between:

- Known risks such as currency gyrations and expected default frequency, and

- Unknown risks due to high leverage, novelty in instrument design, and new markets' behaviour where uncertainty is king.

In financial markets, unknown unknowns have been called *black swans* – a term adapted by economists to mean seemingly inconceivable events that occur only very occasionally. These are nevertheless real happenings. Sometimes they are lionised because their exact nature, timing, and magnitude of aftermath escape us until we feel their after-effects.

To a substantial extent, financial markets face not so much *black swans*, but the more classical *white swans* that start coming along a great deal more often than expected and, because of their number, bring to bear vicious risks with unexpected consequences. Neither is it true that black swans are very rare birds (even if this is what the majority of economists are led to believe), though until the last moment they may be hidden from general view.

Anyone who has been to the southern end of New Zealand's beautiful south island knows that there are swarms of black swans hidden in small lake fjords, and the traveller comes unexpectedly upon them by driving around. This finds its parallel in the policy of those investors, traders and bank CEOs who make it their policy to navigate in the uncharted waters of credit derivatives and other highly risky instruments (and vehicles), devised to explore the long leg of the risk distribution. They fail to appreciate that in the background of unknown unknowns may be not only unexpected events but also (and mainly) correlations of events, which end by bursting a bubble at a time nobody expected this to happen.

For instance, there exists a vicious correlation between rising levels of unpayable debt; spikes in prices which become a steady trend due to speculation (like the barrel of oil at $145 in 2008); and a variety of macroeconomic factors. There may also be correlations created by the after-effect of wars; big political plots that turn on their head; major natural and man-made disasters affecting insurance coverage on a global scale, and more.

The concept of known unknowns underpins the methodology advanced by the Basel Committee on Banking Supervision and by national regulators. But this is not an approach which will allow the authorities to be in charge in the case of black swans. By contrast *quantum logic* might allow this, provided that we do the proper research and we are able to make far-reaching assumptions. These assumptions can be made in spite of the fact that these assumptions are by majority subjective, and the aftermath of these assumptions is typically measured after the fact, which involves a significant degree of uncertainty when the assumptions are made.

The answer to the challenge posed by black swans lies in testing at the long leg of the risk distribution: 10, 20, 30 standard deviations from the mean (section 3) – always remembering that the economic and banking crisis of 2008 saw 25 standard deviation events. In addition, the mission of looking at the long tail must include the fact that *risk characteristics* can change rapidly as reactions by market players induce feedback effects, involve correlation, and lead to system-wide interactions.

Hidden correlations of events tend to dramatically amplify initial shocks, leading to extreme reactions which have so far been given little or no weight in models – particularly those relying mainly on historical data. The management of well-governed banks should therefore question the limitations of traditional risk models and their outcomes, even if these have been approved by regulators.

At the same time, great attention must be put on qualitative expertise through ad-hoc stress scenarios, and on strong linkages to something that should have sudden absence of market liquidity while funding pressures increase. This is the advice given in a recent document by the Basel Committee, which further suggested that:

> Prior to the crisis, most banks did not perform stress tests that took a comprehensive firm-wide perspective across risks and different books. Even if they did, the stress tests were insufficient in identifying and aggregating risks. As a result, banks did not have a comprehensive view across credit, market and liquidity risks of their various businesses.[49]

This is accurate, provided the word "stress" is deleted. True enough, prior to the 2007-2009 economic and banking crisis these were stress tests. Today, at the time of black swans, tests based on the hypothesis of normal distribution of risk events – albeit at 10, 20, and 30 standard deviations from the mean – can no longer be considered as stress tests. They should be normal everyday tests at the long tail of the risk distribution, where the big exposures hide.

---

[49] Basel Committee on Banking Supervision, 'Principles for Sound Stress-testing Practices and Supervision', BIS, Basel, 2008.

According to Steve Schwarzman, the CEO of Blackstone, 40% of the world's wealth has been destroyed in just five quarters (the fourth of 2007 and year 2008). Schwarzman says that to regenerate the financial system again will require an unprecedented amount of capital – hence his proposal to reduce capital requirements for banks (which was voted down by the large majority of participants to the panel[50] of the 2009 World Economic Forum, in Davos, Switzerland.)

In conclusion, capital requirements must be raised and bank regulation greatly strengthened. But also the methods and tools to be used should be much more powerful than those available at present. That's the "10X" factor to which Andy Grove, Intel's former CEO makes a great deal of references in his book *Only the Paranoid Survive*.[51]

Appendix: VIX, the measurement of volatility

1. The underlying concept

The concept of modelling market volatility, and its dynamics through financial time series, dates back several decades and has gained importance rather gradually. Much of the interest in volatility modelling lies in the fact that when it is calculated in a practical manner volatility is a key driver of risk embedded in a portfolio, at least as far as known unknowns are concerned. VIX, the CBOE volatility index, is driven by the perception of risk and prevailing market uncertainty.

Based on options prices, hence on perceived future behaviour of the S&P 500 index, VIX's domain is equities not commodities. It is a

---

[50] Organised by CNBC.

[51] Andrew S. Grove, *Only the Paranoid Survive*, Currency Doubleday, New York, 1996.

measurement sensitive to prevailing liquidity and it addresses the longer run. There are, however, a couple of exceptions to this statement. VIX impacts on gold prices (less so on silver). In addition, the rise and fall of VIX might impact on oil prices, though this is not a strong correlation.

Studies conducted in the 2004 to 2009 time frame have documented the relationship between equity class performance and the volatility index, enhancing the status of VIX and making it a popular modelling tool. A low VIX shows low concern about future volatility; hence, a hefty appetite for risk. But at the same time, appetite for risk tends to revert to the mean over time and this *might* indicate that low volatility is due for a correction (a hypothesis not always proven by the facts).

A low volatility index is generally welcomed by investors because it helps to measure how much traders will pay to insure against future volatility in the S&P 500, from movements in options prices. For example, on 25 January 2007, just a semester prior to the beginning of the deep economic and banking crisis, VIX dropped to 9.89. Its previous low was 9.90, set in November 2006.

By contrast, VIX has been as high as 45, during the Long-Term Capital Management (LTCM) crisis in September 1998, and in the course of the build-up to the invasion of Iraq in 2003. In the May 2006 brief but deep market sell-off it reached only 24; but a year and a half later, in December 2008, it rose to more than 80, and then it fell back to between 40 and 50.[52]

---

[52] During the Russian meltdown of August 1998, VIX hit 60.

Some upwards swings in VIX can be particularly unsettling. According to Goldman Sachs, the 27 February 2009 jump in the VIX took it eight standard deviations from its average. The move in energy prices that caused the collapse of Amaranth, the hedge fund, in 2008, was a nine standard deviations event. If conventional models are correct such events should not have happened in the history of the known universe. Hence, the conclusion is that conventional wisdom can be awfully wrong or, alternatively, as a volatility measurement VIX is imperfect.

A more likely explanation is that while the computation of VIX is objective, the interpretation of its meaning may be subjective. Here is a quotation from an analyst's projection on 2004: "We saw violent swings in investor sentiment which is why low-quality stocks did so well. We went from extreme 'risk aversion' at the start of the Iraq war to significant appetite for risk. We saw the VIX measure of equity volatility practically halve over the year. We saw US high yield spreads practically halve too. We saw investors go from 'above normal' cash levels to 'normal' cash levels, as equities went from 'undervalued' back to 'fair value'."[53] As is to be expected, other analysts came up with other interpretations.

2. The behaviour of VIX

To better understand why VIX surged with the crisis of 2007-2009, the reader needs to know how it is calculated. As a metric, it is derived from the world of options. If we reverse engineer an option price based on the time value of money, the residual factor is *implied volatility* (section 2), which means uncertainty applying to the asset. VIX gives this figure for the S&P 500 index.

---

[53] Merrill Lynch, '2004: The Year Ahead', January 2004.

1. When the markets are calm, the number of people and companies who sell options increases, driving down their prices, and with this the level of implied volatility.

A continuous low volatility, however, is not positive. If it goes on over an extended period of time, it can cause concern for regulators because it encourages investors to downplay the eventual reappearance of high volatility, and makes them underestimate the risks of possible valuation corrections.

2. When the markets go into a tailspin, volatility surges and it becomes much more likely that those who had bought options would exercise them and those who sold options would not cover their losses with the premium they earned.

At the same time, a level of volatility that mirrors the fundamentals is a hallmark of efficient financial markets. Its pattern tends to reflect the intensity of change in underlying market factors, including those relating to exposure. It also helps in assessment of uncertainty as to future developments. In this sense volatility's role is polyvalent, but it is not that easy to uncover volatility's secrets. Nor has there been factual and documented evidence that if volatility keeps within certain values, then all is well in the market.

There is nothing more than a common belief that volatility outside what might be characterised as 'normal limits' – which are arbitrarily set at the 20 to 30 range – creates stress conditions in financial markets. This is described as pressure exerted on economic players by uncertainty and changing expectations concerning losses. Fundamentally, however, the level of financial market stress ultimately depends on the degree of the financial system's vulnerability, and the scale of the shock producing uncertainty regarding future losses, along with a change in risk appetite.

This being said, the ups and downs of the volatility index, hence the behaviour of VIX, help in many other ways than just measuring the cost of buying and selling options. The higher the index, the more investors are willing to pay to insure themselves against big market moves – which is a different way of saying that VIX acts as indicator of *implied volatility*, by reflecting a market estimate based on the weighted average of volatilities for a wider range of strikes.

For instance, information elements on the behaviour of VIX and interest rates are grouped in quartspaces such as: VIX up and rates down, VIX up and rates up, VIX down and rates up, VIX down and rates down; with empirical criteria often used for evaluating obtained results. A combination of falling long-term interest rates and rising VIX levels has historically generated both the worst absolute returns, and the best relative returns for the financial industry.

Combined with stress-testing, VIX can provide a research capability for exploring the limits of risk distribution. Several major institutions which adopted Basel II's AIRB capital adequacy model have been conducting stress tests under different volatility estimates. Asked whether its analysts use the VIX index for volatility tests, the executive of one of the independent rating agencies said: "We look at assumptions and we challenge the results. We don't prescribe an index. But historical VIX values can be of interest in backtesting."

The same rating agency executive added that when he looks at risks embedded in different portfolios, it is difficult to evaluate the underlying model(s). Only with post-mortems is it possible to tell the level of dependability, and that's where the use of VIX can be valuable as a standard volatility index. An even stronger statement can be made regarding the VIX testing in conjunction to the implementation of quantum logic.

Chapter 2: Virtual Economy and Risk Management

1. Real and virtual economy

Edmund Phelps, who won a Nobel prize for economics in 2006, is one of the experts highly critical of present-day risk management practices in financial services. In his opinion: "Risk-assessment and risk-management models were never well founded. There was a mystique to the idea that market participants knew the price to put on this or that risk."[54]

Phelps has aptly added that it is impossible to imagine that a complex modern financial system could be understood in the required detail and with assumed correctness through today's methods and tools. The requirements for information, he says, "have gone beyond our abilities to gather it" – and, it could be added, to analyse what we gather in a way that we can obtain a firm basis for risk pricing, appreciable insight in terms of exposure, and meaningful results pointing to corrective action.

As the complexity of the financial instruments continued to increase, the legacy tools and methods have been unstuck from business reality. Those we have been using during the last three decades were largely developed for a predominantly *physical economy*, not for the *virtual economy* and its agents which are characterised by 'other times, other customs'.

The virtual economy is not only one of novelty in banking and finance but, also, of greater uncertainty than ever. "Watch out for the binary word," said a study released at end of March 2009 by one of the better known European banks.

---

[54] *The Economist*, 24 January 2009.

This research paper advised that by end of 2010 the prices of the following commodities could be at either extreme:

- Gold (then at $940/ounce) at $300 or $2000

- Oil (then at $50/barrel) at $25 or $100

- S&P 500 Index (then at 820) at 400 or 1400

- US 10-year Treasury yield (then 2.70%) at 1% or 5%

- Euro/dollar exchange rate (then 1.35) at 0.90 or between 1.80 and 2.00

It needs no explaining that these wide swings for financial assets make the investor's positioning a tough job. Even the experts are at a loss because they have been trained to deal with largely real, not wholly virtual, assets. Financial assets – particularly derivative instruments – are wholly virtual by definition.

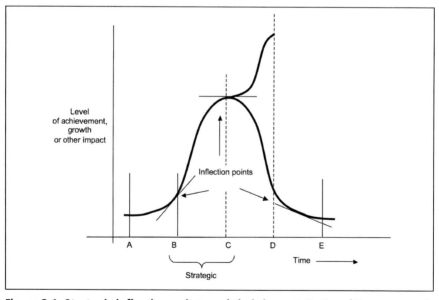

Figure 2.1: Strategic inflection points and their impact. B, C and E are strategic inflection points and D might well become one. The bifurcation in C may be towards growth or decay; it is not yet known whether it is a strategic inflection point.

Most of the old rules are upset because the change from the real economy to the virtual economy was a major *strategic inflection point*.

The term stands for a time in the life of a society, an economy, a company or a person when its fundamentals are changing or about to change. Figure 2.1 presents the pattern in a nutshell.

The impact of a wholesome change can be deadly if its management is not attended to, because strategic inflection points can turn the balance either way. They provide the opportunity to break out of the status quo, and thrust into a higher level of achievement; as with the trajectory C to D in Figure 2.1. Or they lead towards decay because of inertia, lack of leadership, and failure to adapt; as with the C to E trajectory in the same figure.

The latter is precisely what has happened to several economies and many financial institutions (as well as to people) in the course of their transition from the real economy to the virtual economy. The politicians, businessmen and other practitioners of the old art were caught unawares and they got their countries, their companies and themselves in trouble.

In an article published in the *Financial Times* on 25 February 2009, Martin Wolf had good advice for US president Barack Obama and other heads of government participating in the G-20 London meeting. According to Wolf, Obama should have said:

> My fellow leaders. Let me get a big point out of the way: yes, the US has made mistakes. We thought we knew about sophisticated modern finance. We were wrong. On behalf of my country, I apologise. We must learn the lesson and look ahead, not backwards.

Ironically, the more successful a society, economy, company or person was in the old structure and environment, the more threatened they will be by the change, as well as by a slow pace of conversion and reluctance to adapt to the new conditions. This is the so-called *inertia of success*. In addition, very few people understand that leading an organisation through a strategic inflection point is like taking it through uncharted territory, and therefore they should expect the unexpected (see Chapter 1 on the long tail of the risk distribution).

Matters are more challenging because unlike real assets – for instance land, houses, factories, machines – virtual ones do not behave by stereotypes. We know that they exist, and modern accounting rules try to track them, but they may be off balance sheet and they are not subject to depreciation, amortisation or other classical accounting practices. To have an idea about their current value we have to mark them to market, while also keeping in mind that virtual assets are *leveraged* and often overleveraged (Chapter 7). Also, their *fair value*[55] is subject to greater volatility than that of real assets.

Procedures and models currently used for the pricing of financial instruments, and for risk control reasons, do not account for fair value volatility; neither do they reflect the fact that the amount of exposure may increase exponentially with overleveraging and/or depending on the market's mood. These are significant failures in fair value judgments, which should not be allowed to persist. The wealth of financial assets is fragile because they are only a claim on goods and services, and they can be easily manipulated in terms of risk and return.

As the 2007-2009 deep economic and banking crisis has shown, if the value of virtual assets rises a lot faster than gross domestic product (GDP), then either investors expect the GDP to rise substantially or, alternatively, they are willing to pay for grossly overvalued assets. The latter practice, which became quite common in good times, unravels very fast in bad times, turning prices and valuations on their head. Between 2002 and 2007, for example, the US GDP increased by 35%, or 7% per year. Over that same period, American banks' earnings expanded by 200% or 40% per year.

---

[55] Fair value is the price a willing buyer will pay a willing vendor, under other than fire sale conditions.

Then came market judgment time. In 2008 the share prices of wounded banks lost some 95% of their value, and to salvage the economy, through overt and covert action, the American government is in the process of spending more than 150% of GDP.

Measuring, confronting and managing the risks associated with virtual assets requires a great deal of awareness regarding their origin, design, correlations, risk factors, intended market, gearing, concentration and limits which may be reached or exceeded. Moreover because virtual assets (like debt securities) are easily structured, sold, bought and again restructured and resold (section 4), risk measurement and control must be both focused by instrument and entity, and at the same time be systemic and global. This is a formidable task, like hitting two birds with one well-aimed stone.

The power of implementing a tested holistic model like quantum electrodynamics in risk management is that it brings uniformity to the measurement, evolution and control of risk factors' behaviour. We learn how to use quantum theory with one type of risk, and we may practically know how to apply it with nearly all others. That is the beauty of quantum logic. As Victor Hugo once remarked: "You can resist an invading army; you cannot resist an idea whose time has come." This is the case with the sophisticated instruments of QED and of QCD. (See also in the appendix to Chapter 5 the basic notions underpinning them.)

2. Market liquidity and funding liquidity

For a variety of reasons, the virtual economy is more exposed to *liquidity risk* than the real economy has been. A company may be solvent but lack the liquidity to meet its obligations when due – either because of management incompetence, inept cash flow projections, too many exposures, high gearing, a major adversity, or market turmoil which shuts down the pipeline of credit.

The notion underpinning liquidity risk is not new, but in the virtual economy its amplitude and magnitude have changed. Few CEOs and boards of directors have adjusted their managerial policies and practices to this fact, with the result that their businesses may be adversely impacted by their inability to borrow funds or sell assets to meet maturing obligations.

Theoretically, banks manage liquidity risk by maintaining sufficient financial resources to fund their balance sheet. Practically, liquidity needs are met primarily through cash flow (Chapter 7) generated by operations (including deposits), or they are answered by bought money – a challenging proposition when the inter-bank market dries up.

Liquidity risks can be magnified by management's lack of attention to maturities and by failing to prognosticate credit squeezes which usually generate and/or increase liquidity risk. The ability to sell assets may be impaired if other market participants are seeking to sell similar assets at the same time, driving down prices.

This is exacerbated with derivative financial instruments (see the appendix to this chapter) because they soak up liquidity like blotting paper. Country risk or regulatory capital restrictions imposed on the free flows of funds in the global market also work against liquidity.

Other risk factors affecting the bank's liquidity position are: a dramatic increase in client lending; lowering of credit standards; market-making activities (which may reduce liquid resources); structured instruments (with short term and long term imbalances, section 4), and nervous markets.

Downgrades of the bank's credit rating increase its borrowing costs and limit its access to the capital markets. This and other risk factors can have secondary effects. During the financial market turbulence of 2007-2009, for example, banks were faced with a simultaneous disruption of important funding markets. In particular these were the:

- Unsecured inter-bank market,

- Securitisation market,

- Repossession market, and

- Currency swap market.

The result was that all sorts of financial institutions had difficulty accessing longer-term funding. Several banks suffered from the gravity, extent and direction of market disturbances. Even some of the better managed had not included market liquidity disruption in their liquidity risk scenarios. In fact, there are not one, but two, liquidity vulnerabilities:

1. Market liquidity, and

2. Funding liquidity.

Market liquidity includes two main notions: exogenous and endogenous. *Exogenous liquidity* is independent of the bank's actions, relating to the ability to execute a trade order at little or no cost. Such liquidity depends on frequency and size of trades, number of traders in the market, specific market type and cost of transacting. For instance, though perfect liquidity is never attained, the foreign exchange market or a major stock market is normally highly liquid.

Endogenous liquidity relates to the fact that valuation losses may arise due to a large sale of assets. Such risk is mainly driven by the size of the position and liquidation price. If the order to buy or sell is smaller than the volume available in the market at the quote, then the order transacts at or about the quote. If the order exceeds the quote depth, then the bid/ask margin widens and that spread is the endogenous liquidity risk.

Endogenous liquidity risks have added to the after-effects of the 2007-2009 crisis, as banks mistrusted one another and had virtually no information on their counterparties' exposure to subprimes and other toxic instruments. Alternatively their technology did not allow them to know precisely the cash outflows they themselves would face in future. There were also second-round effects leading to an increase in the correlation between the inter-bank and credit markets.

As contrasted to market liquidity, *funding liquidity* is the ability to settle obligations immediately when due. By definition, a bank is illiquid if it is unable to settle its obligations on time over the planning horizon of its operations. The associated funding liquidity risk can take on infinitely different values. In addition, in absolute terms funding liquidity is a yes/no concept, but *funding liquidity risk* is forward-looking within a given horizon.

In the case of the 2007-2009 debacle, off-balance-sheet obligations resulting from transactions in structured products have been the subject of severe funding liquidity risk, including liquidity facilities banks had extended to conduits and structured investment vehicles (SIVs).[56] A surprisingly large number of well-known institutions had not adequately reflected this in their liquidity risk tests, let alone in the pricing of their products (Chapter 3).

Commercial banks, investment banks and financial conglomerates, at large, ran into immense liquidity problems due to poor decisions over the years preceding the crisis. Further liquidity problems arose from the requirements made on banks as an after-effect of credit rating downgrades.

As for hedge funds, their liquidity was hit by redemptions. At its peak in 2007 the hedge fund industry had approached $2 trillion under management, but with the severe banking and economic crisis investors wanted their money back. In December 2008 alone they pulled close to a net $150 billion from hedge funds, in spite of moves by dozens of them to halt or suspend redemptions.[57] To meet investors' demands hedge funds had to sell their most liquid assets, usually equities.[58] They

---

[56] Chorafas, *Financial Boom and Gloom.*

[57] Citadel, Drake, GLG, Farallon, Highbridge, Tremont and Tudor Investments are among the hedge funds and funds of funds that have halted, restricted and suspended redemptions up to the end of 2008. Redemptions aside, on average hedge funds lost roughly 22% of their worth in 2008.

[58] A couple of hedge funds, like Ariel, have been forced to liquidate because of losses incurred through Bernard Madoff's Ponzi game (Chapter 6).

were doing so regardless of which were the best investments, because market liquidity and funding liquidity were so scarce.

Port-mortem it was established that neither in the banking industry nor in other branches of financial services – such as insurance, pension funds, and hedge funds – did liquidity risk tests take into account stress conditions and associated restrictions; nor spill-over effects. Lessons learned on liquidity management suggest that:

- Liquidity dries up completely without advance notice, at the moment when market operations need it most,

- Liquidity risk assumptions which may be valid under normal market conditions can break down under stress, and

- The market's global dimensions are no saviour as challenges emerge all over the place, including cross-border liquidity transfers.

Banks should therefore analyse all liquidity risk factors that arose and are likely to arise under stressed situations. They should also experiment on the interdependency of credit and market risk events, the complexities associated with credit enhancements, adversity in liquidity provision, as well as interaction between exogenous/endogenous market liquidity and funding liquidity.

Quantum logic may well prove to be best tool in helping management understand the depth and extent of possible ramifications of loss of liquidity. But, though necessary, the analytics are not enough. The results must be visualised in a comprehensible way, which follows a pattern. The best quality control charts are discussed in section 5 (briefly introduced in Chapter 1).[59]

---

[59] For a detailed discussion on the implementation of SQC by variables and by attributes in finance, particularly in connection to management control, see D. N. Chorafas, *Reliable Financial Reporting and Internal Control: A Global Implementation Guide*, John Wiley, New York, 2000.

3. CDOs, CDSs and systemic risk

When asked focused questions, few banks bothered to explain how they descended to the abyss by warehousing lots of novel financial instruments whose risks they had not comprehended. Others did publish some accounts, but they largely read like papers in which theorists focused only on a couple of problems they could handle, while failing to elaborate on the after-effect of complex instruments on:

- Market illiquidity,

- Funding illiquidity,

- Company insolvency,

- Effects of high volatility,

- Long tail risks, and

- Other of the virtual economy's deep challenges.

In the first months of the economic and banking crisis of 2007-2009, little was divulged about the fact that not only *collateralised debt obligations* (CDOs) but also *credit default swaps* (CDSs)[60] had been in the eye of the storm. Both are sophisticated derivative financial instruments, theoretically designed for credit risk transfer (CRT), which was generally expected to improve risk management. Practically, however, both CDSs and CDOs had been used in ever greater amounts for leveraging credit.

Textbooks (and traders) say that collateralised debt obligations enable credit institutions and other market participants to readily transfer significant amounts of credit risk to banks, insurance companies and investors willing and able to accept these leveraged transactions. Theoretically, CDOs aim to create value by attracting liquidity towards credit risk in asset classes that, on their own, would be too illiquid or

---

[60] CDSs got the spotlight in late 2008 and in 2009 as the rate of defaults hit a record.

too complex for some investors to consider. However, unlike traditional securitisation the number of assets backing a CDO tends to be rather low, and these assets are often highly heterogeneous, with concentrations of exposure to individual obligors.

Practically, therefore, it is very difficult for both insurers and investors to ascertain (let alone be in charge of) the risk of CDOs, as they need to consider not only the credit risk of individual assets but also correlations between them. This sees to it that a great deal depends on rating agencies assigning a credit score to the different tranches of a CDO, but as the 2007-2009 experience demonstrated these are unreliable, with AAA ratings given to what were no better than the level of junk bonds.

A snapshot of CDO securitisations is given in Figure 2.2. A bank originates, warehouses and administers mortgages – to be used in mortgage-backed securities (MBSs); credit card receivables, auto loans and other assets – for making asset backed securities (ABSs); as well as business loans pools and other debt instruments.

- An investment bank will securitise and distribute these longer-term assets through a securitisation vehicle.

- A rating agency will rate the creditworthiness of the securitisation tranches, and

- A conduit, typically belonging to the investment bank, will provide short-term liquidity using short-term commercial paper.

Once the CDOs move through the transmission lines, they will be warehoused and resecuritised by other investment banks – then resold. Banks originating CDO transactions often use credit derivatives to transfer the credit risk of the underlying pool of assets. This process is known as *synthetic securitisation*. In theory the transaction is flexible in terms of asset mix, as well as in its risk and return characteristics. In practice, investors are poorly placed to choose tailor-made CDOs because the instruments are so complex.

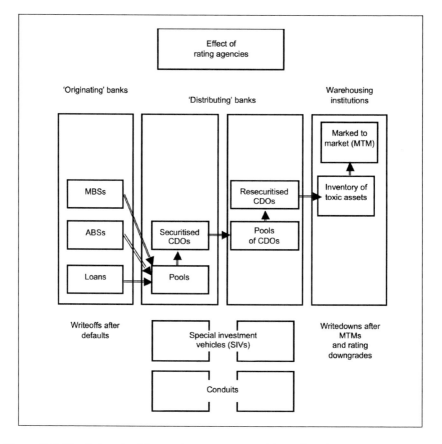

Figure 2.2: The interminable motion money machine of toxic waste.

The assets underlying a CDO remain on the balance sheet of the originating bank, while a structured investment vehicle (SIV) is constructed to hold a pool of credit default swaps (CDSs, see below) that reference the assets. These CDSs generate a premium payment from the originator to the SIV, but in the event that any of the underlying assets default the SIV is responsible for the losses.

Credit default swaps (CDSs) are bilateral financial contracts intended to insure against the possibility of loans, bonds and other debt instruments going into default. The credit default swap is a derivative instrument under which, for a fee, the protection seller agrees to make a payment to the protection buyer in the event that the referenced entity (typically a company or other issuer of a debt product) experiences a credit event like bankruptcy or reorganisation. If the issuer of the bond defaults then the swap (hence the protection seller) provides recovery for that loss to the owner of that bond.

Theoretically, the price of the CDS captures the perceived risk of such a possibility occurring. Practically, this is far from being sure, not only because of the instrument's complexity, but also because of the fact that this is an unregulated market of very large size, which was a major factor in increasing risk throughout the entire financial system.[61] A problem with CDOs and CDSs is that their engineering has reached such heights of complexity that neither the banks themselves nor the regulators can truly calculate the risks associated with them.

Regulators relied on the risk management models of the financial institutions themselves, credit rating companies followed a similar path in rating structured financial products, and the models which have been used were not able to capture the complexities of the instruments' personalised evolution, and their impact on a bank's solvency.

One of the attractions of CDOs and CDSs is that they require no capital reserves from banks because of the way in which they are structured, the practice of carrying them off balance sheet (OBS) through special vehicles and the fact that CDSs mimic insurance policies. These reasons plus easy profits saw to it that since its inception the CDS market for credit default swaps has experienced extraordinary levels of growth, as Figure 2.3 shows. The present and latent systemic risk also skyrocketed.

---

[61] AIG, until September 2008 the world's largest insurance company, lost a fortune selling CDS insurance and has been bailed out by the US Treasury at huge cost.

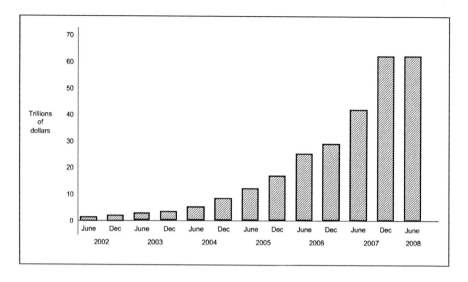

Figure 2.3: Notional principal amount outstanding in the global credit default swaps market over the 2002 to 2008 time frame.

Another attraction of credit default swaps is that their spreads provide a measure of an entity's creditworthiness. Since the financial crisis started, the CDS spreads of many financial institutions have widened significantly, suggesting that banks' default risk has increased. (Practical examples with CDS spreads are given in Chapter 3, section 2).

To gain greater visibility on a counterparty's credit risk, some institutions decompose CDS spreads into:

- An expected-loss component, and

- A default risk premium which reflects the compensation required by investors for accepting exposure to default risk.

An interesting application of this notion is the *joint probabilities of default* (JPDs) for big global banks, computed to capture financial market stress. Current research indicates that CDS-JPDs can offer real-time information on changes in individual banks' default probabilities for which CDSs exist, even if credit spreads may be biased upwards in periods of market upheaval. To progress from individual bank PDs to CDS-JPDs, researchers look at the banking system as a portfolio of banks using as inputs:

- A non-parametric approach, and

- The individual banks CDS-JPDs.

The use of arrows of the QED methodology, explained in Chapter 5, may provide a technical improvement. According to a study by the European Central Bank (ECB) it is possible to derive a measure for banking system stability from joint probability of default estimate (but research is still in progress on this).

Known as *banking system stability index* (BSI), this represents the expected number of bank defaults in the portfolio of banks, if at least one bank defaults. As ECB's *Financial Stability Review* notes, the advantage of the BSI is that it transfers the movements in the JPD to an ordinal measure that is comparable across different sub-samples, avoiding the bias of a larger sample which generally decreases the probability of default.[62]

4. Structured finance is different to classical banking

The virtual economy promoted the market for structured finance. This has opened new markets but also brought up new risks, such as propagating the subprime shocks across broader credit channels and business segments. Post-mortem analysis made by some financial institutions identified three top reasons underpinning the 2007-2009 market turmoil:

1. Loss of confidence in the valuation of complex structured instruments like CDSs and CDOs (section 3).

2. Increase in uncertainty among investors about the adequacy of credit ratings by independent agencies.

---

[62] European Central Bank, *Financial Stability Review*, December 2008.

3. Weaknesses of the originate-to-distribute banking model; for instance the transfer of credit risk led to inadequate assessment and pricing.

As lack of confidence in securitised and resecuritised mortgages, loans and other assets built up, it triggered a sell-off followed by a steady drop in prices of structured financial products. Banks which held such securities were forced into sizeable writedowns. Additionally, links to third parties in the valuation of structured instruments (such as financial guarantors) were found to be inadequate or outright superficial. This further added oil to the fire of a deteriorating credit quality with the result that low credit quality spread from subprime mortgages all the way across the financial system, and, confronted with uncertainty about the value of their own assets and those of their counterparties, banks significantly tightened their lending.

Busy with rebuilding their wounded balance sheets, even those American and British banks which benefited from billions of pounds or dollars of capital injections of taxpayer money have been reluctant to lend. British government plans to break the vicious non-lending cycle by asking banks to pay a premium, for the government insuring their lending, never got off the ground. Instead, banks hoarded more capital, anticipating that a deepening recession would slash asset values further, and that the fair value of derivative instruments they inventoried would be reduced still more.

One of the issues which has not been given enough attention is that very few banks have the staff and flexibility to cope with the restructuring of complex financial instruments. An example is collateralised loan obligations (CLOs) which have an oversized presence and influence in the leveraged loan market.

During 2008 and early 2009, increasing numbers of CLOs failed the tests which relate to the proportion of their loans rated CCC, the number of which has been rising rapidly for most deals. As the economic outlook deteriorated, many highly leveraged companies struggled and tried to loosen the covenants of their borrowing. In turn, such moves presented upfront costs to lenders and called for restructuring at a time when CLO managers had lost up to 70% of their fees and cut staff.

The situation also deteriorated in risk management terms as banks, service companies, and SIVs had big exposures to the same large deals – so that when a borrower hit trouble, the fallout had broader impact. The growing number of defaults sent some vehicles from being comfortable to breaching tests in a matter of weeks. The deterioration in loan portfolios reduced some institutions to near-insolvency; they did not collapse, but hung around with meagre resources.

Computational challenges increased as default risk exposure varies by type of derivative, and it can also occur for the full notional amount of trades where a final exchange of principal takes place. (This may, for instance, be the case for currency swaps.)

Swap agreements and forward contracts are generally OTC-transacted and hence exposed to default risk to the extent of their replacement cost. This much wider range of exposure needs to be compared to futures contracts which are exchange-traded and usually require daily cash settlement, with related risk of loss generally limited to a one-day net positive change in market value.[63]

Confronted with the fact that the OTC-traded $62 trillion credit default swaps market has escaped their control, governments and supervisory authorities have tried, post-mortem, to tackle operational inefficiencies, and bring in some sort of regulation where so far practically none existed. There have also been ideas circulating that dealers in credit derivatives should be urged to tear up some of the

---

[63] Option contracts can be exchange traded or OTC. Purchased options have default risk to the extent of their replacement cost. Written options represent a potential obligation to counterparties conditioned by market risk.

outstanding trades that can pose a potential risk to the financial system. Such belated awareness of the huge dangers associated with the growing mountain of CDSs and other toxic waste heightened market concern about covert counterparty risk and created new worries about the ability of protection providers to face the after-effect of a tsunami in bankruptcies.

Optimists talked of certain estimates which suggested that thousands of trades offset each other, and could be torn up on either a bilateral or multilateral basis. On 16 June 2008, the chief executive of the International Securities Dealers Association (ISDA) said that such elimination or portfolio compression was part of "new housekeeping", but failed to explain who would be paying the costs associated with contract cancellations. A downside in the tear-off process is that most CDSs are custom-made, introvert, and rarely traded.

While a properly endowed clearing house could be instrumental in improving accountability for trading activity in regard to new contracts, it would have little effect for the $62 trillion (in notional principal amounts) already warehoused. Potential dangers associated with such illiquid positions are present and real, but examples which have been published in the financial media about portfolio compression are elementary.

Offsetting CDSs makes sense in the case of (and indeed it might have been a reason for) the bargain basement purchase of Bear Stearns by JP Morgan Chase in March 2008. By becoming the owner of Bear's CDSs, JP Morgan management was within its rights to tear up offsetting contracts in its own portfolio and in that of the bought entity. Things are far from being linear, however, when two financial institutions are or remain independent of one another.

In conclusion, experts have been right to suggest that until all of the complex structured products can be valued in a way that carries conviction when estimating the worth of portfolios of banks – and therefore the survivability of the institutions themselves – predicting the financial industry's future is a hazardous process at best. The only thing that can be said with reasonable assurance is that much more capital will be needed to recapitalise the big banks than was originally thought.

5. Advanced statistical methods and tolerances in the virtual economy

Financial institutions have always been in the business of taking risk, but because both the ways and magnitude of their bets have radically changed they can no longer continue to watch over risk through legacy approaches. Since structured finance is quite different from the classical process of intermediation in banking, and given that it continues to increase its weight in present-day transactions, we have to revamp our methods and tools so that they can confront the new environment.

The more complex the instruments in which we deal, and the wider the expansion of the virtual economy, the greater the attention that we need to pay to the methods and tools which we choose. Another requirement is that new methods and tools must be characterised by overall simplicity – so that their principles, workings and results are understood by everybody who deals with them. This has weighed on the choice of quantum logic for risk pricing and risk control, but not to the exclusion of other time-tested approaches. Advanced statistical methods, for example, have been successfully employed in product and process control, as well as effective visualisation of process behaviour.

The purpose of this and of the following sections is to bring to the reader's attention the fact that while the use of QED and QCD for the control of high level risks (as this book proposes) is a novel idea with great potential, there also exist advanced statistical tools which were actually used during WWII – assuring the quality of weapons systems and their components – and which have been employed in risk screening and risk pricing.

RAROC is a good example. It stands for *Risk Adjusted Return on Capital*, and was developed as a financial application in the mid-1980s by Carmine Vona, for Bankers Trust. At the heart of this process-control model is an operating characteristics (OC) curve (more on this in section 6), which assists the loans officer in making objective, well-documented decisions about a client's creditworthiness. RAROC provides a firm basis for *risk pricing*, and it can be seen as the first product of high technology used by banks for that specific purpose.

The careful reader is by now acquainted with the fact that with structured products, and generally with derivative instruments, risk pricing is more complex than with the classical product line of business and personal loans. RAROC was an 'out of the box' idea which put technology at the service of loans officers and loans committees.

The fact to take notice of is that after 25 years of successful uninterrupted use of advanced statistical constructs, such as RAROC and other expert systems and agents[64], there exists plenty of evidence that technology can be a major contributor to financial engineering. It is indeed regretful that more use has not been made of high-tech means of controlling the risk of structured products.

Most people agree with the concept that, whether in the real or in the virtual economy, true product and process quality is inseparable from right pricing, and this demands a total commitment that begins at the very top of the organisation – but they are at a loss when it comes to choosing a method. Experience in engineering teaches that product quality, process quality and the control of risk correlate; and advanced statistical analysis provides a good method.

But there are prerequisites. If the CEO and the board are committed to risk management, and if executive promotions are tied to it, then this could become a priority and it would seep down to the middle and lower organisation levels – thus inevitably to all employees.

---

[64] D. N. Chorafas and Heinrich Steinmann, *Expert Systems in Banking*, Macmillan, London, 1991 and Chorafas, 'Rocket Scientists in Banking'.

By contrast, if a financial institution treats the quality of its products and the control of risk as an afterthought, then risk pricing will never take hold. When this happens, novel complex instruments, like structured products, have free reign to bring the institution down – as the cases of AIG, Bear Stearns, Lehman Brothers, Royal Bank of Scotland, Fortis, IKB, HypoBank and so many others document.

A beautiful tool for measurement and management of risk over a period of time is statistical quality control (SQC), which has its origins in the seminal work of Walter Shewhart.[65] In the background of its implementation lies the fact that the value of decisions about risk and return is greatly enhanced when there is appropriate evidence of variations in targeted risk factors. Variation is inevitable, but when an exposure stays inside acceptable specifications this means that the system is in control.

SQC tracks variation tick-by-tick and visualises the resulting pattern. This solves a basic problem of any pricing process (and of any quality control process as well) – that of determining whether variation is normal; that is, kept within pre-established tolerances. Nobody walks on a straight line, but excessive variation is disruptive. The statistical tools for solving this type of problem are based on three fundamentals:

1.   Chance causes of variation exist in any process, product, transaction or account.

2.   Measured quality is always subject to variation as a result of chance causes, hence the definition of acceptable limits.

---

[65] The concept of using mathematical statistics for quality control purposes was introduced in 1924 when Dr W. A. Shewhart (who often published under the pseudonym Student) wrote a memorandum on techniques for obtaining better homogeneity of products. This memorandum resulted in the control chart which, in 1929, was enriched by sampling tables, published by Dr Harry Roming and Harold Dodge, based on the normal distribution.

3.   Variation outside a stable pattern indicates a change in the product, process, system (or one of their key risk factors), which must be discovered and corrected.

The role played by sampling plans, frequency distributions, control charts and statistical evaluation techniques is to target the pattern of chance variation, as well as deviations from a wanted pattern. Accounting systems do something similar, but in a different way, in a different time frame and for a different purpose. Hence the wisdom of using sophisticated statistical analysis for process control.

The tool for determining the pattern of variation for a given variable as a result of the system of chance causes is the frequency distribution (see section 6). More specifically, this is the normal frequency distribution of risk of which we spoke in Chapter 1. The spread of a frequency distribution must be less than the total tolerance allowed by the specifications. If this is not true, then there exists a certain percentage of failures in terms of observing established tolerances.

Tolerance limits are set at the time of product or process design. Over time, *confidence limits* are multiples of the standard deviation defined by the object's behaviour – whether in a manufacturing plant or in the market.

Both tolerance limits and confidence limits are very important decision elements because, in conjunction, they tell us whether the product, process or system is or is not in control. Structural financial products are no exception to this rule, except that their developers don't bother to establish tolerances. Yet many economists, bankers, and other financial experts talk of the 'banking industry'. And an industry, whose products have no tolerances, can run wild – the way banking did with the economy in 2007.

6. A bird's-eye view of charts for quality assurance and risk control

Classically, the use of statistics in connection to financial information tends towards the hypothesis that many, though not all, frequency distributions in banking approximate the normal curve. Chapter 1 brought to the reader's attention that the normal distribution's popularity rests on the fact that the theory underpinning it proved to be of significant practical value, particularly because of the existence of rich statistical tables. In fact, we should neither accept wholeheartedly nor reject outright the hypothesis of the normal distribution. We will accept or reject this hypothesis only after we test the population (or sample) of data we work with.

If the hypothesis of a normal frequency distribution is accepted, then the bell-shaped curve presents an excellent opportunity for understanding the basic theory underlying statistical quality control. If not, then we supplement SQC with confidence intervals at the level of 'four 9s' (99.99% – or as a minimum 'three 9s' (99.9%)). We do not have confidence levels at 99%, as with VaR (Chapter 4), because this leaves 1% of all cases out of the study.

Precisely because the normal distribution does not apply to all situations, even with advanced statistics our work is based on approximations. We also know that while we use nonlinear models for financial analysis these too are only approximations of real life since many situations are non-linear. The reason why we do so is that financial rocket science is still in its infancy, but, at the same time, it helps to have an explanatory scenario which assists in providing material for causal analysis (Chapter 4).

Typically, the *description* model includes primary measurements, tabular and graphic presentation of facts and assessment of collective characteristics. The *explanation*, which we make, targets the specification of causal hypotheses and their testing against empirical data, which permits us to draw some meaningful but temporary conclusions (see the appendix to Chapter 5).

Our statistical research is done by in-depth analysis of samples[66] taken out of a homogenous population or, alternatively, samples taken to test the *null hypothesis* of whether the samples on which we work come from the same population (essentially meaning that the population in which we are interested is homogeneous). Typically, sampling plans are classified by:

- Sample size,

- A measure of the amount of inspection required, and

- Acceptable quality level (AQL) of the population (or sample).

The latter is the percentage of defects conditioning the probability of accepting a given level of significance (or confidence).

The Risk Adjusted Return on Capital (RAROC, section 5) is based on a sequential sampling plan of creditworthiness. Scoring substitutes for percentage defective. A prime rate corresponds to the best score. Every successive column in Figure 2.4 has a lower score but a higher interest rate. To the bank, this interest rate differential provides a sort of reinsurance policy. This is an example of quality control *by attributes*:

- 'Go' versus 'no go'.

- 'High score' versus 'non-high score' (all the way to the 20 credit rating scores by independent rating agencies).

There are two types of statistical quality control charts by attributes, *c charts* for defects per unit; and *p charts* for percentage defective. Both serve the process of inspection – whether we talk of assumed risk or of quality levels. The *c chart* can have, to my judgment, a wide area of

---

[66] Nearly eight decades of SQC practice in the manufacturing industry document that the best way to thoroughly identify, measure and study quality changes is through sampling. With destructive testing sampling is, for evident reasons, a must.

application in banking because the number of exposures embedded in a structured product, or other derivative instrument, has direct bearing on risk pricing and repricing due to changes in risk quotient.

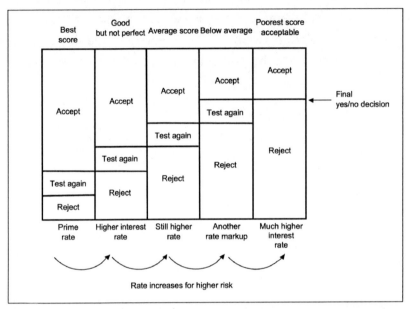

Figure 2.4: A sequential sampling plan permits avoidance of inflexible yes/no answers to a request for loans, taking a reinsurance for higher credit risk.

Statistical sampling procedures are characterised by the rules that must be followed. Such rules contribute to the effectiveness of the controls. For every sampling plan there is an *operating characteristics* (OC) curve, which shows how the plan will perform as lots of different quality levels are submitted to it. The shape of an OC curve is a function of both sample size and percentage of the population. The OC curve visualises the likelihood that a lot of a given level of attributes, percentage defective, or assumed risk may be rejected while, overall, it is of acceptable quality.

This is shown in Figure 2.5, and the corresponding statistical measure is known as α, Type I error, or producer's risk. For instance, α tells *the* level of significance in VaR (Chapter 4) and other tests by presenting the likelihood of such a happening: rejecting what should have been accepted – therefore the confidence attached to test results.

There also exists a probability that a *lot*[67] under statistical inspection may be accepted as satisfactory, while it should have been rejected. This likelihood is known as β, Type II error, or consumer's risk. As we will see in Chapter 4, there are many reasons why VaR is half-baked. The absence of β is one of them. (The β in Figure 2.5 should not be confused with β indicating volatility (Chapter 1), though both volatility and Type II error are conditioned by the standard deviation of the normal distribution.)

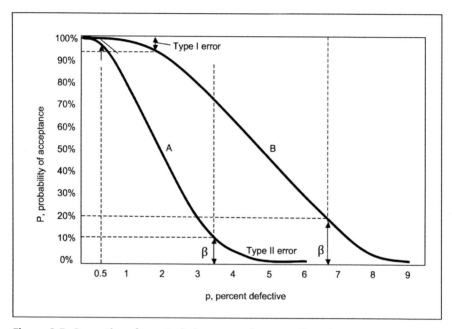

Figure 2.5: Operating characteristics curves for sampling plans.

The message the reader should retain from this discussion is that whether our tests and statistical charts target risks of financial instruments or quality of production, our aim is to provide ourselves with assurance that we deal with fairly uniform items, which abide by

---

[67] In statistics, the word lot denotes a group of items, usually homogenous ones. This term is mostly used in manufacturing, while in finance we talk of a pool of loans.

specifications and tolerances. No two items – rivets, vehicles, loans, people – are exactly the same.

In a similar manner, risk and quality are characterised by significant differences in what superficially looks like being the same products, processes or systems. That's how life works in the real and in the virtual economy and, therefore, being in charge means recognising the existence of such variability, measuring deviations and setting and observing limits.

The sharper the OC curve (the less inclined), the more dependable are the results we obtain. In Figure 2.5, curve A is better than curve B. There are statistical means for decreasing the variance which flattens the OC curve. If N stands for population size, and n for sample size, it is possible to reduce the variance by:

- Decreasing N, while holding n constant,

- Increasing n, while holding N constant,

- Increasing n and N, while holding constant the ratio n/N

In general, the effect of varying the sample size n is more important than the effect of varying N in terms of α and β. The reader should appreciate that Type I and Type II errors exist and they will not disappear, but a higher level of confidence is always welcome and it can be attained.

Statistical quality inspection and its associated accept/reject procedure is based on a pattern of variation inherent to the process we are studying, and hope to keep under control. Attributes, however, are not the only way to proceed. The pattern of change within this process, which is visualised through charting, may be established by *variables* as shown in Figure 2.6. The graph is based on:

- $\bar{\bar{x}}$; the mean of sample means, and

- $\bar{R}$; the mean of sample ranges.

In the upper half of Figure 2.6, the $\bar{\bar{x}}$ chart has both *tolerance* and *quality control* limits with the latter position inside the former. There are also upper and lower limits in this chart. By contrast, in the bottom of Figure 2.6 the $\overline{R}$ chart has no lower control limit because the minimum value a range may have is zero.

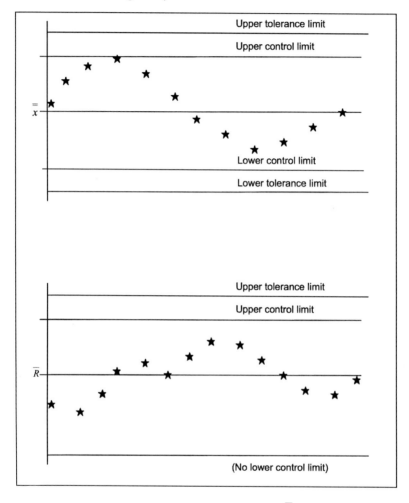

Figure 2.6: Control charts by variables for mean of means $\overline{\overline{x}}$ and mean of ranges $\overline{R}$.

Control charts by variables are based on the rule that variation that is under control will follow a stable pattern as long as the system of chance causes remains the same, which is by no means a foregone conclusion. Once a stable system of chance causes is established, the quality control limits for the resulting pattern of variation can be determined and, using SQC, carefully watched.

Causality may see to it that future data points $(\bar{\bar{x}}, \bar{R})$ might fall outside the upper and lower control limits. Alternatively, at the origin of breaking the limits may not be causality but a change in the population. With financial products and processes, new risk factors might have shown up, making the original pricing algorithm invalid. Based on SQC evidence, a thorough analysis will unearth the reason(s). In principle, the opportunities for risk getting out of control are nearly infinite. This is true even if the probability of major change happening at any point in time might seem to be rather small or fairly constant.

The methods brought to the reader's attention in this section are well established, but poorly used or even alien to many financial institutions. This is unfortunate, because they provide an excellent means to learn and control the pattern of risk by product, process, banking entity and the people working for it.

There is also a powerful 20th century method for enterprise management: Six Sigma. It has been successfully used by JP Morgan and Chase Manhattan (before and after their merger), GE Capital, the engineering operations of General Electric, Motorola (which developed it) and other well-known companies.

The tools available in Six Sigma's arsenal in attacking quality and cost control issues include the aforementioned statistical process control, process mapping, tree diagrams, defect measurements, chi-square tests, experimental design, root cause analysis and Pareto diagrams.

In terms of methodology, GE's keywords in implementing Six Sigma have been:

- Define
- Measure
- Analyse
- Improve
- Control

These are also the keywords of any serious risk pricing and risk management effort. Though the concept of the normal distribution underpins Six Sigma (and SQC), as Figure 2.7 shows its implementation aims to trim the long leg of the risk distribution. Its target is the distance observed between the variability of production and specifications established at the drafting stage. Six Sigma should have been used in the control of risk with structured products, but it was not.

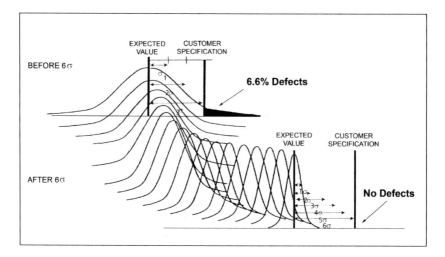

Figure 2.7: Three standard deviations usually fit between quality control targets and customer specifications. But this is not always enough.[68]

---

[68] Included with the permission of General Electric.

7. Know yourself and your institution

In his famous book *The Art of War*, Sun Tzu, the Chinese general and statesman of 500 BC, gives this advice: "If you know yourself and know your enemy, you must not be afraid of the outcome of 1000 battles," adding that "I would surely choose (as assistant) a person who examines an obstacle with prudence." Prerequisites to prudence are analysis, experimentation, prognostication and planning. The methods and tools sections 5 and 6 brought to the reader's attention are of great value in this process.

"All my life I've gone through anticipating trouble," said Charlie Munger in his Commencement address at the University of Southern California Law School, on 13 May 2007. He added "Here I am, going along in my 84th year and, like Epictetus, I've had a favoured life. It didn't make me unhappy to anticipate trouble all the time and be ready to perform adequately if trouble came. It didn't hurt me at all. In fact it helped me." These are words of wisdom from an experienced and successful investor.[69]

Munger has probably learned from Sun Tzu. It is said that Mao, too, had learned a great deal from the policy of the famous Chinese general who would not spend time studying the successful military engagements. What interested him was his analysis of failures. Distilling from these teachings, Mao Tse Tung wrote that it is important to know the situation not only before but also after having established a plan.[70] Had the czars of the financial industry done so, the world economy would not have been brought to its knees in 2007-2009.

---

[69] Charles Munger is Warren Buffett's partner in managing Berkshire Hathaway, now 86 years old (at the time of writing in 2009).

[70] Indeed it is said that Mao's *Little Red Book* essentially paraphrased, or rather unsubtly plagiarised, Sun Tzu's work.

From personal experience, I can confirm that Sun Tzu's ideas in *The Art of War* provide valuable insights for gaining leadership in risk management. If you know yourself, your bank, its board, its CEO and its professionals; the instruments which it uses, its counterparties, and markets to which it appeals; as well as your bank's exposure and financial staying power; that is, if you soundly comprehend all the broad factors and actors in play; then you don't have to worry about the outcome of a 1000 risks. And taking a leaf out of Sun Tzu's book, the most successful people in any job always *accept* and *analyse* their failures, and learn from what went wrong.

Statistical quality control charts are very helpful in learning from past failures. They make walking backwards through time possible, because they map the effects of one's past decisions and moves, help in rethinking one's policies and tactics and assist in developing alternative scenarios (Chapter 4), before starting again with renewed vigour and conviction. Successful people and companies don't shy away from challenges, but they are distinguished by their ability to see further out and anticipate the unexpected by learning from the past.

This is the soul of first class risk management practice, as contrasted with a policy characterised by hiding the facts via lack of transparency and a plethora of false statements. Another valuable concept underpinning the right approach to the control of exposure is that in finance, as in science and in life at large, there exists a chain of events which the SQC carefully registers.

Patterns are revealing. Tracking the exposure assumed with the 'investment of the moment' can be instrumental in learning the risk profile of the investor and of his or her banker. Today, the investments of the moment are complex derivatives (sections 3 and 4); but as the 19th century turned into the 20th century it was Trusts. At the time, Andrew Carnegie signalled his opinion in an article he penned for the *Century Magazine*. He stated that that the Trusts were nothing other than the panacea of the moment, and he envisioned a line of dead Trusts like the ghosts of Macbeth's victims, only much longer.

As a clear thinker and master of risk management, Andrew Carnegie believed all businessmen would eventually profit by spirited competition and the policy of being in charge; but they would lose by falling for the "panacea of the moment." To be ahead of the curve, he capitalised on his ability to make instantaneous decisions, which gave him an advantage over competitors. A believer in the survival of the fittest, Carnegie saw this competition as a contest between fabricators of steel and fabricators of securities, makers of billets and makers of bonds.[71]

More recently, in a shareholder meeting, Warren Buffett expressed his and his company's ability to hold the line as follows: "Well, we do have filters. And sometimes those filters are very irritating to people who check in with us about businesses – because we really can say 'No' in ten seconds or so to 90% of all of the things that come along, simply because we have these filters."

Filtering out and saying 'No!' to business opportunities presented on account of their purposely beefed-up returns and downsized risks, is the key to success. This is not a matter of always being negative. True intelligence – and good business sense – are demonstrated in the skills and guts one has in evaluating things and in rejecting them. This has two prerequisites:

1. Learning from past mistakes, and

2. Dealing only with things one understands.

Finance allows the creation of vast enterprises out of the combined capital of millions of people, supplied at modest cost. It permits entrepreneurs to launch new companies, challenging the power of incumbents. But like anything else that goes wild, runaway finance becomes a destructive force. This is an ethical and political issue, not just one of economics.

---

[71] Peter Krass, *Carnegie*, Wiley, New York, 2002.

Neither are unconventional measures – which are invented as required by governments and central banks – the solution. But they may be part of the problem. "The Fed's move to zero interest rates leaves experts blind, and complicates Bernanke's job," said one of the experts interviewed by Bloomberg financial network on 28 January 2009.

Instead of salvage at any cost, at a cost indeed of trillions of dollars to the taxpayer, what the banking industry needs is a restructured risk management system which has its origin in lessons learned from the recent huge credit and banking crisis. Redressing a bad situation also requires the authority of the state as guarantor of good behaviour – in a way similar to the case where the authority of the state assures its debt notes (the legal tender) will be paid at a rate which is not unfavourable to the holder. At a basic level, this is the goal of risk pricing.

Appendix: derivative financial instruments

Derivatives are the instruments of the virtual economy. In the late 1980s, the Financial Accounting Standards Board (FASB), an agency of the Securities and Exchange Commission (SEC), outlined 14 distinct classes which among themselves constituted the derivative financial instruments available at the time. These definitions were specific, but they soon became obsolete because the world of derivatives underwent dramatic changes. Products once considered exotic became commonplace and new products were rapidly developed. Novelty in product design promoted a rapid increase in trading and this became a major competitive advantage for banks that were ahead of the crowd. (And just for the record, after the 2007-2009 debacle derivatives have been redefined by critics as, more simply, complex financial instruments that can damage your wealth.)

As innovation in the derivatives market went ahead by leaps and bounds, in 1998 FASB took account of the evidence that previous distinctions among the different types of contracts became blurred. Statement of Financial Accounting Standards 133 (SFAS 133) defined derivatives as financial instruments with the following characteristics:

- They have one or more *underlying*, one or more *notional principal amounts*[72], or both.

- Usually, they require no initial net investment, and when this is needed it is smaller than that needed with other instruments.

- They demand or permit net settlements, or provide for delivery of an asset that practically puts the buyer in a net settlement position.

The International Financial Reporting Standards (IFRS) by London-based International Accounting Standards Board (IASB) defines a *derivative* in slightly different terms, looking at it as a financial instrument whose value changes in response to change in the price of an underlying. As with FASB's definition, the latter may be an interest rate, commodity, security price or index.

The IASB definition also specifies that a derivative typically requires no initial investment, or one that is smaller than would be needed for a classical contract with similar response to changes in market factors. In addition, part of the IASB definition is that the derivatives contract is settled at a future date.

The definitions by FASB and IASB converge on the fact that derivative contracts give rise to a financial asset of one entity and a financial liability at the counterparty in the transaction. But contrary to assets and liabilities of the *real economy* which are written, respectively, at

---

[72] A term borrowed from swaps, the notional principal amount is a contractual reference value which (with few exceptions) is not paid to either counterparty but serves for calculation of what is due according to the specific contract.

the left and right side of the balance sheet and stay there[73], the instruments of the *virtual economy* move frequently from left to right (and vice versa) as their market value changes at a moment's notice. The most popular derivatives fall into two classes:

1. Interest rate products,

2. Currency exchange products.

Interest rate products include, but are not limited to, forward rate agreements (FRAs); interest rate swaps (IRSs); caps, floors, and collars; eurodollar futures; Treasury bills (T-bills) and T-bond futures; options on eurodollars; and options on T-bills and T-bonds. Typical currency products are futures, forwards, swaps, options (defined in the following paragraphs), and options on futures.

Interest rates, currencies, and equities are traded in spot positions and forwards; also as options. Examples include foreign exchange forward transactions, forward legs of foreign exchange swaps, and other currency instruments involving an exchange of one currency for another at a future date.

Originally invented by Thales, an *option* is an agreement between a buyer and a seller that, when exercised, gives the former the right (but not the obligation) to require the option writer (seller) to perform certain specific financial duties like purchasing or selling a stated quantity and quality of the underlying commodity (or asset), at an agreed upon price (strike price).

With a *call* option, if the buyer (holder) exercises his rights, he pays the strike price and receives delivery of the commodity. With a *put* option he delivers the commodity and receives the price agreed to, when the contract is first entered into.

---

[73] The way defined by Luca Pacciolo in his seminal work of 1495, which constitutes the basis of modern accounting.

Futures are current commitments that are exercised, as their name implies, in the future. They are traded in exchanges. *Forwards* are like futures but they are not traded in exchanges. They are essentially customised bilateral agreements traded over the counter (OTC) and they have no active market.[74]

A standard *swap* involves period receipt of a predetermined fixed amount, and corresponding period payment of the spot value of a unit of the reference asset. Swaps usually involve two parties that enter into an agreement that, for a certain period, they will exchange regular payments; for instance, swapping floating-rate interest for fixed rate interest. The popularity of swaps, forwards, futures, options and other derivatives derives from two facts:

1. They are flexible instruments.

2. They can be highly leveraged.

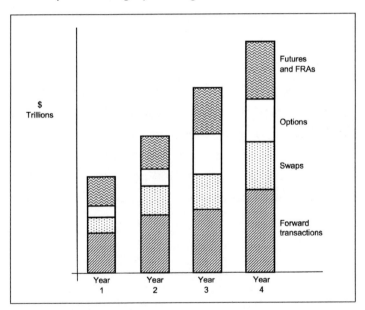

Figure 2.8: Annual increase in notional amounts of derivative instruments, at a major bank.

---

[74] An over-the-counter trade is off-exchange, bank-to-bank and can be seen as part of business contracted by entities in the shadow banking system. Roughly 80% of the deals concerning derivative instruments mentioned in the preceding paragraphs are traded OTC.

Year-on-year the volume and value of derivatives trades continues to increase, the latter at an average rate of about 30%. This is shown in Figure 2.8, based on four years of statistics by a major bank. Accounting rules see to it that derivative financial instruments must be accounted for and revalued on an item-by-item basis. Gains and losses arising from marking to market or marking to model[75] must be recognised, and treated in the income statement in a manner similar to the more classical on-balance sheet instruments.

Derivative contracts in the trading book classified as trading assets arise from proprietary trading activity and from customer-based activity. Changes in realised and unrealised gains and losses, and interest flows, are included in *trading revenues*. The fair value of exchange-traded derivatives is typically derived from observable market prices and/or observable market parameters. Fair values for OTC derivatives are determined on the basis of internally developed proprietary models using various input parameters.

Good governance requires that where the input parameters cannot be validated using observable market data, reserves are established, amortised to income over the life of the instrument, or released into income when observable market data becomes available. This, however, is not a universal practice, and there exist many ways for regulatory arbitrage to take place. It should be remembered that derivative financial instruments are a game of risk, and no policy or model can eliminate this. It is he who limits the risk by controlling its magnitude that wins.

---

[75] As already mentioned, treated over the counter, many derivative instruments don't have an active market. On the other hand, pricing models are not known to be accurate (more on this in Chapter 3).

Derivatives are useful instruments and they are indivisible from the virtual economy in which we live. These is nothing wrong with derivatives *per se*. Rather it is the excesses associated with their use, and the bank-to-bank derivatives trading and warehousing which, when done without commercial foundation[76], creates the Mount Everest of risk whose conquest requires the use of powerful methods like quantum logic.

---

[76] Which is the case with up to 95% of all OTC deals.

Chapter 3: Product Pricing in the Virtual Economy

1. Why the old pricing theory does not apply

Econometrics finds its origins in the seminal work of Vilfredo Pareto and Léon Walras in the late 19th century. Pricing theory is a relatively newer development, with Paul Samuelson and Thomas E. Copeland among its high priests.[77] Another important contribution from the 20th century comes from Irving Fisher, who in his 1911 book *The Purchasing Power of Money* formalised the quantity theory of money.

Fisher held that the supply of money times its velocity (the rate at which money circulates through the market) is equal to output multiplied by the price level. He used this algorithm to explain how changing the velocity of money's circulation affects prices, and could cause real interest rates to deviate from nominal ones.

One of the important observations credited to Irving Fisher is that monetary forces can produce booms and busts, although they do not necessarily have long-run effects on output. He also graphically demonstrated money's role in the economy by using an allegory from water storage:

> Water, moving into the pool at a certain volume per unit of time, is income. The volume of stored water, at a particular moment in the pool, is capital, and when more water runs out of the pool than comes in, capital is depleted. Eventually the pool empties.

---

[77] Paul A. Samuelson, *Economics*, McGraw-Hill, New York, 1951; Thomas E. Copeland and J. Fred Weston, *Financial Theory and Corporate Policy*, Addison-Wesley, Reading, Massachusetts, 1988; (new edition of an original Copeland book of 1946).

The pool can be filled up again through debt, but this will eventually be followed by debt inflation, which increases the public burden of leverage. Fisher described *debt deflation* as a sequence of distress-selling, falling asset prices, rising real interest rates, more distress-selling, falling velocity of the circulation of money, declining net worth and rising bankruptcies, as well as events like bank runs, curtailment of credit and dumping of assets, but also growing distrust accompanied by hoarding.

This is a fitting paradigm of the 2007-2009 economic and banking crisis, putting Fisher apart from other economists – including mathematical economists who have largely worked under the hypothesis of normal markets and willing buyers. The latter do not characterise the first decade of the 21st century, particularly after the double crash of 2000 (equity markets) and 2007 (complex financial instruments). Instead, the situation is one of:

- Exponentially rising and falling prices, all the way to the tails of the risk distribution.

- Prices of derivative financial instruments that get unstuck from those theoretically applying to their underlyings.

- Financial values behaving in ways other than those of a smooth curve, or of sideways movements.

- Change in market prices reaching 25 standard deviations, as Goldman Sachs said in 2008; characterised by sharp downs, rebounds and drawn-outs.

In addition, risk factors have multiplied and their definition has become coarse, limiting the level of accuracy in their assessment. With novel financial instruments and their behaviour scarcely understood by the majority of commercial bankers, the latter are relying on their investment bank counterparties to provide risk information – and all this is leading to inaccurate pricing. Experts suggest that in the market environment of 2008 and 2009, the sell-side had an incentive not to give the right answer. Traders had a direct interest in sustaining value volatility, and pricing volatility has been driving their profits and bonuses, as well as those of their bosses.

The after-effect has defied a comprehensive approach to risk and return in the pricing of transactions. The care needed to ensure that the calculation and inclusion of further-out risk is not superficial has not been on call. At the same time, nobody really knew how the loss of positions involving use of risk capital could or should be discounted. The more instrument novelty proceeded by leaps and bounds the less their designers, traders and supervisors were able to project the worst case probability of loss.

The pricing theory whose foundations have been laid in the years preceding and following the two world wars is at a loss when confronting the complexity embedded in structured financial products (Chapter 2). Risk management completed with obsolete approaches like value at risk (VaR, Chapter 5), is not able to capture events connected to worst case scenarios.

As the economic climate worsened, structured products have shown their capacity to wound well beyond losses typically associated with simpler instruments. In late January 2009, Regions Financial, a medium-size American regional bank, reported a record $6.2 billion quarterly loss on souring property loans. In Europe, shares in KBC, a big Belgian bank, plummeted on concerns that it would take major writedowns on corporate collateralised debt obligations (CDOs).

Even staid custody banks, which theoretically do not assume highly exposed positions, became masters in unpleasant ways to surprise. On 20 January 2009 shares in State Street, a well-known Boston bank, lost nearly 60% of their value as it announced large losses on bond investments. Rumour had it that these involved some complex products which turned into 'troubled assets'.

In research meetings I was told that many market players were disappointed because of the lack of any specifics by regulators on how to solve the troubled asset pricing problem. In their judgment this added considerable uncertainty over the ultimate losses on, and dilution potential of, assets – particularly those that were the least well understood. Supervisors, central bankers and government officials found themselves confronted with the same complexities. Therefore they could contribute precious little in confronting the aforementioned challenges.

In the second half of 2008, some economists and financial analysts expressed their disappointment at the foresight (or lack thereof) of the authorities in regard to risk pricing. This reaction intensified in November 2008 when Hank Paulson, then Treasury Secretary, abandoned his announced intention of auctioning toxic waste inventoried in the portfolios of big banks. The step backwards by the ex-CEO of Goldman Sachs led to a break between the need of banks to minimise, or at least spread out, further losses, on the one hand; and the needs of the potential buyers of distressed assets, who would like to see rock-bottom wounded asset prices before taking positions, on the other.

Copeland, Fisher, Pareto, Samuelson and Walras have not been confronted with the pricing of CDOs, CDSs and other complex derivative financial instruments (Chapter 2). By contrast, as a well-known former investment banker, Paulson should have had the experience to deal with this issue; also he should have known of people able to summon up the courage to attack the pricing problems of structured instruments.

The conclusion must be that new departures are necessary – and quantum electrodynamics may well be the best available way of providing them (Chapter 5). Everything has a price; the challenge is to find it in a reasonably accurate way and be able to adjust that fair price as events develop. Prior to discussing how risk and uncertainty can be monitored through QED, though, it is wise to examine which other methods are available for doing so.

2. Price discovery through credit spreads[78]

Risk is not properly accounted as a cost in the price of financial instruments and transactions. If this were the case, then there would not have been a swarm of firms with major financial deals confronted with extraordinary losses.

Two big name examples are General Electric and Berkshire Hathaway. Through its wholly-owned subsidiary GE Capital, General Electric relentlessly expanded its finance operations (which handled everything from credit cards to leasing and property). On 9 March 2009 GE's stock fell to $6.5 from a high of $38. The market's disapproval was also indicated by the widening of credit spreads. In September/October 2008, GE's 5-year CDS spread hit 600 basis points, then hovered between 400 and 600 bp.

This was previously unheard of for an AAA credit rated company (by late March 2009 GE lost one of its As). Even Warren Buffett's Berkshire Hathaway wrote equity derivative contracts that in 2008 created a big liability in its accounts. The after-effect of CDSs has been unforgiving also in credit terms. In November 2008 it was the turn of Berkshire's 5-year CDSs to hit 500 bp, subsequently trading in the 300 bp to 500 bp range.

As the careful reader will remember from Chapter 2, CDS-based *credit spreads* represent the premium required by the market for a given credit quality. In the first eight years of the new century Dubai was the glamour city of real estate boom, a haven of tax-free merchandising and a developing financial centre. It looked as if nothing could go wrong. Up to and including 2007 its CDS spreads were tiny[79] but in

---

[78] See also the contrarian view regarding the CDSs' credit spreads, in section 5.

[79] For 5-year contracts.

2008 they increased sharply. As Figure 3.1 shows, by 2009 Dubai's CDS spread hit 1,000 bp, then fell to 750 bp and 500 bp, as neighbouring Abu Dhabi underwrote $10 billion of its $20 billion debt.

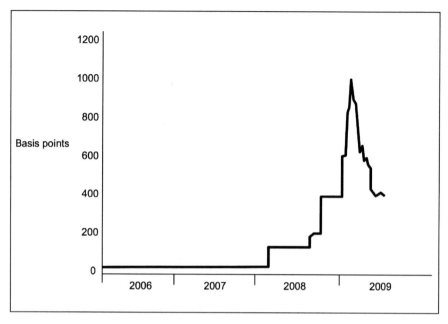

Figure 3.1: Spike in Dubai's credit default swaps (2006-2009).

This is far from being the only case where CDS spreads are used as a measure of instantaneous market response to problems of creditworthiness. A more basic example is provided by spreads on euro zone government bonds versus German bunds. In mid-February 2008 the spreads of the other euro zone sovereign bonds were between 10 and 40 basis points over bunds. A year later the spreads ranged from a high end 300 bp for Greece and 280 bp for Ireland to 150 bp for Italy and 50 bp for Belgium, with the other euro zone members falling between these two.

In the euro zone, monetary policy is established by the European Central Bank, but fiscal policies vary widely among member states, and the same is true about national debt. Governments, other than the German, have been committing themselves to high levels of public expenditure. Recently joined by Ireland, Greece and Italy have been examples of spending beyond one's means.

With the severe banking crisis, Ireland has been taking on risky assets from the financial sector while tax revenues collapse. Not only in Ireland but also in Britain and in the United States, the financial and economic crisis saw to it that sovereign and corporate debt became intermingled in late 2008 and 2009. For several governments worldwide, CDS spreads have been at levels surprisingly above CDS spreads on certain corporate names, suggesting that sovereign bonds are not necessarily a safe haven.

Sovereign issuers, whose creditworthiness has been put in doubt, have to pay the extra yield a debt instrument must offer over a credit risk-free alternative like the German bund. This is essentially the default risk premium over and beyond the expected loss component which represents the main body of the risk distribution and is reflected by the credit rating. No wonder, therefore, that there has been a notable discrepancy between credit rating and CDS implied default rates. On a 5-year time frame:

- The default rate for AAA is 0.0% and for AA also 0.0%.

- But for Spain with AAA the CDS implied default rate was 14.8%.

- For Italy with AA, 19.3%, and

- For Ireland with AA (negative outlook)[80] 31.7%.

This thesis contradicts what many people said, that the difference between default rates implied by credit rating and by CDS spreads is crazy. That is not true: ratings and CDS spreads may be quite far apart and still be valid, because the first looks at the body of the risk distribution and the second at the long tail. Hence, they are bound to be different.

---

[80] Formerly AAA.

In addition, credit ratings are a lagging indicator and, hence, rather static. By contrast, that resting on CDS spreads is dynamic and adjusted to the market's pulse tick by tick. An example is presented by US credit default swaps versus the sovereign credit quality of other countries, which provides a *relative* basis for comparison.

Figure 3.2 shows the relative CDS spreads between the United States and Russia on the 1 May 2008 to 1 February 2009 horizon. Starting in August 2008, the falling line in the chart indicates that investors expected Russia's credit quality to deteriorate relative to the credit quality of the US. A bottom was reached at end of October 2008 at 1.100 bp, as the Russian rouble went into free fall. By December 2008/January 2009 the relative credit quality had stabilised at about 700 bp – still a huge gap compared to the 100 bp that prevailed prior to May 2008.

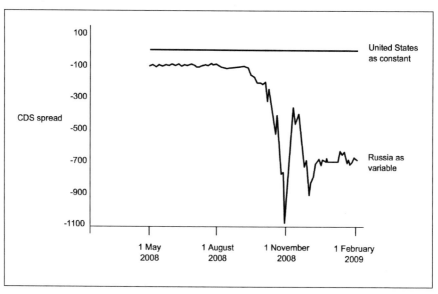

Figure 3.2: CDS spreads: United States versus Russia over a 9-month time horizon (1 May 2008 to 1 February 2009).

A wealth of pricing information can be derived by keeping tabs on CDS spreads within a group of nations, companies or other entities. A recent study by the European Central Bank further suggests that it is important to disentangle credit and liquidity risk, because this provides useful information on developments in the government bond market. The approach advanced by the ECB is to divide the risk premium into two parts:

1. One incorporating the price investors attach to risk,

2. The other related to the amount of risk *perceived* by investors.

This *perception* is influenced by a variety of factors which, while present in relatively calm markets, assume significant weight at times of high market volatility, and they can lead to large departures from fundamentals.[81] ECB's algorithm is:

```
Risk Premium = Quantum of Risk x Price of Risk
```

The principles underpinning CDS spreads also prevail in the corporate sector. Figure 3.3 presents an example with integrated oil firms over a six-month period (1 September 2008 to 27 February 2009), where credit spreads serve as an investment grade benchmark.

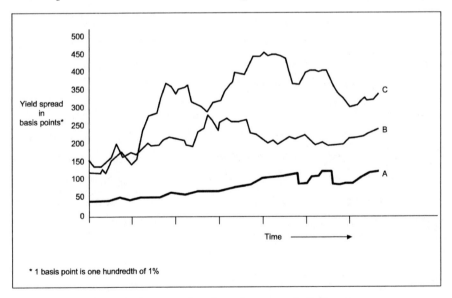

Figure 3.3: Credit default swaps for three integrated oil firms.

---

[81] European Central Bank 'Financial Integration in Europe', April 2009.

From the bunch, company C is the weakest, while company A has the best balance sheet. In the market's opinion, the financial staying power of company B falls between A and C. Notice that during the first month of the period mapped into Figure 3.3, the spreads of companies B and C were practically the same; then the spread of company C significantly weakened.

Among other basic factors, volatility (Chapter 1) has a great deal to do with *credit spread risk*, because it increases the likelihood of a financial instrument's value being affected by outliers and other plausible but low likelihood events. This is significant inasmuch as the effect of novelty in the financial markets has contributed to an increase in volatility which, in turn, affects the credit spreads.

The existence of a market-actuated price discovery mechanism for derivative products is of great value, and the development of market-based metrics is welcome, because dependable measurement and management of exposure is always important.

By addressing themselves to the tail of the risk distribution, credit spreads may permit the calculation of direction and magnitude of the QED arrows, of which we will talk about in Chapter 5, in connection with the implementation of quantum electrodynamics.

Bankers and many investors are fascinated by the possibilities created by new financial instruments, which they think offer almost limitless ways to manage risks. That's not true. In absolute terms, novel products frequently create more risks than they help to manage. But some, like CDS spreads, provide interesting risk management opportunities. (A contrarian view of CDS spreads is presented in section 4.)

3. Discounted cash flow and intrinsic value[82]

Section 2 brought to the reader's attention that the advantage of credit spreads over the more classical credit ratings is that they explore the long leg of the risk distribution. When capital adequacy evaporates, solvency is put in question and liquidity disappears (at least for certain financial instruments), banks are faced with a challenge to their survival which is exaggerated by the fact that sufficient or reliable market data are not available. This is because:

- The complexity of many novel financial products is not well understood by market participants.

- The risks associated with these instruments are most often severely underestimated, and

- In their frustration several banks switch from valuation methods based on market data to those based on models and internal inputs, without assuring the necessary evidence.[83]

Precisely because financial modelling is in its infancy and vital historical data is missing, marking to market is king (no matter what some bankers or regulators may say). But at the same time, it is wise to have alternatives. In the opinion of Alan Meltzer, professor of economics at Carnegie Mellon University, all assets warehoused by banks should be given the *discounted cash flow test*.[84] If an asset does not pass it, then that asset has no value.

---

[82] Discounted cash flow is discussed in this chapter on the supposition that the notion of cash flow is familiar to the reader. If not, please first read the cash flow section in Chapter 8 on super-leveraging.

[83] The Basel Committee on Banking Supervision makes this reference, albeit limiting it to the frequent lack of necessary historical data for modelling. 'External Audit Quality and Banking Supervision', BIS, Basel, December 2008.

[84] As stated in an interview he gave to Bloomberg financial news on 26 March 2009.

The concepts underpinning discounted cash flow and, associated with it, the intrinsic value of an asset, can be better appreciated by returning to the fundamentals: capital, interest rate and net present value (NPV). The amount of *capital* is, so to speak, a photograph of the current financial condition. It is a measure based on accounting rules and it is correct provided the books are right. Interest rates are theoretically set by the monetary authority and practically by the market; NPV is a computed quantity of a very short time-span.[85]

Market uncertainty sees to it that NPV, and therefore the next capital figure, will again be something which is in existence only at a moment of time. Income, on the other hand, is by its nature a flow over time, produced and received per week, month, or year as a cash flow (Chapter 8). This difference in time dimension between capital and income sees to it that under no circumstances can we add capital expressed in monetary units (say dollars) to income flow with the dimension of *dollars per unit of time*.

The market, however, relates capital and income through the *interest rate*, which can also be used to compute *discounted cash flow* (DCF) in evaluating the company itself, its products and its business in terms of future income. This statement is valid of loans, securities and other assets warehoused in a portfolio. The DCF principle, also known as investor's method, is that the value of any of these assets is the value of the future benefits it brings, expressed by the cash flows that it will generate in interest payments, dividends, and so on. This is adjusted for the time value of money and the risk that return on capital will not be what is expected.

Therefore, the discount rate being chosen must reflect the projected interest rate and assumed risk. This is typically expressed through the

---

[85] See also the discussion of solvency in Chapter 7.

concept that the higher the risk, the higher should be the rate used to discount all forecast future cash flows, in order to calculate the net present value of the stream of these cash flows.

- In the case of bonds, investors usually consider the interest rate and credit risk, though market risk is important too.

- With equities most attention is paid to market risk, even if credit risk is also present.

- Structured securities are more complex because they often contain embedded options, futures and other derivatives instruments whose risk is difficult to untangle.

In terms of the pure interest component, there must be a cash flow standard against which return can be compared. Government bonds of Group of Ten nations are considered credit risk-free.

Discounted cash flows could be:

- *Historical*, based on the rate stated on the date a transaction was originally consummated;

- *Current*, as of the date a financial statement or evaluation are being prepared; or

- Of another type, such as *average expected rate* over the life of the asset or obligation.

One should be consistent with the discount rate, because manipulating it biases the financial facts. The same is true about the time horizon of a discount evaluation. The prevailing rough rule of thumb is that an asset that is to be evaluated (or liquidated) within a year is considered as part of current assets (and of working capital), as well as of current liabilities. A time horizon of more than a year is part of longer-term (or fixed) capital assets, or of longer-term liabilities.[86]

---

[86] This may also vary with the law of the land. In France and Italy, the short term is up to six months; while in the US, Britain and Germany it is up to one year.

Discounted cash flow is key to determining the net present value and the internal rate of return of an asset. Notice that the present capital value changes as the payoff from a project or financial instrument is subject to charges not necessarily reflected in the foregoing brief outline. For instance:

• Costs of the transaction, and

• Risk at the long leg of the distribution.[87]

Discounted cash flow and present value can be employed both post-mortem and a priori – the latter case is that of studying alternative investments if the required earnings are chosen in advance. A time-adjusted return provides an estimate of an asset's, or project's, *intrinsic value*; and because of cost and risk outliers the time adjusted return will not be equal to the discounted cash flow.

An asset which has no cash flow over the time horizon being examined has no intrinsic value. To explain the notion of intrinsic value, Warren Buffett uses college education as an example. A simple algorithm ignores non-economic benefits of education, concentrating instead on *financial value*. The ABC is based on three estimates:

A. Future earnings with college degree.

B. Future earnings without college education.

C. All college-related costs, including invested time.

The person's future earnings must be discounted to present day applying the algorithm: $D = A - (B+C)$. If D is positive, there is intrinsic value. In the business world, intrinsic value can be significantly greater than book value if the company generates a healthy cash flow. In fact, book value can be meaningful if the portfolio is valued by marking to market (section 7), rather than through accruals accounting.

---

[87] As well as inflation. With every project or instrument, inflation should be treated consistently. Otherwise, cash flow comparisons are unsound and misleading.

In conclusion, then, the use of intrinsic value helps in managing the business with shareholder value creation in mind. This computation is future-oriented, providing an economic view by reflecting on discounted cash flows which (as we just saw) are not based solely on historical information. The Q ratio works along a similar line of reasoning, incorporating inflation's aftermath.

$$Q = \frac{\text{Present value (cash flow + residual value)}}{\text{Inflation adjusted assets}}$$

Like discounted cash flows, the Q ratio valuation model rests on measures which are relatively well-known, and it particularly serves in connection to studies involving a medium-range planning period. A Q ratio greater than 1 means that the value assigned to the company's net assets by the stock market is greater than their actual replacement. In this sense, Q greater than 1 indicates value creation, while Q less than 1 signals value destruction.

4. Price discovery through auctions

It is always rewarding to have alternative ways of measuring exposure available, because this opens a wider horizon to product pricing, makes it possible to test one method against the other, and allows the dependability of each approach to be evaluated. The importance of alternative paths to the same goal should never be underestimated. Usually, though not always, if there exists one approach to a solution, then there are also others. Alternatives should not be accepted at face value, but should be critically evaluated for accuracy and simplicity. If a better solution is calibrated at an acceptable level of reliability, it should be used industry-wide to support homogeneity in measurements.

The pandemic afflicting financial models is their extreme incompatibility. (This judgment includes VaR (Chapter 4) as each bank uses its own 'improved' version, while regulators have neither the will nor the people to control them). A good example on standardisation is the metre. If one doubts how long it is, all he needs to do is to go to the Musée de Sèvres and measure it.

One could argue, with some reason, that the method for pricing financial instruments need be no other than the free market's classic of supply and demand for products and services. Supply and demand rules, however, are not made for complex derivatives. Their kingdom is the retail market in which consumers buy thousands or millions of small items from a score of different merchandising establishments: grocery stores, drugs stores, department stores, gasoline stations, as well as utilities, airlines and so on.

Already with wages and salaries, supply and demand relations are not always so clear-cut. To the family head, his wage is not simply another price but the difference between luxury, comfort or privation. Hence the drive of labour unions to gain bargaining power; while the use of strikes and lockouts often causes conditions to deviate from competition characterised by classical rules of supply and demand. Is the system of supply and demand working badly in the modern economy? The answer is no, as long as two conditions are fulfilled:

1. It keeps on doing what it is designed to do: putting standard goods in the hands of people without exploiting them and without harming the producer.

2. Politicians do not habitually get involved in the mechanism of providing a price to attract willing parties. (But they did the opposite on 1 April 2009, when they killed marking to market in the US (sections 6 and 7).[88])

---

[88] By twisting the arms of FASB board members.

Derivative financial instruments, of course, are not standard goods, and though they still need to have a price, the discovery process is unlike that of any other commodity or service. Neither is there an equilibrium of supply and demand to be restored, or *factors of production* to account for. But there are other price determinants that need to be addressed.

For instance, the pricing of total return swaps as well as of other credit derivatives depends upon the distribution of the future credit quality of the reference asset. This may be an underlying pool of corporate debt issues or some other underlying, like the nearly worthless subprimes. For pricing purposes the movement and co-movement of credit qualities is of critical importance. The study of such movement requires the understanding not only of credit risk characteristics but also of the way these might change, often at a moment's notice.

For the fixed income investor, it is also very important that capital markets are increasingly used for shifting risks, and this poses challenges. The practice is not new. A stock market shifts business risk from the promoter(s) of a certain company and their banker(s) to thousands of investors nationally or even worldwide. What is new is that this is done on a massive scale and in novel ways where previous experience is thin. In addition, the more sophisticated a financial product is, the more investors are challenged in their view of its risks, the ways and means to value it, and the systems necessary to keep its exposure under control.

The notions behind these three points enter squarely, but at different levels of appreciation, into an auction. One can argue that these three issues have always been present with financial instruments at large. This is true, but classical answers were much more linear and 'evident' than those required nowadays.

Life insurance provides an example on past answers. Insurers are trained to look at years of records of births and deaths to estimate lifespans, create actuarial tables, and set appropriate premiums. Branches of insurance established a long time ago have plenty of statistical evidence available and they use computer models to experiment on the odds of a pandemic; or employ simulation in tracking diseases.

By contrast, with collateralised debt obligations (CDOs) and credit default swaps (CDSs), the statistics are poor and unreliable, and neither the models nor the processes are clear-cut. This is true both in absolute terms and due to the fact that CDOs and CDSs are customised. Therefore, banks and investors at large have to be prepared for a range of risks, including some that were unthinkable not long ago. They also need to note that global supply chains expose them to potential calamities all over the world.

The silver lining in all this huge computational challenge is that new financial instruments are themselves offering a helping hand in areas where old tools and methods prove to be insufficient. An example is the role of credit spreads of credit default swaps in product pricing, of which we spoke at length in section 2.

While my own opinion concerning the use of credit spreads established by the market is positive, contrarians are within their rights when they ask the question: How reliable is the input which they offer? And what about the dependability of CDOs pricing? Experts say that to answer these queries one must distinguish between two classes:

1. About 70% of novel instruments like CDOs are linked to an individual issuer, and though they are more complex than selling a bond short the difference is not inordinate.

2. Complexity, however, increases exponentially with the other 30%, as rocket scientists have developed ways of unbundling CDS indexes, slicing them into tranches of risk and return, and recombining them into new instruments.

This was a popular practice with collateralised debt obligations, which grew out of the market for asset-backed securities (ABSs) encompassing mortgages, car loans, credit-card receivables and more. Not only is the structured CDO a more complex variation than the simple one-company derivative instrument, but it also uses a lot more leverage and employs plenty of bundling sophistication with only a tiny amount of caution.

Unknowns associated with embedded risks make the job of right pricing (and therefore of risk management) so much more difficult, particularly in the absence of a dependable risk measurement method. What about letting the market do that through *price finding auctions*, using a process whose bare outline can be briefly sketched in two terms:

1. The sort of thing to be produced is at least partly determined by investors, and

2. How things are produced is determined by advancements in technology, rocket science and the competition of other banks.

Take, as an example, loan CDSs (LCDSs). The first ever European LCDS credit event auction was held in early February 2008 to settle contracts referring to Sanitec, a Nordic bathroom products maker. These contracts were triggered due to a missed coupon payment on 22 December 2008. Sanitec debt featured both *senior* (1st lien) and *subordinated* (2nd lien/mezzanine) contracts. The auctions resulted in recoveries settled at 33.5% for 1st lien, but at only 4% for 2nd lien.[89]

By comparison, recoveries associated with American LCDS auction results ranged from 52.5% for Masonite International, to 40.12% for Hawaiian Telcom, and 23.75% for the Tribune Company. These are interesting pricing results because until recently LCDS contracts were traded on the standard assumption of recovery at 70%. It needs no explaining that the expectation of loan recoveries has plummeted.

---

[89] Bank of America/Merrill Lynch, 'Situation Room', 5 February 2009.

Like any pricing mechanism, auctions can present unpleasant surprises, as the foregoing examples document. Experts on Wall Street suggest that this was the reason why Hank Paulson, the Treasury Secretary of the Bush Administration, chose to forgo the auctions of toxic waste he had proudly announced in connection with the $700 billion Troubled Asset Relief Program (TARP). Once market prices have been established, banks with similar troubled assets would have had horrendous losses from writedowns they had thus far avoided (more on marking to market in sections 6 and 7).

5. PPIP: example of an imperfect auction

Auctions may be imperfect, and some of them are planned in plain violation of free market principles. Here are a couple of recent examples. The public auction programme announced in October 2008 by Henry Paulson was dropped, but on 23 March 2009 Tim Geithner, Treasury Secretary of the Obama Administration, came up with his own plan, known as Public-Private Investment Program (PPIP).

PPIP included a one-sided incentives plan to motivate private capital, renaming warehoused loans as *legacy securities*. Everybody of course knew that the vaults of commercial and investment banks were full with *toxic assets*, not *legacy assets*.[90]

In a Bloomberg News panel of 27 April 2009, by the Milken Institute, Sam Zell said that the most important consideration is "what your assets are worth". In the opinion of other panellists, government policies such as the Public-Private Investment Program had therefore simply not been providing the confidence the market wanted. In addition, the PPIP was unique in the American economy because it cast the government in the dual role of lender *and* equity partner.

---

[90] Also a bad choice of label because it can be interpreted to mean that all legacy assets classically inventoried by financial institutions are toxic.

So at the same time it leaves aside the true government function of standards-setting and regulation. The absence of an independent regulator guarantees that plenty of people and companies are going to make profits at the expense of taxpayers. "The government creates an unrealistic market," said Sam Zell during the panel meeting. When he said this he was referring to the fact that wounded assets warehoused by banks, which were worth nothing, may suddenly be worth a lot. The reason for the switch would be that somebody, the taxpayer, provides 85% of the financing.

In a more general sense, the market's reaction was mixed. Some people rejoiced at the profits looming on the horizon – but in terms of fundamentals many analysts suggested that PPIP was nothing other than a revival of TARP. In other peoples' opinions, underlying PPIP was not so much a public auction but a covert form of bank recapitalisation – with private buyers getting plenty of help through co-investment by the Treasury, cheap loans from the Federal Reserve, and guarantees from the Federal Deposit Insurance Corporation (FDIC).

Several economists, too, denounced the plan as a disguised subsidy posing as a market-oriented solution. They also said that PPIP's true *legacy loans* would face difficulties as there was nothing in its structure to assist banks in mitigating recognition of very significant losses. These losses would be incurred by exposing their wounded loans to auction. This meant selling them at market clearing prices and being confronted with devastating write-offs.[91]

---

[91] In addition, the Treasury had failed to define how the results of these auctions would be coordinated with capital stress tests, which were underway following another government decision of mid-February 2009.

According to opinions contrary to the Treasury's plan, if the bid/ask for wounded loans was too wide, this would create a gap that could not be narrowed, even with considerable leverage. Theoretically, the introduction of leverage could narrow the bid/ask spread for toxic assets. Practically it is better not to bet on such a thing happening because the introduction of market pricing for toxic loans exacerbates fundamental issues weighing upon regional banks.

One of the ironies associated with PPIP auctions comes from the fact that, unlike the case of toxic *securities*, nonperforming *loans* on bank balance sheets have not been marked to market, but are marked according to management's perception of recoverable value – usually a very optimistic estimate. As if to increase the level of uncertainty, the Treasury and FDIC reserved the right to modify requirements at any time, with the result that participants will be faced with constant fear that the ground may shift.

Critics say that either the PPIP auctions will be fake or there will be a gap between bank assumptions and that of private capital managers participating in PPIP. The average US bank has been posting a 3% frequency of likely default on prime, 1st lien residential real estate loans; and secondary market pricing impliyies a 10% to 20% frequency for a pool of like loans. Compared to statistics from auctions presented in section 4, these are over-optimistic estimates.

Such significant differences in estimating net present value (and financial reporting) are not necessarily due to poor judgment. Most banks are holding assets, particularly loans, at values far above their market price because under accrual accounting losses can be booked over several years. As a result, even with lavish government help bids may not be high enough to tempt banks to deal. Any price below the loan's carrying value would force them to take a writedown, depleting capital that is in short supply.

For instance, as an article in the *Economist* indicated, Wells Fargo has written its portfolio (largely inherited from the acquisition of Wachovia) down to about 70 cents on the dollar. But the market price is roughly 35 cents on the dollar.[92] Even with leverage, a buyer will not be prepared to pay a price close to 70 cents. And unless the bank is really struggling, why should it deal with the PPIP bidder at fire sale price?

Critics also add that the Treasury has tried to encourage investor participation by sweetening incentives like proportional equity stakes, debt guarantees from the FDIC and other goodies – but it has cared very little for the medium sized and smaller banks and their interests. Neither has the necessary amount of attention been paid to so-called *Level 3* assets. Namely, those for which no reliable market price is available for marking them to their fair value. Therefore, they are valued according to model and myth. The Level 3 amounts are staggering:

- For the ten big American banks they represent more than 16% of their assets.

- In terms of equity share, the Level 3 assets range between 300% for Morgan Stanley and 100% for Bank of America, hovering around 150% for Citigroup, Wells Fargo, Goldman Sachs and JP Morgan Chase.

To appreciate how bad these ratios are, the reader must know that these are, by large majority, exposures to structured financial instruments trading at roughly 30% to 35% of their peak; and even this is an overestimate. Cancelling marking to market (section 6) is very helpful for those banks with Level 3 concentration, but it is also clearly damaging to the notions of a free market, transparency, ethical behaviour and government impartiality.

---

[92] *The Economist*, 28 March 2009.

In short, while Geithner seems determined to proceed with auctions – something that Paulson in the end avoided – his plan looks as if it has rough edges. Moreover, as a research paper by Bank of America/Merrill Lynch pointed out, there are a lot of questions about how PPIP will work in practice. Will it be completely voluntary, highly encouraged, or mandatory for all US banks?[93]

Other critical unanswered queries concern whether banks can sell any loans seen as toxic; how much control the government would have over private investors actively participating in PPIP; if regulators view the pricing for loans purchased through PPIP as their *clearing level*; whether participant banks will be charged with servicing the loans sold into PPIP; and, most importantly, if participation in PPIP creates a capital hole for the bank, will the Treasury provide additional capital to beef-up its balance sheet?

* * *

On 3 June 2009, FDIC stated that it was putting the planned pilot sale under the Legacy Loans Program (LLP) on hold. This was originally announced by Treasury Secretary Geithner as part of PPIP, to facilitate sale of loans on banks' balance sheets by providing cheap financing from FDIC.

While the FDIC postponed the use of this plan for open banks' assets as proposed in March 2009, it also said that it plans to test the funding mechanism of LLP for sale of receivership assets and expects to solicit bids. At Wall Street, however, several analysts looked at that postponement as further evidence that PPIP no longer makes sense and should be scrapped.

---

[93] Bank of America/Merrill Lynch, 'US Banks', 24 March 2009.

6. From marking to market, to marking to myth

Thursday 2 April 2009 was a black day for bank regulation in the US and in the world at large. On one side, at the London G-20, the gathered world leaders promised tougher regulation of the financial industry worldwide, to save the world from a second Great Depression. Across the Atlantic, however, under pressure from big banks and politicians, FASB (the Financial Accounting Standards Board of the Securities and Exchange Commission) decided to drop marking to market (M2M) of 'assets' (read toxic waste) warehoused by institutions, substituting it with a management declaration "on their worth". This double talk was unfair to the American public, the global public and the banks themselves. The abandonment of transparency has become so one-sided that systemic risk can now grow by leaps and bounds year after year.

Back to the fundamentals, marking to market was both an accounting standard (originally established by the FASB) and one of the basic principles promoted by Basel II. It was also the accounting standard adopted by the European Union's member states and other countries which implemented the International Financial Reporting Standards (IFRS)[94] of the International Accounting Standards Board (IASB).

There exist several reasons why marking to market, though not perfect, is considered the best possible method for valuing complex financial instruments (whose value is impossible to establish under accrual accounting). The two most important reasons are:

1. Historical values, and therefore the concepts of amortisation and depreciation, are totally unstuck from the current value of a complex financial instrument.

---

[94] D. N. Chorafas, *IFRS, Fair Value and Corporate Governance: Its Impact on Budgets, Balance Sheets and Management Accounts*, Butterworth-Heinemann, London and Boston, 2005.

2.   In a free economy, fair value is established by the market not by the czar and his bureaucrats.

This does not mean that marking to market is an ideal approach; rather, the reason for adopting it is that with structured instruments and other products propelled by financial technology, it is the only one which can claim some accuracy. There exist, nevertheless, certain issues which work against marking to market.

Derivative instruments traded over the counter (OTC) only have a market price in two instances: when they are sold and when they mature. One might therefore think that it is enough to carry them in the books under original value (which happens under US GAAP *if* management intent is to keep them to maturity). This approach, however, would be highly unstable and unreliable, because banks would use totally fake values in pricing their assets, some of which show up in their capital reserves as big ticket items. (See also Chapter 6 on legal risk with creative accounting.)

The US financial industry lobbied for marking to market accounting in good times, in order to realise 'the value of its assets' by leveraging balance sheets based on these high valuations. This lobbying was a major force behind the global credit bubble. Bank profitability, top salaries, options and bonuses reached for the stars as an ingeniously manipulated market continued to produce fake prices. After the crisis hit and the bears settled in, the process reversed, valuations hit the wall, and big banks' bosses used their political patrons and lobbyists to kill marking to market accounting. This opened a Pandora's box of wild estimates.

In the absence of a market price, estimates are made by marking to model, which involves a significant amount of model risk. The use of quantum logic may improve model dependability by making available an analytical approach which provides not only a better documented risk pricing mechanism, but also a platform for experimentation in conjunction with auctions, CDS spreads and risk charges discussed.

Being a scientific method, QED will also assist in correcting other current shortcomings – for example, the ultra-light interpretation of risk charges and their impact on capital adequacy in the globalised economy.

Indeed, the credit and banking crisis of 2007-2009 has documented serious difficulties in the comparison of capital adequacy across banks, because of the many differences in assumptions made, and methods used, to value exposures. This was bad for the financial institutions themselves and for the economy at large; and the problem lies with the lack of a universal, reliable methodology.

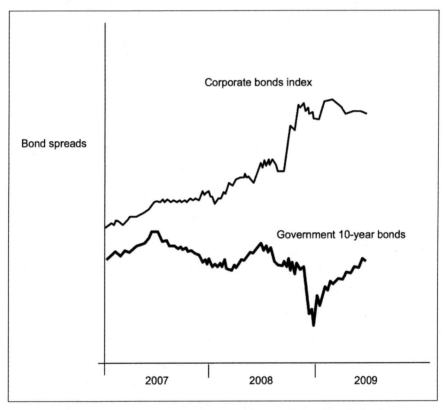

Figure 3.4: Spread between corporates and government bonds in the 2007 to early 2009 time frame.

The absence of a powerful universal risk model and associated standard procedures confuses market participants, who find refuge in large yield buffers, exemplified in Figure 3.4 with bond spreads. It is also confuses the regulators, who are expected to analyse valuation losses, compare those suffered by financial institutions in different jurisdictions, and come up with corrective steps, as well as general directives, distinguishing between:

- Valuations and changes connected to inventoried assets, and

- Increases in credit and market impairments; the writedowns.

No serious action can be taken by marking to myth. In the absence of a universal risk pricing standard such as quantum logic can provide, a serious error by regulatory authorities was the amount of discretion which they gave to credit institutions in terms of valuing their assets. To better appreciate this statement the reader should keep in perspective that, according to Basel II, at time of recognition banks can value their securities (both good and rotten) according to three alternative accounting procedures:

1. Fair value through profit and loss, by marking to market,

2. Held to maturity by *management intent*, using accruals, and

3. *Available-for-sale*, where bank management is given a free hand in making its own rules.

For securities included under the third class, decline in value and resulting loss is not taken through the income statement until the asset is sold. This has proved to be a huge loophole and banks have exploited the system by using management's discretion in deciding whether available-for-sale assets are impaired and by how much.

Moreover, banks which marked to market their own liabilities issued by themselves soon discovered that, curiously enough, deterioration of their credit rating had a *positive effect* leading to an increase in equity. The miracle happened by way of assigning a lower value to these liabilities. It is indeed quite interesting that through legalised creative accounting the impairment of assets can be turned around and become another 'asset'.

By contrast, marking to market has revealed the horrendous contents of portfolios belonging to many big banks, insurance companies and investors. This was unavoidable given the creative accounting practices that became widespread. Therefore, it is not surprising that fair value accounting mandated by US GAAP and IFRS has received a lot of blame (section 7), while politicians who do not understand (or don't want to understand) how the market works, mandated a change to accounting rules.

Marking to market and fair value accounting are pillars of truthful financial reporting. The goal is *transparency*, which enables investors, bankers, regulators and government officials to put things right by identifying specific causes of exposure. These causes can include bad lending practices, fraud, fake financial reporting and poor risk management.

Severe mistakes in judgment and in banking practices should not be hidden from public view. The job of accounting standards setters is to promote transparency, assure a way of measuring materiality and upholding accountability. In that sense, they should be independent of political pressures, while they collaborate with *prudent regulators* to enhance their work by providing better measurements of the quality and quantity of portfolios' true positions. It needs no further explaining that fair value accounting is also indispensable for effective risk management policies and practices.

7. Conflicts of interest in opposing marking to market

While he was CEO of American International Group (AIG), the former giant of the insurance industry, Martin Sullivan argued that it is wrong to force companies to mark to market in an illiquid market. This view was shared by many bankers who wounded their institutions through plenty of excesses, and who conveniently forgot that they themselves designed and traded very risky instruments OTC. In fact:

- Most of the securities which in the 'good years' were marked to market should not have been issued in the first place, and

- As Kevin Bailey, of the Office of the Comptroller of the Currency deposited to Congress on 11 March 2009, only 25% of securities warehoused in big banks are being marked to market.[95]

In May 2008, when Sullivan made the aforementioned statement, AIG had taken an $11 billion hit by writing down some of its overvalued securities. This was the biggest quarterly loss in its history and it was followed by more large losses, the firing of Sullivan, its nationalisation and the injection of taxpayers' money to keep the financial carcass alive. By March 2009 its equity became a permanent penny stock.

Many of the bankers and other investment specialists who severely damaged the net worth of both their institutions and their clients, hang all their hopes on reducing transparency by suspending marking to market accounting rules. Fair value established by a free market has become their enemy because it has helped reveal that they are failed bankers. If they were not failed bankers they would have thought of risk and exposure at the time they designed, sold, bought, accumulated and manipulated all this toxic waste.

In addition, it would have been much better for the reputation of CEOs of wounded banks, and for their institutions, if they had admitted that they were wrong when they loaded themselves with toxic assets. They should have learned about sound management from Sam Walton, one of the most successful businessmen of the post-World War II years, who remarked: "When I decide that I am wrong, I am ready to move on to something else."[96]

---

[95] Just for this 25%, on 1 April 2009 the Obama administration cancelled the marking to market accounting rule.

[96] Sam Walton, *Made in America: My Story*, Bantam Books, New York, 1992.

A product, project or process may prove unable to deliver what was promised, and as Walton aptly aphorised on another occasion: "One should never underwrite somebody else's inefficiencies" – or his own. Lesser individuals, however, don't have the foresight to take that position. Instead, they try to make the taxpayers pay for their mistakes and for their inefficiencies.

On 28 January 2008 Robert Rubin – a former treasury secretary, former boss of Goldman Sachs, and the man who as member of Citigroup's corporate office saw America's biggest bank reduced to ashes under his watch – was quoted by Bloomberg financial news as having said that fair value accounting had damaged the banks. This is not true.

What has damaged the big banks on an unprecedented scale is very poor governance and the weaknesses resulting from persistent conflicts of interest by high-placed individuals – not the inanimate world of accounting and accounts. Since the time he worked for Goldman Sachs, Rubin should have known that toxic waste could kill. The toxic waste big banks accumulated from 2003 to 2007 was absolutely worthless since the time of securitisation and resecuritisation of subprimes.[97] The reason for the big banks' downfall is not fair value but the creative accounting practices adopted to maximise bonuses and satisfy egos.

Moreover, the ex-big bankers who took position against fair value have the experience to appreciate that since this was the accounting law of the land, one day the horrendous bleeding of their portfolio (due to highly risky derivatives trades) would become public knowledge. They are also old enough to understand that time and again transparency has shown itself to be of tremendous importance in restoring market confidence.

---

[97] Chorafas, *Financial Boom and Gloom.*

Both at Goldman Sachs and at Citigroup, the long-favoured off balance sheet vehicles were the enemies of transparency. This should not be repeated again. Supervisors must be able to oversee the financial institution's whole range of exposure including off balance sheet pseudo-assets stuffed-up in special purpose vehicles (SPV), structured investment vehicles (SIV), and conduits. Also they should be eager to integrate all off balance sheet positions into the balance sheet.

Profound conflicts of interest have not allowed this to happen. On 11 March 2009 the CEO of JP Morgan Chase was talking to the New York Chamber of Commerce saying things other bankers were eager to hear. Orwell would have characterised it as *Newspeak*, because on one side the CEO asked for a regulator of systemic risk (without really specifying what sort of authority he would have, over whom, and from where the funds would come); and on the other he promoted (in disguise) the cancellation of marking to market.

Though marking to market is not perfect, it has proved to be the better alternative to providing information on fair value to investors and the supervisory authorities. It has also assisted in avoiding misinformation and tricky selling practices that harm market confidence. As section 6 has noted, overall dependability can be improved through a robust and comprehensive approach to disclosure requirements using QED, but until such improvement materialises there are no other valid options. Contrary to what Rubin and some other bankers say, fair value accounting is a direct way to counter mistrust in the marketplace. When disclosure requirements are strengthened everyone would be obliged to come clean about their exposure – including wounded financial products, distressed portfolios, latent liquidity risks and plain solvency.

* * *

After the results of the so-called stress tests of February to May 2009 were released, the market thought it knew the real reason for striking marking to market out of the US accounting standards. "The universe is not what it used to be, nor what it appears to be," said Frank

Wilczek, the physicist, in regard to our knowledge of the cosmos. The same applies to stress-testing, and to our knowledge about the survivability of the self-wounded big banks.

On 8 May 2009, when the findings of balance sheet analysis of 19 US banks came to the public eye (with two exceptions: Bank of America and Wells Fargo) their equity cushions were said to be comfortable and their capital adequacy easily attainable, and the effects of changed US accounting standards came squarely centre stage. Killing marking to market was a trick to whitewash the deep-red balance sheets of banks.

Part Two

Using Quantum Electrodynamics for Risk Control

Chapter 4: Not Everything that Counts Gets Counted

1. The Basel Committee's proposed revision of the 1996 Market Risk Amendment[98]

The Market Risk Amendment to the first Basel capital accord (Basel I) came to life in 1996. A dozen years later, in July 2008, the Basel Committee on Banking Supervision issued two consultative documents with impact on risk management policies and practices in institutions under prudential supervision: 'Proposed Revisions to the Basel II Market Risk Framework' and 'Guidelines for Computing Capital for Incremental Risk in the Trading Book'.[99] Cornerstone to both documents is the fact that regulatory authorities have decided to:

- Account for *market illiquidity*, which can turn the models and risk measures used by banks on their head when market conditions are stressful;

- Implement an *incremental risk charge* (IRC, section 4) which would capture price changes due to defaults and other sources of price risks, as well as those resulting from credit risk migration.

While changes in regulatory thinking – particularly those concerning adaptation to evolving market conditions, and novel financial instruments – are welcome, a careful study of the aforementioned

---

[98] For the rules of the original Market Risk Amendment see D. N. Chorafas, *The 1996 Market Risk Amendment. Understanding the Marking-to-Model and Value-at-Risk*, Irwin/McGraw-Hill, Burr Ridge, IL, 1998.

[99] Both documents have been reissued in January 2009 respectively under the titles 'Revisions to the Basel II Market Risk Framework' and 'Guidelines for Computing Capital for Incremental Risk in the Trading Book'. Also, both documents make reference to an agreement reached between the Basel Committee and IOSCO (the International Organisation of Securities Supervisors) in July 2005.

consultative documents leads me to the belief that they are not radical enough. They essentially revolve around a primitive and largely irrelevant model which we have come across before – *value at risk* (VaR, see the Appendix) with its low 99% *level of confidence* (Chapter 2), which greatly contrasts to the level of confidence of 99.99% required for Basel's new concept of IRC.[100]

Even if this was the only failure, it would make Basel's new market risk framework a house divided against itself. Moreover, as the consultative Basel documents themselves state, value at risk measurements ignore differences in the underlying liquidity of trading book positions and put too much emphasis on modelling short-run profit and loss (P&L) volatility at the expense of medium to longer trends.

The longer-term view recently taken by Basel, and the fact that its level of confidence is by an order of magnitude higher than that of VaR, makes the integration of results to be obtained by the two models dubious at best, and at worst awfully misleading. It would have been much better to start anew, placing emphasis on exposures associated with transactions and positions created by novel financial products such as long lists of debt securities, re-securitisations of commercial and consumer liabilities, collateralised debt obligations (CDOs), the daily appearance of new structured credit instruments, credit default swaps (CDSs), and more.

In addition, a primary preoccupation of a new supervisory methodology should be the layers of structure characterising each of the novel financial products and the way in which these can be reverse-engineered for marking to market and for risk allocation reasons. It

---

[100] IRC has not yet been fully developed, let alone tested. However, from the Basel document it transpires that it may well be an improvement over previous methods.

must be faced; there is an element of complexity in practically every financial entity. Risk control measures could be effective if they account for the fact that:

- A bank's risk policy concerning exposures being assumed is rarely revealed.

- Each portfolio reflects the strategy, selection criteria and marketing policies of each individual bank, and

- Derivatives and other contracts warehoused by an institution are not a random sample of their total population.

Therefore *everything that counts must be counted*, which is not being done today. Risk identification and measurement should not be superficial (the way VaR goes about it) but timely, accurate and detailed. The aforementioned two documents by the Basel Committee seem to recognise this fact, but between the lines they make the point that no methodology for doing so exists at the present time. The answer is QED.

To count everything that counts, we must make use of the growing body of knowledge gained during the events of the 2007-2009 credit, banking and liquidity crisis. New regulation should capitalise on this knowledge in order to make the risk control system as foolproof as possible.

In addition, since Chapter 1 the thesis of this book has been that we must use quantum electrodynamics (QED)[101], the first class modelling approach from physics, to its full potential. Many of the rocket

---

[101] Quantum electrodynamics describes all phenomena of the physical world except those gravitational and radioactive (which involve nuclei shifting in their energy fields). The development of a grand unifying theory in physics is still under research.

scientists employed in the banking industry during the last 20 years are physicists; therefore, they should be knowledgeable about it. Chapter 5 will show that as a method QED could be instrumental in providing holistic management for credit risk, market risk and liquidity risk.

These are the three *strong forces* in risk control which must be addressed in an integrated way, and not through fractional and parochial approaches as has been done so far. Correspondingly, operational risk and business risk are weak forces in a global sense because they are dependent on the specific institution. (Part Three addresses the challenges connected to legal risk, overleveraging and weak supervision, which varies most significantly by jurisdiction, through quantum chromodynamics or QCD.)

The institution of the *global sheriff* proposed by George Soros during the 2008 World Economic Forum in Davos, Switzerland[102], can be viable if the three strong forces of financial risk go through a process or *recertification* and *integration*. Today, nobody knows how to do this properly; or how much it would cost. Costs matter[103], but the cost to the economy and the banking industry of the 2008-2009 hecatomb has been so high that no effort should be spared to bring a sense of reality in risk management, even if the cost is significant.

Particular emphasis must be placed on product design and the technology necessary to address the three strong forces in financial management in an integrated way. The task is challenging because, since the time of their original definition, credit, market and liquidity risks

---

[102] Chorafas, *Financial Boom and Gloom.*

[103] The measurement of costs of legislation and regulation for society as a whole, and the business community in particular, is a controversial issue that has received, so far, little attention. The classical assessment of these costs gives no insight into the total compliance burden and, most importantly, the cost to the community and the nation of big bank failures.

have not been projected to work in unison. To redesign them, we need to reduce them to the level of their basic components and examine them closely prior to redefining them and restructuring them.

(Let me add a word of caution as a conclusion to section 1. It has not been an intention of this book to present to the reader the details of a methodology and its tools, through which QED can be effectively applied in financial risk control. This is a major project to be undertaken by the regulators. Instead, what the text offers in Chapter 5 is proof on how a successful theory from the physical sciences could be adapted to financial and market conditions in order to be meaningfully applicable to their realities – and, by so doing, improve the effectiveness of risk measurement and management.)

2. Underrating risk is bad management

The structure of an organisation matters and so do its products, but they matter less than the quality of the people who lead it: from board members to the CEO, senior managers, traders, investment specialists, accountants, auditors, risk controllers and other professionals.

At the same time, in terms of structure, as far as end results are concerned, the organisation's size can be a negative. There is a good reason why, in late April 2009, Sheila Bair, the FDIC chairwoman, asked for authority to break up the mammoth financial organisations the Federal Deposit Insurance Corporation may have to salvage.

In addition, legacy risk control practices and inability to challenge 'the obvious' are negatives because the financial world is always evolving and old approaches often turn out to be counterproductive. The same is true of what is imprecisely called common sense.[104] Exercising common sense may be good, but it is not sufficient. Today's

---

[104] Which, as a French proverb has it, is most widely distributed – this being the reason why each of us has so little.

mammoth financial supermarkets require much more than common sense to be in charge at managerial and professional levels, because they are both harder to lead, supervise and keep on track, and they impose much greater costs if a firm falls over a financial precipice.

The thesis of this section is that even if regulators and legislators manage to put together the best possible rules for keeping risks under lock and key, their efforts will fail unless and until they involve together the personal accountability of board members, chief executive officers and (say) the top 30 people in any and every financial organisation under their watch. Risk control must be written in the genes of an organisation's top people. Otherwise it will never become an effective function.

Precisely for this reason, the careful reader of the two July 2008 Basel documents, referred to at the beginning of section 1, would be deceived by the fact that no mention is being made to senior management's responsibility and accountability in regard to implementation of the revised market risk framework and incremental risk charge. Nor are there rigorous rules designed to ensure that plain bad management – of 2002 to 2009 style – will be severely punished because it ends up by defrauding the economy, taxpayers, and the financial institution's stakeholders.

Alert business people know that they must closely watch over exposure because of the lessons that experience has taught them, but not everybody is alert. Getting the debt level right was so crucial that executives at well-managed institutions ran worst-case scenarios (section 5). They knew that they would have to live for years with the debt levels that they and their colleagues patched in, hence they asked themselves and those around them critical questions:

- What would happen *if* interest rates shot up?

- *If* the national economy entered a deep recession?

- *If* there is a global contagion?

- *If* the cold war starts again and the market splinters?

- *If* the national debt skyrockets to 170% of GDP, as happened in Japan, or beyond?

"Such questioning sessions were a crucial part of KKR's success over the years; they prevented the buyout firm – for all its ambition – from embarking on overly risky deals that could lead to financial disaster down the road," said George Anders. "Kohlberg asked the questions then, as a way of teaching his younger partners. In later years, Kravis and Roberts would assume their old mentor's role, posing similar questions to younger men working for them."[105]

One of the key reasons why underrating risk is bad management is that large organisations act as accelerators of their own risk appetite. The recklessness of investment bankers at AIG, Bear Stearns, Citigroup, Lehman Brothers, Merrill Lynch and UBS, among others, has made these banks the credit crunch's biggest loss-makers to date. At Citi, Merrill and UBS, clients of their lucrative private banking operations have been nervous, switching their wealth to other institutions. Regulators have also been uneasy but, as the facts proved, powerless.

Neither is effective risk management a matter of making trading and investment decisions which are always 'right'. No decisions are foolproof; sometimes, even the best ones look as if they were based on what later appear to have been false assumptions or estimates. Market conditions change and certain major events may overtake even the most carefully laid plans.

---

[105] George Anders, *Merchants of Debt*, Basic Books, New York, 1992.

Therefore, rather than simply classifying decisions into right and wrong, it is important to know the:

- Hypotheses which went into them,

- Level of analysis which preceded them,

- Responsibilities which have been assumed,

- Contrarian opinions which were considered, and weights given to them, and

- How the logic of dissent has been incorporated into the decision process in reaching a conclusion.

Doing so requires specific knowledge associated with instruments and business models. The management skills needed to excel at investment banking are different from those in retail and in corporate lending. The universal banking model may sound great on paper, but when the tough times come the men at the top of big and well-known financial organisations find that the measurement of outstanding exposures is elusive. The 2007-2009 evidence is that:

- They did not know which problem to tackle first (Citigroup, Merrill Lynch, UBS).

- They discovered the hard way that the people reporting to them were not easy to police and bring into line (Société Générale, IKB).

- While they thought they were diversified, their risks were concentrated in a few instruments (CDOs, subprimes, commercial paper) and names (Bear Stearns for JP Morgan Chase), and

- Their 'one type fits all' approach to risk management was totally inadequate given the diversity of instruments they were using, their wide distribution of exposures, and the global nature of their operations.

There is plenty to learn by studying the lessons from the credit and banking crisis which started in July/August 2007. Practically every institution which suffered heavily from this crisis and its after-effects had in place a risk control organisation, but it did not function as effectively as expected. They also employed thousands of risk managers (UBS had 3400 of them); but they did not deliver.

In several of the banks, the lack of corrective action was due to sprawling bureaucratic practices. Internal walls built by bureaucrats can be as deadly as risk-taking without limits. "If you put the Federal Government in charge of the Sahara desert," Milton Friedman once said, "in five years there'd be a shortage of sand."[106] Friedman's dictum fits the events of 2007-2009 precisely because, as far as risk control is concerned, there has hitherto been a disturbingly large amount of inaction by the authorities – while the policies that were announced were hollow (Chapter 3).

3. Lessons from the credit and banking crisis can help in risk control

One of the after-effects of the severe credit and banking crisis of 2007-2009 is the documentation it provided on how poorly risk is managed among financial institutions – big and small. The board, CEO and senior executives of commercial and investment banks which lost tens of billions and went first to sovereign wealth funds (SWFs) and then to their governments for loans, are the first to blame for the lack of oversight.

Lessons must always be learned from past failures. The first lesson is that of personal accountability. In the US the Sarbanes-Oxley Act of 2002 presses this point for CEOs and CFOs – but it has never really been applied.

---

[106] *The Economist*, 9 August 2008.

The second lesson is that failure to act on the basis of early indicators should translate into an increase of capital requirements for the institution. Retrospectively, several top executives said that they should have paid more attention to the first signs of trouble. Some even admitted that they were not really in charge of what was happening under their watch. Yet they should have known better. Long years of experience teach that no crisis comes completely out of the blue. There are always clues and advance warnings if one watches out carefully for them, and interprets them correctly.

For instance, well before the blow-up of the credit markets in July/August 2007, there was a crisis in the structured credit market in May 2005, which indicated the likelihood of unexpected consequences. In that month, bonds of General Motors were marked down by rating agencies from investment grade to junk, but that signal got lost in the prevailing general high spirits. Banks and investors took no measures to reposition their portfolios and they increased rather than reduced their exposure to CDOs.

This higher and higher exposure to structured instruments and asset-backed securities at large was part of a one-sided risk-and-return strategy. Banks were eager to buy pools of assets (mainly loans and bonds), warehouse them in the balance sheet, structure them once again and sell them to end investors at a profit – no matter the level of exposure assumed by their clients and by themselves.

During the explosion of structured debt instruments in the Greenspan years,[107] commercial and investment bankers expected the pseudo-AAA tranches of subprimes and other junk debt to rise in value and showered

---

[107] Particularly in the last years Dr Alan Greenspan was chairman of the Fed: 2002 to 2006.

themselves with bonuses from the not-yet materialised profits. What actually happened was the reverse of what was projected. Bankers who thought they knew what they were doing were eager to sell non-investment grade tranches (equity, mezzanine) to investors[108], while keeping those that were highly rated. However, AAA tranches went down in price and, curiously enough, the price of non-investment grade tranches went up.

Plenty of bankers had bet the wrong way, and they were at a loss in interpreting the reasons and in working out what to do next, whilst they lost themselves in the complex world of cross-correlations between tranches. One of them, whom I met, stated that there had been a short squeeze in junk tranches driving their prices up; another spoke of a general non-publicised selling of the senior structured tranches, including the best AAA and super-seniors.

The lesson learned by this market twist is interesting for two reasons: it documents how superficial some of the analyses on financials are; and demonstrates how new financial instruments can be a confidence game, while their risk management is in its infancy. Liquidity started to disappear, but, confused by their wrong bets, even senior bankers did not interpret this as a danger signal. (Eventually the mid-2005 mini-liquidity crisis returned on a very big scale in the summer of 2007 and beyond.)

Many banks thought that they could find protection in their models, but the models proved to be awfully biased. Here is a practical example on how wrong VaR estimates can be. Year-end 2007, at Merrill Lynch, excluding CDOs and residual securities, value at risk was computed

---

[108] In many cases, new approvals for risky structured instruments were conditioned to reducing the equity tranche (highest risk tranche) to zero.

equal to $65 million; by contrast, real life losses had hit a dazzling $8.4 billion. The error between model-based and real exposure was 12,923%.

Even worse, if subprime and residual securities positions at the same bank were included, then VaR-based losses were $157 million. This is very small compared to the end of 2007 real-life losses which hit $24.9 billion and nearly brought the institution to its knees. The difference between marking to myth and real life was equal to 15,605%.

It is not only that VaR is so much of an irrelevant risk management model – even if it is the regulators', commercial bankers' and investment bankers' darling – it is also that nobody seems to have bothered to study cause and effect. Yet a good way to be in charge of risk management is to examine the causes as well as the most likely effects of a growing exposure.

The crisis of 2007-2009 provided plenty of evidence that old methods for risk measurement were and are not valuable. Models for risk reporting and supervisory policies associated with them have become inadequate because of the mass of money being traded, and the complexity of instruments developed, sold, bought and warehoused in the 21st century.

It is because of these same reasons that the safety net put in place in the 1930s, after the Great Depression, is far from being adequate. The treasury of the US Federal Deposit Insurance Corp (FDIC) is a case in point. On 27 August 2008 the FDIC said its 'problem list' of banks increased by 30% in the second quarter of 2008 to 117 institutions – an inevitable result of the fact that a growing number of residential and commercial real estate loans were overdue. (By the end of April 2009, some 20 banks had been taken over in the preceding year alone.)

The FDIC, which for 75 years performed greatly, seemed to be overtaken by the wave of failures of American mortgage institutions and giant banks. In addition, while this scenario was still unfolding, medium-size US commercial banks were not far behind. "Pretty dismal," was the description of their state by Sheila Bair, who chairs the FDIC.[109] Pretty soon her agency will have to replenish its deposit; the question is how – or, more precisely, who – will be hurt.[110]

4. Incremental risk charge and stress tests[111]

Rules and regulations are not cast in stone. As their implementation is monitored and their effects evaluated against what was intended and planned, changes have to be made to adapt the prevailing rules to developing circumstances, to better the protection they provide and to stop regulatory arbitrage. A good example in this direction is provided by the *incremental risk change* (IRC) decided by the Basel Committee, as the results of the major economic and banking crisis brought the message that Basel II needed to be recalibrated.

In retrospect, several experts expressed the opinion that one of the flaws in the new capital adequacy framework had to do with the fact that while (theoretically) there existed a fairly clear distinction between credit risk and market risk, in practice this has changed. If credit and market risk were seen independent of each other, then the pricing of each exposure, and capital requirements associated with them, could be computed almost independently of one another. By contrast, today, even with classical financial instruments, credit risk and market risk correlate up to a point. With securitisations and derivatives correlation significantly increases, with market risk morphing into credit risk, and vice versa.

---

[109] *The Economist*, 30 August 2008.

[110] By the end of the first quarter 2009, experts suggested that over the next 12 months deposit insurance would require payouts of about $200 billion and this is no time for FDIC to raise premiums. Therefore, it will have to go to the US Treasury to cover the shortfall.

[111] See also in Chapter 5 some of the problems present with IRC.

When Basel II was still at the drafting board, to deal with the likelihood of correlation between credit risk and market risk increasing with securitisations and derivatives, regulators introduced risk weights into the calculation of capital requirements. With the standardised approach, risk weights have been rather simple – except that in addition to the more classical weights of 0%, 20%, 50% and 100%, a new weighting factor of 150% was introduced, applicable to borrowers with poor rating. The use of weights was believed to make the computation of capital charge for a loan fairly straightforward, but the economic and banking crisis of 2007-2009 demonstrated that this is far from being the case.

More sophisticated than the standard method, the two internal ratings-based (IRB) solutions were projected to favour a high-quality portfolio, with low quality being penalised. The wrong credit rating of debt securities, like the AAA attributed to worthless subprimes, has proved that this was ineffectual.

External rating grade	Probability of default (%)[112]	Risk weights	
		Standardised approach	IRB approach[113]
Floor	0.03	20	14
AAA to AA-	0.03 to 0.05	20	14 to 19
A+ to A-	0.06 to 0.11	50	21 to 31
BBB+ to BB-	0.12 to 1.33	100	33 to 149
B+ to B-	1.34 to 20.00	150	150 to 625
Unrated		100[114]	

Table 4.1: standardised and IRB approaches for corporate credits[115]

---

[112] According to KMV Corporation data.

[113] Based on maturity assumption of three years, loss given default of 50% and exposure default of 100%.

[114] Which is very curious because 'unrate' may be B or even CCC.

[115] European Central Bank (ECB), Monthly Bulletin, May 2001.

Table 1 offers a bird's-eye view of standardised and IRB risk weights. Between the lines there is some ambiguity as Basel II provides two options for claims on banks, leaving it to national supervisors to decide which one will be applied to banks in their jurisdiction.

- Under the first option, banks are assigned a risk weight one category less favourable than that given to claims on sovereigns.

- According to the second option, a bank's risk weighting is based on the maturity of the loan.

As the significance of complex and illiquid credit products in the trading book has grown steadily, this formalisation of risk weights, which dates back to 2001, proved to be unsatisfactory. Capital put aside for credit risk and market risk charges became unstuck from assumed exposure by banking institutions. In addition trading volumes in complex products rose significantly, and capital charges in the trading book become more favourable than those in the banking book, leading to a new wave of regulatory arbitrage.

Knowledgeable bankers who care for their institution's survival suggest that the aforementioned system of risk weights is fine as long as normal conditions continue to prevail. But in a crisis, and most particularly in a deep crisis, it is worth practically nothing. This did not escape the attention of the Basel Committee, which in 2005 introduced new capital charges for *specific price risk*, by requiring that additional capital is held for default on existing exposures – the *incremental default risk charge* (IDRC).

However, during the severe economic and banking crisis this incremental default risk charge did not capture losses of asset-backed securities (ABSs) in CDOs, and of other securitised financial instruments held in the trading book. The reason is that the stress did not come only from actual defaults but also, and primarily, from credit mitigations.

In consequence, the Basel Committee extended the IDRC charge to cover migration risks. Another modification to the 1996 Market Risk Amendment was that of stress periods, to be used when determining capital requirements. By closing one of the loopholes in Basel's capital adequacy, the new *incremental risk charge* (IRC) aimed at ending the manipulating of banking book rules by employing, instead, the trading book.

In addition, stress tests need to be performed at varying degrees of aggregation, from that of individual instrument to the institutional level. They must take place for different risk types including market, credit and liquidity risk; as well as benefit from a methodology which allows exposures to be identified and aggregated across the bank. Quantum logicians make a significant contribution to this process.

Contrary to the opinion of many bankers that statistical data and relationships allow accurate assessment of risk, the events of 2007-2009 have in fact revealed serious flaws with relying solely, or even mainly, on historical information. Backward-looking historical data sets tend to indicate benign conditions, so that an incremental risk analysis does not pick up the possibility of vulnerabilities or severe shocks. They are built in such a way that they prove to be unreliable once outliers and extreme events begin to unfold.

As the Basel Committee points out, stress-testing alerts bank management to adverse unexpected outcomes related to a variety of outliers. It provides an indication of how much capital might be needed to absorb losses in case of large shocks, and it can be used as a tool supplementing other risk control measures. Stress tests are particularly valuable in:

- Focusing attention on the banks' risk tolerances,

- Overcoming limitations of historical data,

- Supporting better internal and external communications,

- Contributing to a forward-looking assessment of risk, and

- Assisting in the elaboration of risk mitigation and contingency planning across a range of conditions.

The Basel Committee also points out that stress-testing is particularly important during and after periods of benign economic and financial developments, when fading memory of negative conditions can lead to complacency – and therefore to the under-pricing of risk.[116] The regulators might also have added that the severity of stress-testing should be increasing with time as:

- Stressed conditions of the past tend to become normal, and

- It is necessary to test further out in the long leg of the risk distribution (Chapter 1).

In addition, the point which was made in Chapter 3 about the use of quantum logic in conjunction with auctions and CDS spreads is equally valid with the incremental risk charge. The fact that risk weights were manipulated by the banking industry, and IDRC proved an incomplete approach in mapping risk, is even more evidence of a need for method improvement and the implementation of QED.

In conclusion, the analysis of past shortcomings is always most helpful in learning what to avoid and what to do better. For somebody who is eager to learn, errors and failures can be of precious assistance. Also a vital element of progress is the interdisciplinary transferring of experience; for instance from physics to the domain of finance and other areas of activity.

---

[116] Basel Committee on Banking Supervision, "Principles for Sound Stress-testing Practices and Supervision", BIS, Basel, January 2009.

5. The contribution of scenarios to realistic estimates of exposure

Section 4 brought to the reader's attention the importance of stress tests in conjunction with an incremental risk charge. A stress test can be made in any of the following ways:

- Scenario writing,
- Sensitivity analysis,[117]
- Statistical inference under extreme conditions,
- Drills for a meltdown.[118]

The latter are engineered by assuming the occurrence of the worst conditions that are plausible but unlikely.

A scenario reflecting worsening conditions was implemented in 2009 by the Bank of New York Mellon, when it initiated the policy of including statement figures in its earnings showing what could happen to its capital base under various hypotheses. This was an excellent initiative, using *what if* scenarios to help all stakeholders – from board members to regulators and investors – to think through how the institution copes with periods of pressure and adjust the risk appetite accordingly before the bank becomes another Lehman Brothers, AIG or Bear Stearns.

Statistical inference under extreme conditions is instrumental in analysing the quantitative effect of events in the long leg of the risk distribution – which was the theme of Chapter 1. In contrast to this, a scenario is a qualitative elaboration of a plausible future outcome, taking into account a number of potential happenings and developments. The aim is to analyse the outcome of mostly uncertain

---

[117] I am not particularly fond of sensitivity tests because they only shock one single parameter, holding constant all other factors and therefore largely underestimating exposure.

[118] D. N. Chorafas, *Stress-testing for Risk Control Under Basel II, Elsevier*, Oxford and Boston, 2007.

events and their impact. Scenarios can be developed for strategic planning, capital management, pricing decisions, risk control and other areas of activity.

As a result of stress tests through scenarios a company can anticipate events that otherwise come as surprises. The information scenarios permit management to engage in mitigation strategies and develop contingency plans for a wide range of impacts. Therefore, scenarios are an important mechanism for evaluating multiple risks as well as for communicating opinions, subsequently distilling them in an orderly manner and producing to 'a sense of the meeting' (see section 7 on the Delphi method).

In my experience I have found the use of scenarios instrumental in breaking the communications barrier that classically exists between traders and risk managers. Elaborating them not only serves as an eye-opener, but also, within the same firm, person-to-person communication is not always effective because of:

- Background differences,
- Difficulties in bringing a point across,
- A policy of departmental secrecy,
- The spirit of being each one on his own, or
- Lack of a common language appreciated and understood by everyone in the organisation (which QED could provide).

According to *Metcalfe's Law* (named after Bob Metcalfe, the inventor of the ethernet standard for traffic in networks), the *value* of a network – defined as its *utility* to a population – is roughly proportional to the number of users squared. An example is the telephone network. One telephone is useless; two telephones are not much better. It is only when most of the population has a telephone that the power of the network reaches its full potential.

The common language running on a network which interconnects people sitting at opposite sides of a risk-and-reward divide may well be scenarios referring to an outline (or synopsis) of a plot, play or other work. The scenario sets a sequence of scenes, which may or may not involve decisions, and provides for specific estimates, measurements, references, influences or updates connected to a developing situation.

It can also serve to elicit responses to specific issues of interest; for example, by conveying evidence on:

- Even small price movements on instruments like CDOs, and

- The large marking-to-market losses for the bank, into which these translate.

Practical experience teaches that online scenarios can have a tremendous communications potential. One of the lessons learned through the 2007-2009 crisis is that Pareto's law is always present. The 20% of holdings which escape careful scrutiny typically represent the 80% or more of total losses. Hence the need not only to steadily analyse balance sheet and off balance sheet positions before and after one hedges them, but also before and after they are marked to market. Such information should be made instantaneously available to senior management through scenarios, and permanently stored in a database so that walkthroughs and post-mortems can properly pinpoint personal accountability for exposure and for inaction in terms of risk control.

The nature of scenarios makes them suitable for representing behaviour in a way that allows people with dissimilar views to provide different opinions, which may be diverging, converging or overlapping. One of the best methods presently available is Delphi (section 7). One of Delphi's most interesting uses has been in connection to elicitation of systems specifications and model parameters.

The reader should, however, be aware that scenarios are tests, and tests always require careful planning. This is not yet generally appreciated in the banking industry or anywhere else. Here is what the Basel Committee says on that matter:

> Most bank stress tests were not designed to capture the extreme market events that were experienced. Most firms discovered that one or several aspects of their stress tests

did not even broadly match actual developments. In particular, scenarios tended to reflect mild shocks, assume shorter durations and underestimate the correlations between different positions, risk types and markets due to system-wide interactions and feedback effects.[119]

The result was a counterproductive widespread complacency. Far from being stress tests, these misdirected scenarios resulted in totally erroneous estimates of losses that were no more than a quarter's worth of earnings and typically much less, as the Basel Committee pointed out. Professional people should know of the existence of multiple risk factors, feedback effects and risk concentrations – and account for them.

The aforementioned January 2009 document by the Basel Committee identified a number of specific risks which were not properly covered (let alone in sufficient detail) in most stress tests done by the banking industry. Examples include:

- Funding liquidity risk (Chapter 3);
- Behaviour of complex structured products under stressed liquidity;
- Securitisation risk;
- Basis risk in relation to hedging strategies;
- Contingent risks, and more.

In conclusion, scenarios are a powerful tool, but if they are not sufficiently researched, properly planned and well-executed, then they suffer from the same problems as other risk control tools and methods. They fail, for instance, to recognise that risk dynamics for structured instruments, and derivative products at large, are different from those

---

[119] Basel Committee 'Principles for Sound Stress-testing Practices and Supervision,' BIS, Basel, January 2009.

for similarly-rated cash instruments, like bonds and loans of classical banking; or present other shortcomings like lack of flexibility.

6. The scenarios' flexibility

A scenarios' flexibility comes from the fact that it revolves around the interplay of human decision-makers and real or emulated events concerning people's behaviour and the aftermath of their decisions. The active participation of managers, traders, investment advisors and other dealers in investigative processes is the characteristic that distinguishes scenarios from other models and information carriers, opening the way to a framework for experimental purposes.

The reader should however notice that:

- Good scenarios aren't created randomly, and
- The results provided by the best of them resemble exploratory science rather than operational analysis.

The best stress programmes integrate not one but a range of scenarios and take into account both individual risk factors and system-wide interactions. This dual approach helps in deepening management's understanding of vulnerabilities, making senior executives aware of switches between expected and unexpected outcomes, as well as non-linear loss profiles.

Moreover, the benefit derived from scenarios is so much greater when they are administered flexibly and imaginatively, since an inflexible approach leads to underestimation of the likelihood and severity of extreme events. This gives a false sense of security about a bank's resilience to shocks. It is also advisable to supplement historical scenarios with forward-looking modules incorporating:

- Changes in portfolio composition,
- Significant variations in prices, and
- The possibility of emerging risks not covered by relying on previous stress episodes.

The elicitation of expert opinions and experimentation incorporating the above references results in focused tests on performance, the output of which can be valuable to pricing decisions. One of the domains in which stress scenarios deliver interesting results is the formulation of alternative strategies for more effective risk management by assessing:

- Correlations of risks in extreme cases,

- Exogenous shocks to a portfolio of assets,

- Major stresses affecting specific business lines, and

- The after-effect of increases in leverage (or contemplated increases).

Here is an example, from a recent Merrill Lynch study, on who needs scenarios in connection to financial leverage: "...it has to be remembered that financial leverage played a significant role in influencing the recent parabolic profit cycle. We are not just talking about the financial services sector, but industrials and retailers too, as practically everyone became a 'financial' this cycle – GE, H&R Block, GM, Ford and even John Deere!"[120] The able use of scenarios has prerequisites:

1. The first, and foremost, is understanding the problem.

Curiously enough, this requirement is very often violated, because the problem seems to be 'so obvious'. The integral part of understanding the problem is appreciating the importance of free expression of opinion, as well as communications requirements, documentation prerequisites and problem constraints.

2. Identifying all factors influencing the problem, and their range of variation.

This is a tall call and the challenge increases exponentially with detail. Therefore scenario designers must resist the general tendency to include more detail than really necessary. But at the same time, they must be

---

[120] Merrill Lynch, 'Economic Commentary', 22 August 2008.

careful in their identification of risk factors, since their characteristics may be not be evident; and some events may be present not in the problem's regular run but at its extremes, as Figure 4.1 shows.

Rating all risk factors which have been identified in terms of correlations and impact.

Because complexity is the enemy of accuracy, and a scenario's goal is to provide results of acceptable and proven accuracy (not detail), choices must be made based on pertinence and materiality – judged in terms of the sought out goal. This statement is valid in terms of both normal and extreme conditions, and is particularly important in the latter case.

Situations, intentions, attitudes and other qualitative factors must be given a role in the scenario.

These will usually involve alternative paths of development affecting physical and play conditions, iterative processes, force structure(s), likely actions and reactions by players, a limit or range of limits, measurements of market effects and after-effects, market psychology, and risk control aims. A flexible scenario will be structured to make the online exchange of information and opinions clear, timely and efficient.

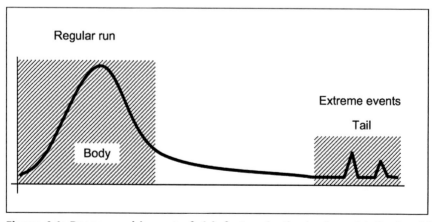

Figure 4.1: Ranges and impact of risk factors in the body and tail of a risk distribution.

Structure and comparability are required because a scenario is a multi-way communications means; not a game whose result each player keeps to himself.[121] In addition, the scenario needs a *sponsor*. In risk management scenarios, the sponsor may be the board, CEO or another senior executive. Requests flow from the sponsor to the designer to the players and responses, including documentation, go from the players to the sponsor.

Precisely because sponsorship typically targets one focal issue, scenarios have locality in terms of goals and results. A credit risk scenario focuses on creditworthiness and probability of default. If the results being obtained are subsequently used for market risk purposes where instrument liquidity, volatility and market psychology hold the upper ground, the scenario's output will be irrelevant at best. In terms of its design, therefore, crucial questions are:

- What is the theme the sponsor wants to examine?

- What kind of questions should the players answer?

- What is the level of confidence they should observe?

- Should the session manager be allowed to set rulings? To strike out rules?

- Should anyone have the right to disregard controversial or adverse hypotheses?[122]

Nobody, including the president, should have the right to veto scenario assumptions and options, because this is impairing one of the main benefits – to stimulate discussion and use the information to reach a specific goal. Worst case scenarios are not played to accuse anybody,

---

[121] Whether trader, investment expert, risk controller or manager each individual decision-maker using the scenario is a player. Scenarios which are multiplayer represent a number of different opinions. One-player scenarios are non-essential to the references made in this chapter.

[122] A flat answer is he should not, yet companies do allow this to happen.

but to allow a critical assessment of the bank's ability to react to unexpected severe events, including its vulnerability to changes in economic and financial conditions.

Scenarios are impaired when CEOs, CFOs, risk managers or any others are given the freedom to affect the results or screen the output. Under no condition should there be interference with the acts of experimentation and communication. The scenario's players must not only be but also *feel free* to transmit their own concerns, insights, questions, interpretations and findings back to the sponsor. The Delphi method provides an excellent example of this policy.

7. The Delphi method[123]

As sections 5 and 6 have explained, scenarios are interactive tools (typically textual and graphical) helping in the description of an environment, product or process for *elicitation* of opinions, development, integration, verification and validation of plausible events, specifications or assumptions. It is therefore also for *anticipation* of actions and reactions. The arguments and counterarguments developed by scenarios enlarge perspective and challenge established notions.

The qualitative nature of scenarios is particularly well suited to financial studies, as well as for prognostication and evaluation in the sciences and in engineering, making people alert to non-quantifiable conditions or characteristics. Combined with a system of rewards for right estimates verified post-mortem with walkthroughs, it is possible to avoid systematic bias whatever may be the cause.

---

[123] The original Delphi in Greece is generally thought to be the temple which could tell the future, but there are many tales about it which do not add up to that assumption. One of them mentioned by Thucydides, the famous ancient historian, is that Delphi served as a money-lending centre at usury.

An example is provided by qualitative *model validation* through scenarios, in which domain experts participate. According to the Basel Committee, model validation should be systematically applied for both internally designed and vendor-provided models and this should include not just its numerical results but also the model's:

- Theoretical soundness,
- Appropriateness of assumptions,
- Mathematical integrity, and
- Consistency of treatment with market practices.[124]

Basel also suggests that sensitivity analyses are performed to assess the impact of variations in modern parameters on fair value, including stress conditions (with the aggregate being subject to backtesting). Scenarios are an excellent way to ensure that management understands the conditions under which the model performs, and judge whether or not these are realistic and acceptable.

All this is written on the understanding that scenarios and numerical analyses complement one another, with the former providing a systematic and direct use of expert judgment, which is examined and presented dispassionately; and the latter based on hard data, but also subject to *data insufficiency*. Different approaches can be employed in obtaining this result; the one I like best is the aforementioned *Delphi method*.

Delphi makes use of a process that might be seen as *expert arbitration* with deliberation steered by a control group through feedback. Its predecessor methodology in 1948 had targeted horse racing, while the current method was developed in the early 1960s in the US in conjunction with the Apollo program.

---

[124] Basel Committee on Banking Supervision, 'Supervisory Guidance for Assessing Bank's Financial Instrument Fair Value Practices', BIS, Basel, November 2008.

A fairly accurate way of looking at Delphi is that it essentially consists of an interactive, virtual roundtable discussion with feedback. The participants to it are networked rather than being physically present in the same place.

Its strength lies in the fact that:

- Events and their likelihood are often subject to a conditional probability (Bayes' theorem); something is happening *if* something else takes place.

- The elicitation of expert opinion is systematic, open and more forthcoming than opinions expressed in a committee, and

- The experts' prognostication is subjected to iterations, with the responses being obtained and presented to the same experts in order to confront them with *dissension*.

In principle, problem solving becomes better focused when more minds are put to the task, though there exist limits to the number of participants. Delphi uses interviews and/or questionnaires to extract estimates or prognostications on a specific event (or issue) from a sample of experts and it attempts to improve the panel approach in arriving at an estimate by subjecting the views of individual experts to each other's opinions – which might be divergent.

Dissension helps the participants in the virtual roundtable to focus their judgment. Dissension is a sort of criticism, but the conveyed message is anonymous, and face-to-face confrontation is avoided because of this anonymity of opinions and of the arguments advanced in their defence. The flexibility of the method sees to it that there are different ways of implementing Delphi. In one version the participating experts are asked not only to give their opinions, but also to make annotations on the reasons for their opinions. Direct debate is replaced by the interchange of information, of stated opinions and of annotations, through a carefully designed sequence of questionnaires, graphs and feedbacks.

At every successive questioning, each participant is given new and refined information, in the form of the other participants' evolving opinions. The process continues until further progress toward a consensus appears to be negligible. The remaining conflicting views are then documented and presented in a form which shows the relative weight of each opinion within the group.

One of the better examples of using Delphi in finance is an opinion-based estimation of correlation coefficients.[125] My years of experience with a number of institutions and risk management projects documents that (sometimes because of data insufficiency, and most often due to plain bias) correlations can be awfully wrong.

8. Refining judgmental opinions through Delphi

Progressively refining judgmental opinions through successive iterations is not only a good approach for taking some of the subjectivity out of the system; it is also the way the market works. Combined guesses by market participants tend to be more accurate than just one person's estimates. Ask a small crowd, rather than a pair, and the average is often close to a given measurement, correlation or other statistic.[126]

Not only the wisdom of crowds created through an iterative process leads to greater accuracy in projections, but also more recently psychologists have found that two guesses made by the same person at different times are better than one. Psychologists also noticed that the interval between the first and second estimates determined how accurate the average was.

---

[125] Correlation is a statistical concept referring, for example, to the co-movement of two variables such as risks or prices over time.

[126] A phenomenon called the wisdom of crowds by James Surowiecki, a columnist for the *New Yorker*.

It is *as if*:

- The brain is constantly creating hypotheses about a given process, checking them against reality, and

- Those that pass are adopted, or once more recycled in search of what the 'right' answer ought to look like.

The network's first and foremost contribution is that it obliges knowledgeable people to think of adversity and its after-effect – something they don't usually do as a matter of course. Someone recalled a conversation with Warren Buffett on this subject. "Warren Buffett said: 'What do you think the odds of this thing making it are?' I said, 'Pretty good. One out of two.' He said, 'Do you think that's good? Why don't you go in an airplane with a parachute that opens one out of every two times and jump?' "[127]

Estimating the likelihood of an event is one thing, evaluating whether or not that event is rational, sustainable or of acceptable risk, without being subject to tunnel vision, is another.

Rationality, sustainability and acceptability are frequently blurred because of tunnel vision. This happens more frequently than one expects, and when it does it has disastrous consequences on estimating, modelling, computing, choosing and using correlation coefficients. The mathematics of correlations is straightforward[128]; by contrast, company politics associated with a decision on correlations can be most convoluted.

Back in 2003, a working group by the Basel Committee found little consistency in methods employed by the surveyed credit institutions, as

---

[127] Roger Lowenstein, *Buffett, the Making of an American Capitalist*, Weidenfeld & Nicolson, London, 1996.

[128] D. N. Chorafas, *After Basel II. Assuring Compliance and Smoothing the Rough Edges*, Lafferty/VRL Publishing, London, 2005.

far as the calculation of *correlations*[129] based on diversification benefits were concerned. Basel's Joint Forum report pointed out that: "At one extreme some institutions estimate correlations among all risk types using data or synthetic indices. At the other extreme, some firms do not attempt to estimate correlations."[130] Both extremes disregard the fact that the computation of critical correlation coefficients is of fundamental importance to properly estimating risk concentrations. Also, a policy of arbitrarily choosing correlations by board decisions is counterproductive because it exposes the bank to very bad surprises.[131]

Leaving aside the case of regulatory arbitrage and the misuse of correlations associated with it, banks do not dispute Basel II's premise that correlations must account for major dependencies between different activities and risk types, but neither are they objective in their calculations. What they frequently say is that future correlations will be benign (therefore, low) because senior management pays so much attention to diversification – which, in my experience, is a chimera.

In the aftermath, the board, an executive committee, or some other decision-making entity, decides that historical correlations are more or less irrelevant. Instead it sets a low correlation as a sort of policy to be followed in computing exposure. This is, of course, nonsense but it is found in several cases in the banking industry – particularly among institutions where the quality of management is wanting.

A way to improve upon correlations accuracy is to use a method of refining quantitative estimates and judgmental opinions through iterative queries to known domain experts. In the example given in Figure 4.2 a statistically valid number of professionals in corporate

---

[129] Correlation is a statistical concept referring to the co-movement of two variables such as risks or prices, over time.

[130] Banking Committee on Banking Supervision. The Joint Forum "Trends in Risk Integration and Aggregation", BIS, August 2003.

[131] More on correlation risk in Chapter 5.

banking were asked to estimate a correlation coefficient of single name exposures where original opinions put it in the range of 20% to 40%. Delphi made it possible to shrink that range to manageable proportions, also making a histogram of expert opinions available in the last iteration.

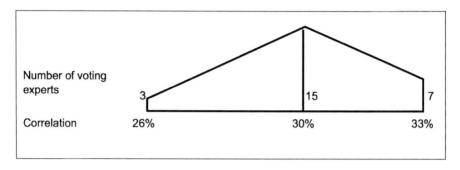

Figure 4.2: Voting by experts on two instruments correlation by using Delphi, an established methodology.

(Contrast this to the case of a well-known global bank where the board 'decided' that the correlation coefficient for *all* exposures will be 25%, no matter what the specific case. At that time, following an analytical study, another better managed global bank with fairly similar transactions found that the correlation coefficients of its warehoused positions ranged between 17% and 80%.)

An example of how the process of refining judgmental opinions can be effectively used in risk management is provided by the way the European Central Bank's (ECB's) Survey of Professional Forecasters (SPF) works. Given the diversity of the panel of participants, aggregate SPF results may reflect a relatively heterogeneous set of subjective views and assumptions. (This survey typically gathers information on expectations for euro zone inflation, GDP growth and unemployment.)

SPF participants are also asked to assess the likelihood of future outcomes falling within specific intervals. The aggregate probability distribution obtained by combining forecasters' responses provides a pattern of their assessments; as well as information about how they gauge the risk of the actual outcome being above or below the most likely range.[132]

The reader should notice that the wisdom of crowds can work only when no dictator, expert, or group of experts is exercising dominance over the people expected to express their honest opinions. In a panel or survey, this happens when the panellists are subjected to a herd syndrome which is self-defeating given that:

- Experts form their opinion largely on personal experience, which has been built over years of practice, and into which has been integrated a great deal of their training.

- The divergence existing in this personal experience, like the estimated likelihood of an event, is precisely what we wish to capture in an unbiased but productised form.

The essence of productisation is the ability to merge scenarios and partial results into an aggregate. This helps to produce a script that provides, so to speak, 'the sense of the meeting'. Experts, of course, can be wrong, as happened with the timing of the Apollo program.

In the early 1960s, the Rand Corporation asked experts around the globe which year man would land on the moon. The answer with highest frequency was the early 1990s – roughly three decades hence. But the Soviet space challenge led to a race, and man landed on the moon in 1969. Nothing is foolproof, and nothing is as prone to failure as human opinion. This strengthens rather than diminishes the importance of Delphi because, even if the main body of experts moves in one way, some outliers may well indicate the exception which eventually becomes the rule.

---

[132] European Central Bank, Monthly Bulletin, August 2008.

Appendix: why the value at risk model is irrelevant

Value at risk (VaR) is a model developed in 1990-1991 at the request of Morgan Bank's CEO. What he had asked for was a brief, summary report (if possible in one number) able to show the exposure his institution had assumed by noon over the last 24 hours; and he wanted to have this report at his desk, as well as in the hands of a selected group of JP Morgan executives, by 4.15 pm.

The 1996 Market Risk Amendment by the Basel Committee on Banking Supervision followed upon this concept and adopted Morgan's model. It also identified two alternative approaches:

1. One is *parametric* (VaR/P), based on historical analysis (assuming a normal distribution of risks) and on correlation (variance/covariance).

2. The other, non-parametric, is based on *simulation* (VaR/S), and typically uses the Monte Carlo method.[133]

Banks have been free to choose the approach they want, but the results are not necessarily comparable.

Provided all other conditions which enter into risk control are fulfilled, Monte Carlo simulation (the better of the two approaches) allows exposure embedded in a number of instruments to be analysed. Results rely on the generation of a distribution of returns. These may be asset price paths or exposure estimates.

• By means of values drawn from a multivariate normal distribution, rocket scientists develop future risk hypotheses.

• They do so by employing a pricing methodology to calculate the value of the portfolio, based on computed VaR estimates.

---

[133] Chorafas, *Chaos Theory.*

This method is *non-parametric*, because it makes no assumptions about the population's parameters. Though the *outputs* might have the pattern of a normal distribution, this is not taken to be so *a priori*. VaR/S, however, has three downsides:

1. The first and most serious one, shared with VaR/P, is that only half to two-thirds of warehoused financial instruments offer themselves to risk analysis by VaR.

2. The second is that simulation is computation-intensive, therefore time consuming. This is particularly so for banks which still use low-spec technology (which is more than half of institutions).

3. The third constraint (also shared with VaR/P) is that while plenty of people in the financial sector masquerade as rocket scientists, few really know what they are doing. Those who are knowledgeable appreciate that though the Monte Carlo method is an excellent tool, it should be used only when it is supported by appropriate expertise, computing power, and the company features a large database bandwidth.

Alternatively, a bank can employ the more limited variance/covariance method and the correlation matrix which it implies. Its results, however, are even more limited and unreliable than those of VaR/S in the ever expanding universe of novel and complex derivative instruments. Moreover, VaR/P has two other major deficiencies which see to it that the measure of exposure it provides is not really appropriate:

• The most talked about is the approximation resulting from the undocumented assumption of a normal distribution. In an analytical sense, this assumption of normality reduces the value of VaR's output, even if it features the benefit of simplifying VaR calculations, because it permits the use of statistical tables.

With this approach, all percentiles are assumed to be known multiples of the standard deviation, a process which is unrealistic; it also provides only one estimate of exposure.[134]

- Less talked about, but just as serious is that – as Dr Alan Greenspan has underlined – we are still at the infancy of variance/covariance computation in finance. Behind this second and most important constraint of parametric VaR lies the question of serial independence of observed values. To make matters even less reliable, the VaR method makes a mathematically incorrect assumption about the reporting period. The '√10 x daily holding algorithm', for a 10-day period, advanced by the Basel Committee, presupposes serial independence – which means that one day's risk results do not affect the next day's. Evidently, this is not the case with risk embedded in a portfolio of securities.

In addition, the fact that VaR focuses on exposure in the course of a single day is in itself a major negative. Its downside also includes an inordinate amount of clumsiness, over-reliance on historical data and evidence that it works best when markets are stable. Other weaknesses include:

- It does not capture the effects of highly stressed markets, and

- It does not tell what would happen if assets could not be quickly hedged or liquidated.

Do not blame the model, however; rather, blame the people who use it and do not appreciate that what they are doing is misleading. As if what has been mentioned was not enough, another major weakness shared by both VaR models is the lack of *confidence intervals* which

---

[134] Researchers from the Federal Reserve of New York, and Princeton University, have proposed a metric COVaR, for 'conditional value at risk'. Its aim is to capture the risk of loss in a portfolio due to other institutions being in trouble. It takes account of spill-over effects to increase the VaR results. This is better than classical VaR, but since VaR is unreliable so is COVaR.

minimise the outliers and exceptions. The supervisory authorities say that for financial reporting reasons the confidence interval must be 99%. However, 99% is too low because it leaves the long leg of the risk distribution wholly outside – the most dangerous 1% of all exposures is located in this long leg – and it is also incompatible with the newer Basel regulation on incremental risk charge (IRC, section 4). Furthermore, while banks do report VaR to regulators at 99% confidence intervals, for internal decisions they may use 97.5%, 95%, 90% or some other figure.

	2002	**2003**	**Increase of Exposure**
UBS	180	260	50%
JP Morgan Chase	120	180	50%
Citigroup	50	70	40%
Morgan Stanley	50	60	20%
Goldman Sachs	45	60	33%
Crédit Suisse First Boston	40	50	25%

Table 4.2: Year-on-year VaR exposure at six global banks at end of 2003 (in $billions)[135]

---

[135] *The Economist*, 21 February 2004.

Worst of all, nobody really understands what VaR is saying. Table 4.2 provides an example. When 2003 VaR results for big banks were made public, I asked senior financial executives and regulators what could be the reason for the most significant jump in VaR exposure between 25% and 50% year on year. The answer I invariably received was: "Well, we don't exactly know. Many things might have provoked it."

It is ridiculous to use metrics when "we don't exactly know" what they tell us. Either commercial bankers, investment bankers and regulators are not concerned about systemic risk – which may well be the case, because had they acted aggressively to right the balances in 2004 we would not have had the deep credit and banking crisis of 2007-2009 – or they know very well that VaR and other currently available tools for measurement of exposure have lost contact with reality and they have become irrelevant. Hence the need for networking the wisdom of crowds through the Delphi approach, and for developing a high level risk measurement by using the best method science can offer: QED.

Chapter 5: Applying Feynman Diagrams in Risk Management

1. The probability of an event

O ver the last three decades the complexity of financial exposure has increased by leaps and bounds. To cope with the esoteric features of novel instruments and their unknowns, modern risk management has become a heavy user of mathematics and formulae from physics. Theoretically, *computational finance* evolved as a sort of second nature to economists specialising in macroeconomic models. Practically, however, this thesis is unsustainable.

Though it rests on great spirits like Léon Walras and Vilfredo Pareto of the 19th century and John von Neumann of the 20th, computational finance is still in its infancy or, at best, at its early stages of development. Many models, including some adopted by supervisory authorities are way off the mark, and are characterised by:

- A very narrow viewpoint,

- Resting on limited time series,

- Using algorithms unfit for the problem at hand, and

- Being utterly misunderstood by those employing them.[136]

It comes as no surprise, therefore, that not only the Basel Committee and national supervisors, but also the 15 November 2008 and 2 April 2009 international economic conferences, held respectively in Washington and London, stressed the need to "develop processes that provide for timely and comprehensive measurement of risk concentrations and large counterparty risk positions across products

---

[136] Chorafas *Chaos Theory*; and Chorafas and Steinmann *Expert Systems in Banking*.

and geographies." They also emphasised the requirement for new stress-testing models and procedures.[137]

There are two ways to look at the use of models in finance. The one espoused by this book is as the *mind's eye*, a tool to transform one's culture. The other is the narrow approach of mapping a product or process into the computer through mathematical formulas. Both have a place in economics and finance, but it has been a deliberate choice to stick to the broader, cultural perspective, and use the most powerful concepts science can provide.

A basic reason for this choice is that the central theme of this book is not risk management *per se*, but ways and means to avoid a repetition of the descent of finance and of the economy, through sound governance and effective supervision. This makes it most important to define in the best possible way what sort of methods and tools we need to measure risk in an unambiguous, reliable and universally understood way; and I believe that quantum electrodynamics fulfils this objective.

The way Richard Feynman, the physicist, relays it in his book *QED: The Strange Theory of Light and Matter*, the most important process in physics (which is the foremost exact science) is that of calculating the *probability of an event*. "Nature permits us to calculate only probabilities,"[138] he says. Let me add that the same is true of banking, financial products, markets and many other domains.

Chapter 1 brought to the reader's attention the fact that there is always a distribution of events, and this is true in banking, in the sciences and in any other field of life. Risk distribution is an example.

---

[137] Chorafas, *Stress-testing*.

[138] Richard P. Feynman, *QED: The Strange Theory of Light and Matter*, Penguin Books, London 1985.

In addition, this distribution of events happening in the real and in the virtual economy can be seen as composed of two main parts:

1. Those of high frequency but relatively lower impact (HF/LI) which constitute its body, and

2. Those of low frequency but plausible and of significantly higher impact (LF/HI) which are found in the tails, where we need to calculate both probability and after-effect.

Subsequently, Chapter 2 explained the nature of novel financial instruments which create mountains of risk, and it suggested that the 'rocket scientists' who develop them should be put to task to devise advanced risk control tools and methods.[139] It also made the reader aware of the fact that presently available statistical quality control charts provide excellent means for gauging whether a product or process is *in control*, particularly in reference to the body of the risk distribution.

SQCs are also instrumental in visualising trends, which is crucial because in finance, as in science, we are dealing with events that exhibit an alternation of relatively smooth behaviour and sudden changes or transition. When transitions regard an object's or entity's state, for example the velocity of a body hitting a surface, they are called *impacts*. If they concern the rules that determine the events we observe, like those underpinning CDS spreads, they are known as *switches*.

For its part, Chapter 3 presented practical examples to document that risk is all over the place, and it must be properly priced. The point has also been made that any pricing solution which does not pay a great amount of attention to the *probability of adverse events*, as well as of lack of events expected to happen, will provide results on the wrong side of the balance sheet.

---

[139] See also Chorafas *Rocket Scientists in Banking*.

All this is highly relevant to risk management because banks are complex and opaque firms. Working out the risks they take (and they have been taking) proved to be beyond their regulators, their managers and their shareholders. The recent crisis has shown that all three populations were incapable of understanding the nature and level of assumed exposure. This led to poor governance and weak supervision, making the credit institutions fragile and bringing the economy to the edge of an abyss.

Feynman's statement that the most important process in physics is that of calculating *the probability of an event* very much applies to banking and finance; the event we are after is *risk*. As we will see in this chapter, for reasons of calculation, and in order to gain insight, we can capitalise on the notion of *vectors* underpinning the *Feynman diagrams*.

The Appendix refreshes the reader's knowledge of vector quantities, one of the pillars of calculus. The use of vector diagrams in risk management is a new contribution, one which had to be made because they transform the risk control process into a better, understandable form.

Vectors (labelled 'arrows' in a Feynman diagram) can be computed and mapped into a risk space very easily; the addition of vectors is straightforward; and their graphical representation is enlightening. Moreover, there exist libraries of computer programs dealing with vector analysis[140], which can be very profitably used in computation.

---

[140] As well as with matrices and with numerical analysis at large.

2. Feynman diagrams[141]

Richard Feynman's *QED* consists essentially of four lectures he gave at UCLA. These were mainly addressed to the general public and to other scientists, but not necessarily to physicists. Therefore the lecturer had to start in the simplest possible way, with something that the audience already more or less knew. That approach is excellent in introducing the QED method to the realm of risk management.

Feynman's choice in making his subject comprehensible was an experiment to measure the *partial reflection* of light, first by a single surface of glass then by two and eventually by multiple surfaces. Let us take two surfaces. The theme is *photons*; think of each of them as a little lump of light.[142]

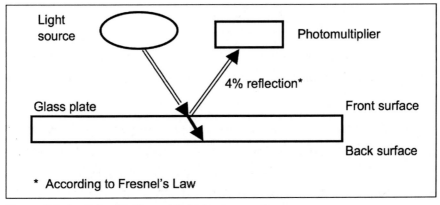

Figure 5.1: Partial reflection of light by two surfaces.

---

[141] Murray Gell-Mann has pointed out that these diagrams were first employed by Ernst Stueckelberg, the physicist, who devised a similar notation years earlier, motivated by the need for a covariant formalism for quantum field theory. Stueckelberg, however, did not provide an automated way to handle symmetry factors and loops, although he was first to find the correct physical interpretation in terms of forward and backward in time particle paths.

[142] It is an interesting hindsight that both photons and electrons behave somewhat like waves and somewhat like particles. Light was first considered to be travelling in waves; then it was accepted that it travels in particles. By contrast, radiation was originally thought to travel in particles; the notion now prevailing is that it travels in waves.

As shown in Figure 5.1, the input received from the light source by the glass is reflected to a plate. The feature of partial reflection by two surfaces led physicists to calculate the probability of an event using an approach quite different than that of making absolute predictions (keep this in mind when we talk of risk). Physicists proceed by drawing little arrows (vectors) on a piece of paper similar to those in Figure 5.2. Feynman repeatedly stressed in his lectures that, on their way to gaining a PhD, graduate physicists should spend time in learning how to draw these arrows.[143] (It should not be that complex in risk terms though considerable work still remains to be done.)

Drawing these arrows may not be so easy to learn, but it constitutes a well-established methodology in physics. The process is known as computing an event's *probability amplitude*. The probability of an event is represented by the area of the square on an arrow[144]. This method could be adapted to the probability of a risk event because the concept of vector calculus is powerful and flexible, and the way Feynman diagrams are used has the potential to represent each possible way an event could happen.

In QED, a physicist draws arrows on a piece of paper. In the example of partial reflection of light two arrows will be drawn, each representing the way a reflection can happen from one of the two surfaces. Stated in a simplified way, the photon bounces off the front surface and/or the back surface to get to the plate. It is important to determine the direction of the arrows. This done, the physicist can combine any number of vectors by adding them.

---

[143] In finance, too, no graduate (master or doctorate) should get a degree if he does not learn how to apply vectors and matrices in risk control.

[144] Or, in different terms, the square of the probability amplitude is the probability of observing a given configuration.

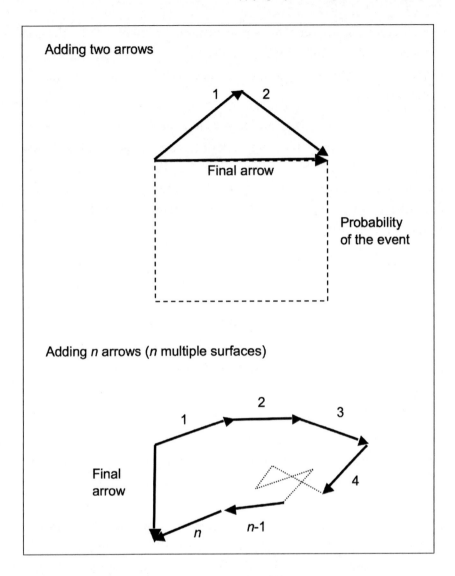

Figure 5.2: Vectorial representation of the probability of events.

The computation of vectors is an integral part of the process of *analysis*, and QED's arrows provide a compelling metaphor in regard to the way the modern financial industry works. What we do in finance is very similar to what is done in physics. We examine the key variables, their sensitivities, potential for reward and embedded risks not only through spot measurements but also, if not mainly, through predictions of future behaviour – a process which has a *probability amplitude*.

Another common background is that, whether in finance or in physics, the most important aim of prognostication is not really future events, but the *future impact* of current events (and in a business environment, of current decisions).

The reader should further notice that it would not be the first time business and finance employ concepts and tools originally developed for studies in physics and in engineering. Levels of confidence and the operating characteristics curves underpinning them (Chapter 2) were a breakthrough of the Manhattan Project (the Allies' atomic bomb effort during World War II).

The premise is that, just like confidence intervals, the notion of vectorial representation, and the way it is implemented in QED, can be effectively extended into the so far poorly understood domain of assumed exposure. Such an approach will provide an analysis of risks and opportunities as well as a way of measuring in a reasonably dependable manner the future effect (positive or negative) of our current commitments.

This is, after all, one of the goals we aim to reach with risk control. Dr Harold D. Koontz, my professor of business policy at UCLA, often talked about the importance of reading tomorrow's newspaper today – albeit at the cost of lower precision and greater uncertainty than might be the case the day after. In any prognostication a basic premise is that the future is no longer unique, unforeseeable or inevitable. There is a multitude of possible futures, with associated likelihood that can be estimated through the probability amplitude Feynman talked about.

The task of prognostication and measurement of likelihood is made so much more complex in times of turbulence, because by definition turbulence is nonlinear, irregular and erratic. Therefore we need *analytical financial models* on which we can depend. For instance, we need to know about trends, study pockets of risk and return, pinpoint inefficiencies, short-lived anomalies and test prevailing hypotheses. This can barely be done with old methods. They key to a successful, forward-looking financial analysis is non-traditional research. Non-traditional research is synonymous with the development (or adaptation) and use of more powerful methods and tools for reasons of prediction.

These two points bring our discussion back to quantum electrodynamics. Most valuable in the case of vector analysis is the fact that, once the representation is done, QED provides an easy approach of combining any number of them, by adding them up into a 'final arrow' from the tale of the first arrow to the head of the last one (see second half of Figure 5.2). This integrative ability is a fundamental reference in connection to the development of a new risk management methodology.

In conclusion, there is beauty in this general rule of quantum theory that the probability of an event is found by adding vectors for *all the ways the event could happen*; and the final arrows square gives the probability of the entire event. This 'computational grand principle' of QED fits with risk management at large, and most particularly exposure associated with complex and obscure instruments like collateralised debt obligations (CDOs) and credit default swaps (CDSs, see Chapter 2).

3. A broad field of QED implementation

The use of quantum electrodynamics for credit, market and liquidity risk – the strong forces – will not be the first type of interdisciplinary implementation. Quantum information technology provides another example on the application of quantum theory, with projects aimed at doing things that classical IT cannot manage.

Quantum computing underpins the research and design machines that can execute lots of calculations in parallel.[145] Quantum cryptography

---

[145] Though this is still at the stage of laboratory projects.

has promised unbreakable codes for messages. For example, the approach taken at the Toshiba research laboratory at Cambridge is that of a photon detector which counts single photons at room temperature. That's the kind of equipment already used to detect multiple photons by relying on the fact that when a photon hits a semiconductor it often knocks an electron out of place. This generates a positively charged hole in the crystal lattice in the place where the negatively charged electron used to be. It also prepares the stage for applying an electric charge to the crystal, in which case these holes and electrons move in opposite directions creating more holes.

Quantum cryptography relies on the fact that an eavesdropper intercepting the message changes the quantum states (giving himself or herself away as being on the line). Hence the emphasis placed on building repeaters that do not destroy quantum states. A crucial development of quantum cryptography is that of a photon counter, making it possible to build quantum repeaters preserving the states of polarisation.

Along a similar line of reasoning, I would suggest that concepts associated with QED are researched for their ability to correct a critical deficiency in risk assessment – consisting of the fact that nearly all current models implicitly assume individual events occur independently of each other (see section 5). Insurance models, for example, make insufficient allowance for the fact that floods often occur in clusters, in spite of the existence of Hurst's coefficient.[146]

This failure to consider 'fat tails' sees to it that expected losses are undervalued in a pricing sense, especially in stop-loss and second event covers. In nature, many supposedly independent events are correlated

---

[146] Hurst was a British engineer who, while working on the floods of the Nile, observed that a flood will be followed by another flood and a drought by another drought next year.

in time, and this has played a key role in the series of floods in 2000 and 2007 in Britain, as well as in flood events that took place in continental Europe during the summer of 2002. Something similar happens in finance, as the deep credit and banking crisis of 2007-2009 indicates.

Another significant improvement that I expect from the use of a method like the QED vectors in risk management, is the elimination of false assumptions and hypotheses which bias models and make their results undependable. What has been basically missing, as the presence of modelling in finance has increased, is a methodology for making and testing tentative statements. Such a methodology could be used to explain some facts or lead to the investigation of others.

Like photon reflection from surfaces, market conditions change, altering the basis on which our assumptions are formulated. In turn, undocumented hypotheses can raise havoc. It is not very often appreciated that assumptions and statements on which analytical finance is increasingly based may be shaky or outright illusionary. Mathematics is inappropriate for solving problems if we are not careful with what we do, and if we are too theoretical, hard-headed, or fail to provide proof.

As an article in *The Economist* put it: "The people at Goldman Sachs lost a packet when something happened that their computers told them should occur only once every 100 millennia." Not only is financial model-making to a significant extent still in its infancy, but there is also a need for processes that can be tested rather than accepted as self-evident truths. When hypotheses are unstuck from reality, it is impossible to estimate gains and losses engineered by events such as:

- Risk embedded in complex instruments,

- Asymmetric market behaviour,

- Switches in market sentiment,

- Risk concentrations among major players,

- How long market liquidity may last, or

- Whether the central bank will be taken as hostage.

By far the best test of a hypothesis is experimental, the principle being that a theory is valid only when it is verified by the results of experiments. When this is unfeasible because (as it often happens in finance) data is unavailable, the methodology is weak or the tools are substandard, the use of interactive scenarios such as the Delphi method might provide a substitute.[147] (Delphi provides no consensus, but a framework for interactive dissent (Chapter 4).)

An item in Bloomberg News in mid-2008 highlighted that the accuracy of analysts' profit prognostications had fallen to its worst level since 1992. This was considered to be important because advocates of the Fed model of the economy were out in full force laying the claim that equities had never been so attractively priced relative to Treasuries. Critics answered that the problem with the Fed model was that it employed consensus earnings forecasts, irrespective of how unrealistic they may be.[148]

All this is bad news for present-day risk management, but good news for a new methodology's implementation potential. Let me add one more thought. When the revolutionary ideas of quantum physics were evolving, many physicists tried to understand them in terms of the then prevailing old-fashioned concepts, like the idea that light goes in straight lines. Clear-minded physicists, however, pointed out that to appreciate the new approaches it was necessary to break with theories of the past; and practice proved them right. The same thing will happen with risk management.

---

[147] But as Chapter 4 has underlined, this should always be subject to verification by post-mortems.

[148] Merrill Lynch, Economic Commentary, 22 August 2008.

4. Are we planning for failure?

One of the expectations associated with the use of a high level approach like QED is the liberation from the narrow principles and practices of today. An old concept used by the new incremental risk charge (IRC) set forth in Basel's 'Guidelines for Computing Capital for Incremental Risk in the Trading Book' – which was introduced to the reader in Chapter 4 – is that this model would or should be based on the assumption of constant level of exposure over a one year capital horizon with *constant level of risk* (emphasis added). However, as the January to December 2008 events in the stock market proved, this is awfully wrong because:

- It does not account for risk volatility measured by VIX (Chapter 1), which on 20 November reached 75.6% – the third highest level in its history.

- One year's time slots have had highly diverse risk characteristics, and

- Spikes and lows in IRC are being represented by averages, which are meaningless.[149]

What I am suggesting in connection to using quantum electrodynamics for IRC, and more broadly for measurement and management of financial exposure, is basic research in risk management. As every scientist knows, basic research is a hard slog for small reward in terms of the number of projects which succeed, but big reward is reaped from projects which are successful. To succeed, we must avoid the traps which currently exist – which is the purpose of the following paragraphs.

---

[149] This Basel document makes reference to correlations approaching the extreme values of 1 or -1 for several days at the height of the disturbance, which does not match the guideline of constant level of risk.

Chapter 4 also brought to the reader's attention the fact that old metrics such as VaR have no place in a modern approach, but that is not what the Basel Committee's aforementioned consultative document states. On page one, reference to value at risk is made nine times, while reference to the incremental risk charge (which is the discussion paper's central theme) is made only four times. Additionally, for neither IRC or VaR, are the following explained:

- Supervisory guidelines for out of control conditions flashed by the models.

- Penalties associated with the lack of senior management's watch and corrective action.

There is a clear lack of attention to methodology. An example of how even an obsolete model can flash out alarm signals when the methodology is rigorous is provided by Wall Street's equity-related value at risk, which estimates the amount a bank could lose in a short period *if* markets fall sharply. In mid-2007, in one of the better known financial institutions, equity-related VaR soared. That was a danger signal, but no action was taken. The methodology was deficient and senior management had other priorities.

If the methodology *was* rigorous, then corrective action would have followed without delay, because management would have got the message that something was going to be wrong with the bank's balance sheet. In this particular case, because profits appeared to be rising faster than VaR, management took no action in controlling the proprietary trading desk. Eventually the profits evaporated, but the losses increased.

This does not mean that the Basel Committee's 'Proposed Revision to the Basel II Market Risk Framework' is totally short of new ideas. One of the best ideas in it (§3(a), page 6) is that factors deemed relevant for pricing should be included as *risk factors* in the VaR model. The VaR model cannot effectively handle this challenge however, and it should be met through QED rather than falling backwards into VaR.

A solution using the QED arrows (discussed in section 1) should also incorporate the guideline, in the above named document, regarding the need that "the model must capture non-linearities beyond those inherent in options". This makes sense with QED but not with VaR, promoted by the discussion paper in reference, for the simple reason that value at risk has not been designed to capture and handle non-linearities, and non-linear challenges cannot be effectively approached through patches, or in the absence of a rigorous mathematical framework.

From algorithms to computer programs, any one who has experience with patches knows that the result is a cumbersome, error-prone, inelegant system, which it is preferable not to touch. Quite to the contrary, though, QED boasts elegance and simplicity. Nature tends to prefer simplicity, and so should first class designers, conscious regulators and users of risk control systems who are keen to be ahead of the curve.

Another old concept that must drop out of sight, unless of course we plan to fail, is the traditional sort of hedging which often turns on its head. In the Basel document in reference the liquidity horizon is represented as the time required to sell the position *or* to hedge all material risks in a stressed market. That's wrong because, by doing so, little attention is paid to short-term illiquidity, which can morph into insolvency, and the fact that even a year would not be enough to liquidate highly illiquid positions, as proven during the period from July 2007 to mid-2009.

As it will be recalled, following the credit crunch and banking crisis the only way for commercial and investment banks to get rid of their structured CDOs was to unload them into the coffers of central banks[150]. While several bottoms of the market were called, massive

---

[150] Chorafas, *Financial Boom and Gloom.*

uncertainty persisted over each big bank's exposure to illiquid securities. Even after having taken $15 billion in writedowns, when it reached the edge of bankruptcy (on 12 September 2008) Lehman Brothers had $53 billion of mortgage 'assets' and leveraged loans in its books.

VaR, or any other of the currently available models, is not capable of handling such perilous and complex cases. QED, by contrast, might provide a solid basis for computing incremental risk, if the prerequisite basic research is done in a learned, dedicated manner – and there is the necessary political will and managerial commitment to apply it.

5. Promoting contrarian opinion

In many banks, the risk control and compliance departments have traditionally been mocked as 'business prevention units'. After the 2007-2009 debacle, however, they started to be seen as critical in an effort to keep weakened banks and other troubled financial services companies out of further mischief. The problem is that while bankers and financial experts have finally started to pay more attention to risk, they are not necessarily able to properly assess their exposure. This is a failure the QED solution aims to correct.

After reading the text which preceded this section, it should be evident to the reader that there is absolutely no intention of *eliminating* risk through the implementation of QED or any other method. Risk is an integral part of the financial system. Even if it was possible to weed it out, which is far from being the case, it would not have been our objective because *risk in the system* is what actually makes it work. But there is a great difference between:

- Measuring risk and, by contrast, having no way of knowing the level of assumed exposure;

- Managing risk and letting it grow, until the banks and the economy collapse under the burden.

Measuring and managing risk is precisely what we should aim to do with quantum logic. A parallel goal is to provide a platform (see Chapter 4 on Delphi) which makes it possible to inject contrary opinions into the process of exposure control. QED's contribution is that of a methodology, tools and an output that everybody involved with risk in the system can understand. It also allows the output to be shared by means of scenarios, and the development of contrary opinions, because when all experts and forecasters agree it is quite possible that something unexpected will happen.

A 2005-2007 example of widely shared opinion based on a weak conception was the lack of appreciation of the connection between liquidity horizon and concentrations. Most banks incorrectly thought their risks were diversified, while in reality they were concentrated in a few names, industries or instruments.

Indeed *correlation risk* (Chapter 4) is one of the most critical factors in computing exposure. Many financial instruments like CDOs and collateralised loan obligations (CLOs) are structured on the basis of an assumption about the degree of concentration and diversification of an underlying pool. Estimating the correlation of defaults among loans in that pool is a key input to the model employed in designing, pricing and subsequently valuing the CDOs. Basel says that correlation assumptions must be supported by analysis of objective data, but the appropriate definition of what is and is not 'objective data' is missing. Also, supervisors are surely aware that, since Basel I, a very liberal choice of correlations has been used for regulatory arbitrage.

The development of, and reference to, contrary opinions is important because correlation risk is elusive, and false correlations often underpin risk management failures. Indeed, this is one of the most challenging domains for QED implementation.

The reader must furthermore appreciate that what particularly matters in the performance of a structured investment, and in general of any committed position, is the *worst-case correlation* because it generates the largest losses in the underlying pool. At the same time, however:

- The difference between average and worst-case correlation is often opaque,

- Wishful thinking has detrimental effects on correlation estimates, and

- Even if the correlation is reasonably evaluated, it may be difficult to incorporate it into present-day models.

The reader should be aware that another major challenge is the case of extreme events. While outliers are being addressed through stress-testing[151], stress test regulation is left to national supervisors and from there to each commercial or investment bank. The outcome is that results of stress tests are totally heterogeneous and it is practically impossible to compare them with one another.

Additionally, stress test results usually integrate very poorly, if at all, with those obtained through normal tests of exposure. In this case, too, both individual banks and the supervisory authorities have a great deal to gain by promoting contrarian opinions in the interpretation of stress tests results.

Exactly because correlations are subject to estimates that are rather poorly documented and very differently interpreted, the better managed banks identify *stressed correlations* for component parts of a portfolio, and for pools, that may experience higher than expected defaults if the financial environment comes under pressure – and in case of panic. By contrast, less well-managed banks rely on third party analysis and assessment of correlation risk, such as made by a helpful broker who has conflicts of interest in correlation estimates.

---

[151] Chorafas, *Stress-testing*.

Reliance on third parties is also misplaced because for ABSs, CDOs and many other products, even 'objective data' correlations have been based on short historical records on default history. Apart from other shortcomings, this has a very negative impact on the study of extreme events. (When Dr Brandon Davies was treasurer of Barclays, he put his assistants to work analysing the British economy, dating back to the Napoleonic Wars, in order to obtain a reliable pattern with outliers.)

Last but not least, even if stated to be temporary, the elimination of crucial elements in the modelling of exposure such as foreign exchange risk, changes in commodity prices and term structure of default-free interest rates – significantly weakens a bank's governance as well as supervisory control.[152] One day this takes its toll, and therefore QED implementation must be careful enough not to repeat such shortcomings.

6. Quantum electrodynamics and compound events

What regulators should look for is a homogeneous basis for risk measurement in all areas of exposure, with particular emphasis on calculating the probability of *compound events*. This means events that are by their nature integrated, as risk exposure usually is, but which consist of a number of things or steps happening (supposedly) independently yet still affecting one another. In this effort, the computational method of quantum electrodynamics can be of significant help.

In QED, a compound event can be analysed as a succession of steps; a procedure which fits perfectly with requirements posed by risk studies. Each of these steps may be studied separately to produce a vector (or arrow, see sections 1 and 2) through a process of successive shrinking and turning, known as multiplying arrows.

---

[152] For instance, IRC (Chapter 4) suffers from such simplifications, collectively known as non-IRC market factors.

Adding arrows and *multiplying arrows* are the two most important operations which could find a wealth of applications in risk control. A broader horizon in implementation will be opened by applied research, a step further than basic research on the use of QED in financial risk studies suggested in the beginning of this chapter. The aim should be that of simplifying our understanding of what makes an objective estimation of exposure so elusive, and how a Feynman diagram of *probability amplitudes* and correlation functions can enhance understanding through graphical presentation.

To a significant extent the power of this approach of adding and multiplying vectors is akin to that of logarithmic calculus: reducing multiplication to addition and exponentiation to multiplication – with the added advantage of experience from physics.[153] As it should be remembered, the QED methodology did not evolve out of theoretical considerations alone. To a substantial extent, it was a practical development based on the fact that most physical phenomena involve the interaction of light and electrons, and a large part of the job of the modern physicist is to calculate the probability that a particular event will happen.

Something quite similar can be said about the risk manager's role, with the additional reference that the latter has to associate a financial impact with the likelihood of a given event happening. As section 1 reminded the reader, there is a most significant difference between high frequency/low impact (HF/LI) and low frequency/high impact (LF/HI) financial events.

- HF/LIs tend to be normally distributed.

- LF/HIs find themselves at the long leg of the risk distribution.

---

[153] Logarithmic calculus has become, so to speak, second nature in connection to financial studies.

To calculate the volatility of prices of a given commodity or derivative financial instrument in the market, analysts usually take percentage price changes. For any given commodity these are thought to form a normal distribution, which is, of course, an approximation. A better approach, popularised in mapping actual price changes, is the *lognormal* distribution used by the Black-Scholes algorithm for option pricing, and shown in Figure 5.3.

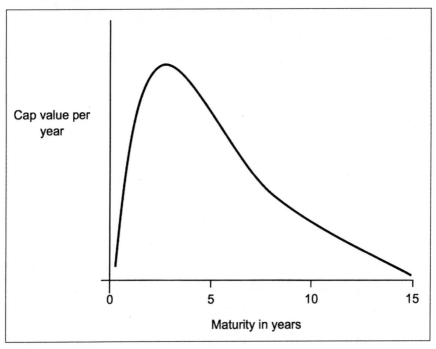

Figure 5.3: A lognormal distribution for option pricing reflecting volatility and maturity.

As a refresher of underlying concepts, a given variable has a lognormal distribution if its natural logarithm *ln* is normally distributed. When it is said that a bond price is lognormally distributed, what this means is that the *rate of return* of the bond is normally distributed, and this rate of return is a function of the natural, or Neperian, logarithm of bond price.

The focal point of a more powerful approach to the study of compound events should be the financial impact of risk, which does not fit into current lognormal models, and its integration has not attracted the attention it deserves. The *space-time* diagrams of QED (discussed in section 7) should target the monetisation of risk over the longer term – a need plainly documented by the banking crisis.

Critics of the current system point out that precisely because the magnitude of a medium to longer-term financial impact has not been properly included in the pricing of instruments by those who designed and marketed them (if it has been addressed at all), banks sustained huge losses from subprimes. This is closely connected to the repeated failure in judging end effects – particularly in the case of nervous markets.

The reason for the aforementioned failure is not just oversight but also the fact that such studies don't go deep enough. If they had done so they would have found that at the heart of the issue, beneath the apparent chaos of the world as we perceive it, there exist underlying laws, and such laws can help in the study of likelihood and impact.

This is practically what Mitchell Feigenbaum said when he advanced the principles of *chaos theory*.[154] What we perceive as the random movement of submicroscopic quantum physics (or their financial counterparts) are simple regularities and symmetries which tend to occur – while systems move from stability to chaos and back to stability.

Based on concepts underpinning chaos theory, it may be possible to address in an objective manner the cost of risk – in cases ranging from simple to compound events. Verifiable risk and associated pricing procedures require the correct calculation of the probability and impact of each risk event, and its component parts, including initial conditions and expected final status. This is a common requirement of practically all scientific studies.

---

[154] Chorafas, *Chaos Theory*.

Provided then that the appropriate homework has been done, we may be well positioned for the estimation of probabilities and analysis of impacts. With QED we are also able to capitalise on an existing and proved methodology, because there is a striking similarity in terms of the computation of probabilities between studies in physics and risk control. In physics the chosen approach rests on the so-called *rules of composition*:

- *If* something can happen in alternative ways we add the probabilities for each of the different ways.

- *If* the event occurs as a succession of steps, or depends on a number of things happening independently, then we multiply the probabilities of these steps or things.

Reliability engineering uses (nearly) the same approach. Moreover, because no system is more reliable than the weakest link in the chain, reliability engineering proceeds by identifying a chain's weaker component parts with the objective of strengthening them.

Taking an example from finance, the meltdown of the CDOs market happened in a number of ways, which produced a joint effect. Banks starved themselves of liquidity through the malpractice of financing longer-term investments (CDOs based on subprimes) through short-term sources (the asset-backed commercial paper (ABCP) sold through conduits). This was a major mistake in judgment and a violation of a basic principle of finance.

The curious thing is that this mistake was made by senior bankers and it was repeated with auction-rate securities (ARS).[155] Banks exercised very poor judgment in investing in junk structured instruments whose underlying was non-investment grade mortgage

---

[155] Chorafas, *Capitalism Without Capital*.

loans, without appropriately evaluating exposure, studying the downside, identifying and computing probabilities of each negative event which may happen, and being able to say whether these factors wore independent or correlated.

In a corresponding example in physics, if we have two detectors of a light source, each one of them could go off independently of the another. Therefore, the physicist calculates the probability of each as a separate complete event. In finance it is more complex than that, and therefore one has to be more humble and much more careful.

7. A space-time graph

One of the most fundamental concepts to be borrowed by risk managers from quantum electrodynamics is the mapping of events in *space and time* (vector spaces are explained in the Appendix). Physicists have simplified the space reference which, though three-dimensional, has been reduced to one dimension in a *space-time* graph and is mapped into the horizontal axis (abscissa). Time is mapped on the vertical axis (ordinate), as shown in Figure 5.4.

Let's first look at the upper half of Figure 5.4. To get a visual image, assume that a tennis ball is going up then down at time t_0 to t_6, doing so vertically. Essentially, this means staying at the same place A in the space dimension. We can replace this physical concept with a logical one, using *risk* rather than the tennis ball but keeping exactly the same physical trajectory. In this case:

Risk is steady over time t_0 to t_6.

Things are different in the lower half of Figure 5.4. Risk increases from time t_0 to t_4 and changes position in space from A to B. At B in the abscissa it hits a wall; for instance, a limit established by the board on counterparty risk (which must be observed by traders and loans officers). After this, at time t_5 to t_6 risk bounces back to position C on the abscissa. In other terms, from time t_0 to t_4 risk is drifting (increasing) towards the limit. After hitting the limit it bounces back but at a higher level (place) than its original position (as measured in the abscissa, not in the ordinate).

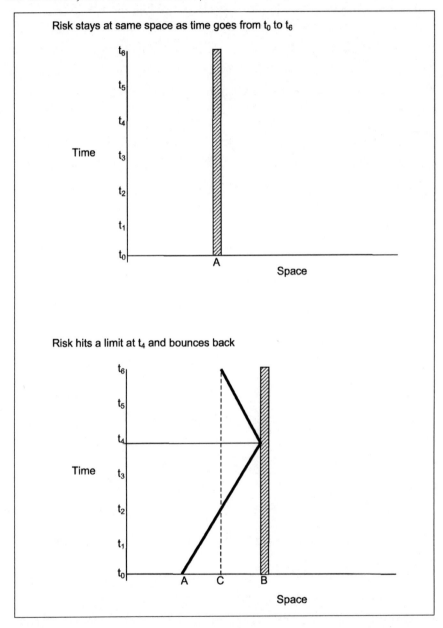

Figure 5.4: A space-time diagram maps the stage on which all actions in the universe take place.

The tennis ball could have made a similar trajectory in space-time. Replacing the assumption of a tennis ball and its position in space with that of risk, we get a *risk-time* diagram. Risk may stand at the same level at different times (which is unlikely), but it may also move to higher impact values practically instantaneously (as in the upper half of Figure 5.4), because of new commitments, compound events and spikes.

Underpinning this change in level of exposure is the concept of extreme values shown in Figure 5.5. Financial instruments reach extreme values because of a stressed market, unexpected consequences, or their own propensity to drift – which happens with increasing frequency.

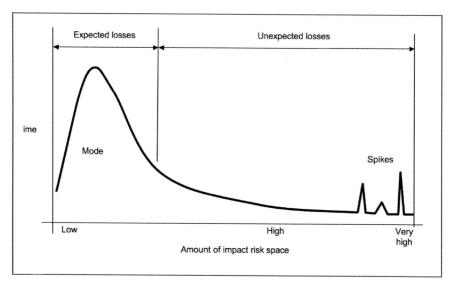

Figure 5.5: A space-time diagram for risk exposure with extreme events.

I emphasise the role of extreme events because no market always works under normal conditions; if anything, nowadays normal conditions tend to be the exception. Indeed, one of the most crucial issues in exposure control is the management of *time* as a risk factor because it cuts across and affects all other risk factors.

With the exception of spot deals, financial transactions are typically longer term, and in terms of risk and return their effects have a material half-life making *time* a most essential variable in any risk management procedure – as well as in simulation, scenario writing or experimentation. The *time management of risk control* determines the extent of a financial transaction's after-effects; and therefore its impact. Moreover, each transaction hedging has its own time frame and subsequent hedgings have a further-out time commitment. Hence the need to:

- Carefully think, rethink and revise changes in relevant time frameworks, likelihood and impacts, and

- Model this process in such a way that time management parameters can be autonomously observed and reset as new deals are made and warehoused positions evolve in terms of their characteristics.

In the Prologue it was mentioned that Sigmund Warburg used to evaluate his fellow bankers, treasurers of corporations, major investors, ministers of finance and chiefs of state on the basis on whether or not they knew the difference between *Kairos*, or short-term time, and *Chronos*, the long-term time. Important events happen in *Chronos*, thus in the longer term.

With that notion in mind, financial exposure in a space-time QED diagram must go from point-to-point just like a photon goes from point-to-point in a space-time graph. In principle, equations developed for the latter can be applied to the former after some adaptation. Though this book does not pretend to provide a complete method for this but, rather, to stimulate research in what promises to be a very interesting domain.

Less likely, but not impossible, is that the third basic action in QED – that an electron which emits or absorbs a photon, and indeed can go backwards (known as junction or coupling) – could also be of service in risk control. Particularly interesting in this connection is the path of the photon, or of the electron, which in Figure 5.4 is going from point A to point B and then to point C, resembling random walks which can be studied with the Monte Carlo method.[156]

The tools of physics developed for the analysis of partial reflection by dividing a layer of glass into a number of sections, as well as the handling of exceptions in emulation which can and do happen in a physical process, may also prove to be instrumental in risk management. For instance, an electron can emit and absorb two photons. In this the electron may be seen as the financial instrument and each photon as a top-most risk factor, or some other key variable chosen by the experimenter.

Risk control applications can also benefit from other cases connected with the behaviour of photons and electrons. One of them is the scattering of light, which corresponds to the scattering of risk. The scattering of light involves a photon going into an electron; say, a risk factor going into a financing instrument after it has been structured and sold. Or a photon (risk factor) may be coming out – though these events will not necessarily happen in that order.

Other notions which can be profitably borrowed from quantum electrodynamics and used in establishing a high level system of risk control are those of index of refraction and compressibility. Let me conclude this section with the statement that whether bank managers like or dislike the concepts underpinning the theory of QED is not the essential question. What is important is the adaptation to finance of the best scientific theory currently available, through:

- An experimental (not just theoretical) method,
- Intense testing and backtesting, and
- Using market results to confirm the results arrived at through the experimental model.

---

[156] Chorafas, *Chaos Theory.*

Though the development of a sophisticated method using models that replicate risk behaviour more accurately than VaR will by no means be an easy undertaking, encouraging the banks to develop metrics for incremental risk charge (IRC), and manage their accuracy, is not an option; it is a 'must'.

To be in charge the Basel Committee must establish in its premises a laboratory equipped with the best brains to be found in the market. QED studies for risk control should become one of the top projects of this laboratory.

8. The risk control structure beyond QED[157]

In *QED*, Richard Feynman writes: "when some fool scientist gives a lecture and says 'this is the way it works, and look how wonderfully similar the theories are,' it's not because Nature is *really* similar; it's because the physicists have only been able to think of the same damn thing, over and over again."[158] Feynman is right. Progress requires three things:

1. New departures,

2. Challenging the obvious,

3. A new culture commensurate with the job to be done.

The tougher the job, the more solid must be the criteria this new culture uses in judging 'right' and 'wrong', and the greater the penalties for breaking the rules. Behaviour matters. It takes much more than an advanced method like quantum electrodynamics to guarantee meeting

---

[157] Where quantum chromodynamics (QCD) can make a unique contribution, because of its essence of physical perfection.

[158] Feynman, *QED*.

the goals of holistic risk management and of avoiding the major errors made by bankers and regulators in the 1990s and early years of the 21st century that led to a tandem of bubbles.

The culture of obsolescence, half-baked approaches and hiding the errors (and the facts) should not be allowed to persist. A bank's reliance on diversification, and on liquid markets, to value its transactions and its inventoried positions invariably leads to neglecting the more fundamental analysis of risk embedded in those transactions and positions. This happens every day and for huge sums.

Ironically, the active use of credit risk transfer (CRT) and imperfect hedging by nearly every market player has generally increased vulnerability in case of rapid change in market sentiment, or a protracted decline in market liquidity.

What are the overall criteria a sound risk management system should fulfil? Here is a list of the most important:

- With over the counter (OTC) transactions it makes no sense to regulate counterparty behaviour; it's the *products* that should be regulated.

- Risk by instrument, counterparty, institution and market must be transparent; therefore it has to be clearly defined, observable and quantifiable (which should be the role of QED).

- Commonly understood and properly measured risk values should be published without delay so that all financial players within and outside an entity are informed about exposure, adjusting their behaviour accordingly.

- Risk control should be properly priced not only in terms of *Kairos* (current conditions), but also in regard to *Chronos* (the longer term).

- Risk metrics should be accurate, reliable, and subjected to as little revision as possible while being adjustable (by regulators acting in unison) to the evolution taking place in the market.

- Grim prognosis about an institution's financial staying power should raise the supervisory authorities attention on personal accountability, applying a legislation similar to the 2002 Sarbanes-Oxley Act for fraud.[159]

This evidently goes beyond QED and it involves new legislation, including regulatory rules which assure that wrongdoers are brought to justice. No valid risk control structure can be built without *ethical values* upheld at least partly by the fear of the judge, and supported by an effective administrative infrastructure.[160] Models are made to supplement, not to substitute, personal judgment and the accountability that goes with it.

Walkthroughs, backtesting, post-mortems and other real life tests must be one of top management's preoccupations. They are a good feedback control policy. Unlike something like linguistics, say, the formal rules of which are codified in a grammar which is taught and is generally well understood by literate people, *simulation* through scenarios, algorithms and heuristics has no universally accepted rules or formalisms. Like chess, market moves are dominated by individual style; and as in a game of chess it is in the interest of each player to obscure the mechanisms characterising the play's background logic, and keep the opposite party in a state of growing uncertainty regarding his or her own guesses about the risk of the next move and its likely impact.

This is true not only in a market-wide sense but also within the same organisation, leading to a constant interplay between traders and risk controllers. The silver lining is that one party's effort to unearth the

---

[159] D. N. Chorafas, *IT Auditing and Sarbanes-Oxley Compliance*, Auerbach/CRC, New York, 2005.

[160] This is written in full understanding that there is personal responsibility associated with the duties of board members, CEOs and CFOs, as well as with the job of risk managers.

hidden side of the other, leads to a process of investigation and discovery, which ends by enriching the outcome of risk evaluation – provided that the bank has endowed itself with bylaws and a first class internal control system (which is far from always being the case).

In the global market, discipline can also be assured (albeit never perfectly) through laws and a network of bank supervisors using QED risk measurements as their common language. As Chapter 4 demonstrated, scenarios help because the next financial crisis will be different in origin and impact; and community intelligence is a good investigative tool. (Laws and rules adopted to close today's loopholes will not necessarily plug tomorrow's.)

Most significantly, without legal action against wrongdoers – which in a global market should be administered globally – bad news will be coming thick and fast, time and again. It is also wise not to adopt a stiff line between right and wrong, but an approach which has been very successfully used for over six decades in statistical quality control, as Chapter 2 brought to the reader's attention.

Nothing works on a straight line, and so legislators and regulators must establish upper and lower *systemic risk tolerances* for all institutions. Breaking the upper tolerance line should have severe legal consequences for board members, the CEO and CFOs in a way similar to what happens with the Sarbanes-Oxley Act in case of fraudulent financial statements. A graphical image is presented in Figure 5.6, which the reader will recognise as a statistical quality control chart. Breaking the lower tolerances would work to the detriment of shareholder value. In addition, financial globalisation requires that these tolerances are established and applied cross-jurisdiction, with the goal of diminishing systemic risk to a practical minimum.

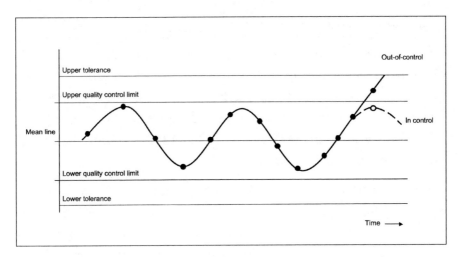

Figure 5.6: Using a statistical quality control chart to track daily exposure.

Both in elaborating and in revamping these tolerances it is necessary to remember the diversity of systemic risk factors which cut across historical functional boundaries. Their triggers depend not only on leverage but also on the type and novelty of financial products, and on the people manning them. This underlines the need for a common quantitative language for risk measurement; and my suggestion is that it should be provided by QED.

Within the aforementioned tolerances exist the *upper and lower control limits* shown in Figure 5.6. These are set by the institution's top management to ring-fence everyday banking and trading activities and assure that excesses do not break the bank as happened with Bear Stearns, Citigroup, Countrywide, Lehman Brothers, Merrill Lynch, UBS and Washington Mutual, as well as Northern Rock and HBOS among others.

In real life, while breaking the upper tolerance should be punished by law, living in the area between upper control limit and upper tolerance must be a matter of market discipline. If this had been done since the first years of this century, then Chuck Prince, Stan O'Neal, Dick Fuld, Marcel Ospel and a host of other big bank bosses would not have taken their institutions to the abyss.

9. Risk fever blues

When it opened for business in 1784, the obstetric clinic of Vienna's General Hospital had a mortality rate of 1.25%, a statistic which prevailed for nearly forty years. But in the 1820s the number of fatalities due to puerperal fever began to dangerously increase, reaching 9.92% in Ward I and 3.38% in Ward II. In 1842 in Ward I the fatality rate had climbed to 29.3%.[161]

According to the majority opinion of Viennese doctors there was an epidemic. But Dr Ignaz Semmelweiss rejected this hypothesis, if for no other reason than because of the significantly different mortality statistics between the two adjoining wards. He performed post-mortems himself every morning, and the findings were always the same: limphatitis, meningitis, pericarditis, peritonitis, phlebitis and pleurisy.

Using the method of *elimination*, Semmelweiss considered each of the hypotheses which assumed that puerperal fever was some sort of epidemic.[162] He also worked on the basis that the significant difference in mortality between the two wards was a crucial element in diagnosis, since both employed the same therapeutic methods, but the doctors attending the patients were different.

That was the *risk factor*. Doctors and medical students of Ward I were also working with corpses; while those of Ward II did not. Matter from the corpses, Dr Semmelweiss recognised, was entering the patients' bloodstreams. Washing hands with soap and water did not remove the invisible matter. A disinfectant was needed, and after experiments with a number of chemicals he decided in favour of chloride of lime.

---

[161] J. Antall and G. Szebelledys, *Pictures from the History of Medicine*, The Semmelweiss Medical Historical Museum, Budapest, Corvina Press, 1973.

[162] Compare this to the April/May 2009 craze over swine flu, which showed a similar pattern and was characterised by the World Health Organisation as a pandemic.

Does this sound familiar? The difference between water and chloride is analogous to the difference between VaR and QED. In the case of Vienna's General Hospital, the change was dramatic. In Ward I the mortality rate went down to 2.38% and then to 1.20%; in Ward II the statistics were even better. The patients were saved, but two odd opponents turned against Semmelweiss:

1. His colleagues and students resented having to wash their hands with chloride of lime.

By analogy, in 2009 this was the reaction of big banks, which used their lobbyists and political patrons to kill marking-to-market (Chapter 3). The messenger was wrong not because the message was incorrect, but for the simple reason that it revealed things they did not want to hear.

2. The international authorities on obstetrics rose against Semmelweiss, his findings and his methods, because he had disturbed the status quo.

This is precisely what has happened with those who laboured to improve risk management, whose status was waning until a long list of excesses brought the financial industry to its knees in 2007 and the economy of Western countries into deep recession. Not only was the measurement of risk through VaR substandard because the model had lost its accuracy and punch (Chapter 4), but also the meagre results it gave were set aside by bankers and regulators. With this, *risk fever* went on unabated with:

- No treatment,
- No medicine,
- No close follow-up and, worst of all,
- No corrective action.

Like the 'international authorities on obstetrics' in the case of Semmelweis, George W. Bush turned against William Donaldson, the chairman of the Securities and Exchange Commission (SEC) and former investment banker, when the latter voted with the Democratic members of the SEC's board to regulate hedge funds. The firing of Donaldson was a milestone in increasing *risk fever* and in bringing the whole banking industry to a crash.

In 2007-2009 in America and Western Europe the financial industry went through the horror of more than a trillion dollars in direct losses and writedowns. This huge amount of money was eventually paid by taxpayers in America, the European Union, Britain, Japan, Canada and Switzerland, as the central banks of these countries injected trillions into the coffers of banks in an attempt to calm the market.

Inflated by huge egos, corrupted by self-interest and with plenty of political backing, the parties opposing the supervision of investment banks and hedge funds, as well as the institution of a sound global risk control system, turned the economy on its head. Niccolò Machiavelli wrote about that resistance in *Il Principe*: "There is no more dangerous thing to manage than the introduction of new order, because one would have as enemies all those who profited from the status quo."[163] This is true in all walks of life, from politics, to medicine and banking.

Political obstruction to sound governance and strategic uncertainties increased the episodes of turning a blind eye to increasing risk, revealing for one more time that the real danger with any control system is that of losing confidence in its deliverables. In hindsight, physicists deal with similar sources of difficulties in studies such as reconciling the various characteristics of subatomic particles. Biologists, too, confront strategic uncertainties; for example, when the Bush Administration forbade stem cell research in the US.

---

[163] Niccolò Machiavelli, *Il Principe*, Einaudi Editore, Milano, 1974.

My years of experience in establishing and in auditing risk management systems at major financial institutions document that what they have lacked the most is *realism* in connection to challenges posed by the business environment on which they were expected to keep a close watch. The second critical failure was the inability to convince that the results being provided were meaningful and helped the different players' profitability rather than providing unwanted obstacles.

In conclusion, in a manner similar to what happened at Vienna's General Hospital, subprimes, CDOs, CDSs and fraudulent credit ratings poisoned the economy's bloodstream. The spin doctors who ran the wounded banks resisted the strong disinfectant in the form of rigorous risk management. Even bank supervisors showed themselves in favour of the status quo, because nearly everybody was making good profits, the market was liquid and it was thought that nothing could go wrong.[164]

Appendix: vectors, linear vector spaces and polygons[165]

The study of phenomena in physics requires mathematical laws and tools such as arithmetic, geometry, trigonometry, statistics and calculus.

- *Mathematical systems* are man-made, with the purpose of making it possible to measure and compute areas, volumes, masses, moments, means, ranges and variances.

- *Calculus* is a fundamental tool of the physical sciences, and it is also increasingly used in macroeconomics and in financial

---

[164] What I find particularly objectionable is the policy to let any financial firm succumbing to its self-made wounds, to convert itself into a bank and unload into the central bank its 5 cents to the dollar securities at their original value. For example, on 20 November 2008, GMAC did so to the tune of $38 billion as first instalment.

[165] In mathematics, vectors and matrices are twins. It was, however, a deliberate decision not to include matrices in order to keep this supplement to Feynman diagrams as short as possible.

analysis – in short in the study of all systems characterised by limiting processes.

The concepts that permitted the organisation and implementation of the process of calculus date back to the great 16th/17th century minds of Newton, Leibniz and Gauss. But other contributions, too, have been outstanding, particularly those by Fermat and Descartes which preceded them and made possible the *arithmetisation of geometry*. Numbers were attached to and coordinated with geometrical objects, and the Cartesian system served to characterise an object and its movement in a plane, as well as to map arithmetic operations affecting objects.

Known as abscissa and ordinate, the X and Y axes in the upper half of Figure 5.7 are number axes frequently (though not always) measured with the same unit. To each point A are assigned two coordinates x_A and y_A. The diagram in the lower half of Figure 5.7 maps a straight line AB (the distance between two points), also in a planar (2-dimensional) system.

> Velocity, acceleration, force and momentum are vectors of the Cartesian plane that have an algebraic structure.
>
> A vector is described as a quantitative element of a system satisfying the postulates of addition, and admitting all real numbers as multipliers.

The introduction of coordinates, to which can be referred different mathematical objects, and their components, was a major stepping stone in the development of calculus. If the picture of the object identified as AB in Figure 5.7 maps a quantity which has magnitude and direction, then this directed line segment is a *vector* similar to those used in the Feynman diagrams in the main body of this chapter.

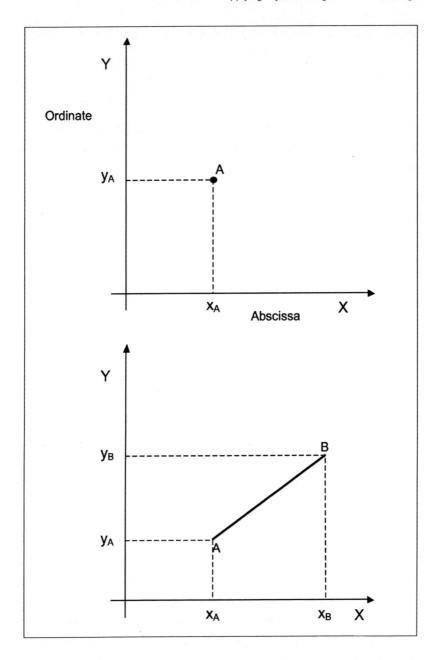

Figure 5.7: Cartesian coordinates and the mapping of points and lines.

In an algebraic sense, vectors can be defined by means of their components, but with complex systems this approach becomes restrictive. A better approach is to capitalise on the concept underpinning a coordinate system (into which the components are mapped as geometric objects) to develop a sufficiently general framework able to contain the possible extension of the concept underpinning a vector. This is known as a *linear vector space S*.

Let's consider a space S into which exits a collection of elements we denote by x, y, z, w; let's also employ the symbol of the operation of addition +, known from arithmetic.

Basic operations in the linear vector space have the following properties:

$$x + y = z$$

$$x + y = y + z$$

$$(x + y) + w = x + (y + w)$$

$$x + 0 = x$$

$$x + (-x) = 0$$

Elementary operations such as those are constituents of those more complex in a Feynman diagram (they also document how simple mathematics is, once you gain the sense of it). The space S with the set of vectors (we can also say which *is* the set of vectors) can be multidimensional. In it any vector x, y, z can be a set of real numbers:

If $x = (k_1, k_2, k_3, \ldots k_n)$

And $y = (l_1, l_2, l_3, \ldots l_n)$

Then $x + y = (k_1 + l_1, k_2 + l_2, k_3 + l_3, \ldots k_n + l_n)$

This, too, speaks volumes on how simple are the vector operations in quantum electrodynamics necessary to handle control diagrams. If a, b denote the *scalar numbers* of a field, then we can obtain the product of the vector and the scalar.[166] All we need to do is follow a set of rules.

---

[166] Simply speaking, scalar multiplication is multiplication by a factor which changes the scale, thereby producing magnification or reduction of the measurement of a variable, or of the length of a line.

$$a(bx) = (ab)x$$

$$(a+b)x = ax + bx$$

$$1 \bullet x = x$$

$$0 \bullet x = 0$$

Matters become more complex in quantum field theory, where Feynamn diagrams represent a probability transition mapped into a space, the S-matrix, between the initial and the final states of the quantum system. The resulting diagram is a contribution of a particular class of particle paths. (Quantum field theory represents the transition amplitude as the weighted sum of all possible histories of the system, from the initial to the final state, in terms of either particles or fields.)

All this sounds wholesome, but it gets simpler the moment we appreciate that a *field* is a collection of numbers which contains the sum, difference, product and quotient of any two numbers in that field. "Although they begin as mathematical devices, the fields leap out of the equations to take a life of their own," writes Frank Wilczek in *The Lightness of Being*.

Conversely, any space S which satisfies the rules of addition and multiplication of vectors by a scalar, is a linear vector space. (Making measurements and handling objects in vector spaces works by analogy with operations on vectors on a plane.) Operations on vectors follow the very simple rules outlined in the preceding paragraphs of this Appendix. Take as an example a 2-dimensional space with vectors $\overline{A_1 B_1}$ and $\overline{R_6 R_1}$ where:

$$\overline{A_1 B_1} \longleftrightarrow (x_1, y_1)$$

$$\overline{R_6 R_1} \longleftrightarrow (x_2, y_2)$$

The rule is:

$$\overline{A_1 B_1} + \overline{R_6 R_1} \longleftrightarrow (x_1 + x_2, y_1 + y_2)$$

$$a \; \overline{A_1 B_1} \longleftrightarrow (ax_1, ay_1)$$

$$b \; \overline{R_6 R_1} \longleftrightarrow (bx_2, by_2)$$

The directed line segments in the space are best considered as an intermediate space model following the triangle law of addition for composition purposes. Consider two forces $\overline{P}$ and $\overline{Q}$ acting upon a given point of the coordinate system, where:

$$\overline{P} \longleftrightarrow (3,4)$$
$$\overline{Q} \longleftrightarrow (-6,5)$$

Which is the resultant force? Applying the mathematical laws outlined in this Appendix:

$$\overline{P} + \overline{Q} \longleftrightarrow (3,4) + (-6, 5) = (-3,9)$$

This can be easily mapped into Cartesian coordinates, as shown in Figure 5.7. More complex cases, like that given as an example at the beginning of this chapter in Figure 5.2, used directed line segments known as *legs* (not to be confused with the long leg of the risk distribution). Legs are used to form *polygons*.

Think of a polygon as being created by a sequence of line segments. The north-south component of a leg is known as *latitude* and the east-west component as the leg's *departure*. An example with a polygon is found in Figure 5.8. With a Feynman diagram it is also necessary to calculate the projection of the vector $\overline{R_6 R_1}$ which closes the polygon, as was already stated in section 2.

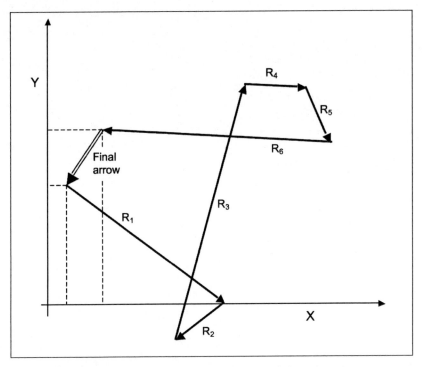

Figure 5.8: Examples of a polygon of vectors in a linear space.

Part Three

Three Themes for Quantum Chromodynamics

Chapter 6: Legal Risk and Ponzi Risk

1. Using quantum electrodynamics for legal risk

Beyond what Chapters 4 and 5 have suggested by promoting the use of scenarios and quantum electrodynamics (QED) as a universal standard for risk measurement, come the domains of exposure described in this and the following two chapters. Auditors must qualify accounts if there is no adequate record of preparation for confronting legal risk in connection to factors motivating court action, such as failure in compliance. This, however, does not exhaust the legal challenges confronting an organisation.

The realm of legal, overleveraging and regulatory issues which can bring an institution to its knees cannot be comprehensively mapped with only QED. In a way paralleling QED's application in physics, the challenges which they pose can be better approached through the wider framework of quantum chromodynamics (QCD), as we will see through examples. In physics, QCD's domain is the strong nuclear force. A good way to look at QCD is as an expanded version of QED, the latter having preceded the former.[167]

The greater sophistication of QCD is brought into the modelling pattern of finance and management because integrating risk factors of a legal nature into assumed exposure requires a greater representational capability than what is offered by the quantitatively oriented quantum electrodynamics. It helps to enrich the holistic risk control methodology through the added value of quantum chromodynamics.

---

[167] As a mathematical construct, QED dates back to 1930, but its effective usage is much more recent, after some hurdles with equations were overcome. There are few critical differences between QED and QCD, but this is neither the subject of this book, nor it does it greatly change the basic concept discussed in these pages.

The concept underpinning this approach is to capitalise on QCD's richer set of ingredients, some of which have qualitative aspects able to amplify and supplement core processes. The most important to retain (for a non-physicist) are quarks and bosons (gluons).

Murray Gell-Mann is the atomic particles theorist who came up with the concept of *quarks*.[168] The term identifies a charged elementary particle in the domain of the strong atomic force (for a definition see the Prologue). As charged elementary particles, quarks are the 'feel' of strong forces. Protons and neutrons are composed of three quarks.

- Each quark comes in six *flavours*: up, down, strange, charmed, bottom and top, and

- Each flavour comes in three *colours*: red, green and blue.

These colours identify the three kinds of charges that appear in QCD, and they can be seen as an analogy to electric charges (the reader will recall from the Prologue that the word 'colour' is a misnomer; but it is also an established term).

As for the six different flavours, or species, the two most used in physics are up and down. (Notice that up and down are labels, implying no connection to directional issues in space-time.) Each of the flavours (up quarks, down quarks, etc) has a unit of colour charge.

Physicists believe that the strong nuclear force is carried by another party, the *gluon* (bosons), which interacts only with itself and with the quarks. More precisely, gluons are part of a class in the strong force which holds the protons and neutrons together in the nucleus of the atom, as well as the quarks together in protons and neutrons. The prevailing hypothesis is that gluons have no mass.

---

[168] Legend has it that when Gell-Mann's fertile and creative imagination came up with the new particles he also conceived that they have "quirky properties". According to another hear-say, Gell-Mann chose that label because in German it means "nothing" (they carry only fractional electrical changes).

QCD has eight colour *gluons*, instead of QED's one photon responding to an electric charge. Colour gluons respond to one another and to different colour charges; and they can also change one colour charge into another. (There exist some interesting properties, in this context, which can be exploited to express qualitative characteristics in legal risk. A red quark has to be joined to a green and a blue quark by gluons; and red + green + blue = white).[169]

The message this brief *tour d'horizon* in modern physics aims to convey is the existence of a very imaginative and extremely rich methodology in quantum chromodynamics. Its wealth of descriptions and flexibility of usage presents enormous possibilities in tracking, measuring and controlling risks in domains which have so far been uncharted territory in the management of exposure – not only in legal matters but also in leveraging, governance, internal control, regulation and more.

A particular challenge is to use QCD to establish a universal model for *risk pricing*, the results of which cannot be massaged to hide the facts (see Chapter 8 in the outcome of the 'stress tests'). A risk pricing model which cannot be easily biased, is able to account for both quantitative and qualitative risk factors, is comprehensible, and is not too complex, can have global appeal.

"Modern physicists consider quantum chromodynamics an almost ideally simple theory," said Nobel prize winner Frank Wilczek, who however warns that "profound simplicity contains an element of its opposite, profound complexity, but its resolution is profoundly straightforward".[170] Another important point Wilczek makes is that the central idea of QCD is *symmetry*, and symmetry means that we have "a distinction without a difference". This phrase is often used by

---

[169] Another pattern is the pair of a quark and antiquark, which makes up particles known as gluons. Of particular interest in quark-antiquark combinations seem to be the mesons.

[170] Frank Wilczek. 'Profound Simplicity', *The New York Academy of Sciences Magazine*, Autumn 2008.

attorneys at law to mean saying the same thing in different ways, and thereby pressing a point or, alternatively, confusing the opposing party.

The symmetry of QCD makes it possible to mix colours, continuously forming blends while preserving the set of basic rules which provide the modelling system's framework. If we know an object has symmetry then we can deduce some of its properties, and this can have a tremendous after-effect on the study of legal risk.

The concept of symmetry, the pattern of which is integral to QCD, constitutes an unprecedented facility in representing legal issues – from civil and penal laws to jurisprudence. But can we really sustain the argument that legal risk is characterised by symmetry? Since I am not a lawyer, allow me to answer this query by quoting Oliver Wendell Holmes (1841-1935), one of the most renowned judges in the history of the Supreme Court of the United States.

The law, Holmes said, is not about right or wrong, or rational judgment, but a system of sanctions. The law and its aftermath is best seen from the viewpoint of a person who asks not what is written in law books, or what reasons judges give in their rulings, but only what a specific court is likely to do to him if he is caught. This is, as well, the definition established by the lawmakers of Sparta, in ancient Greece.

The laws of nature, for which scientists have developed QED and QCD, are universal. They are independent of the jurisdiction in which the lawyer works. By contrast, the laws of men vary from one jurisdiction to the next (and sometimes within the same jurisdiction). But this does not mean that they lack symmetry.

If physicists found it necessary to descend to subatomic level in order to unearth and describe the polyvalence of nature, then governments, lawmakers, judges, lawyers and their clients – confronted with jurisdictional differences in a global economy – can be even greater beneficiaries of QCD's power of expression. At the start, the implementation of QCD in the domain of legal risk should ignore minor details and concentrate on the essential features. Eventually, however, detail will be indispensable; and the devil is in the detail.

2. Legal risk is a disruptive force

Legal risk is more qualitative than quantitative. It is also one of the most critical factors of uncertainty connected to the normal or expected functioning of operations, because its dimensions both expand and change over time. Companies have numerous lawsuits filed against them, asserting various reasons and including class actions as well as stockholders' actions (section 3), which end by being very costly. In addition, legal risk can be a disruptive force because it absorbs an inordinate amount of management attention and the results of complex legal proceedings are difficult to predict.

Many of the complaints being filed do not specify the amount of damages that plaintiffs seek, making it nearly impossible to estimate in advance the likely expense of a financial settlement that might be incurred, should these lawsuits be resolved against the bank. An unfavourable outcome or payment for damages resulting from one or more lawsuits could have a material adverse effect on the company's:

- Reputation,
- Liquidity,
- Financial position, and
- Results of operations.

Even if the outstanding lawsuits are not resolved against the bank, the uncertainty and expense associated with legal cases could seriously harm its market standing. (The board's risk management committee has full responsibility for business risk and risk to reputation.) Experiences teaches that when something goes wrong, the aftermath seems twice as bad as might be the real case.

Theoretically, no great uncertainty should exist in connection to legal risk because starting circa 1700 BC with Hammurabi, the Babylonian emperor, the laws are written in books permitting one to know what he wants to defend or to achieve. Hammurabi's laws, however, were written for a physical economy in its early stage of development. In a virtual economy the sense of risk is much more complex, as Chapter 1 documented. When it looks like legal exposure cannot get worse, it does just that, while in many instances laws, rules and regulations are being manipulated.

Laws are not written on stone. Their letter changes by action of parliament, and their interpretation evolves through jurisprudence. An example is deceit. *Deceit* originally had a narrow meaning of swindling in some way, and one of its forms was that of abusing legal procedure. That concept of deceit, however, expanded over time. Another example is *defamation*. Lawyers say that no domain is more fertile for litigation than defamation, because its meaning is elastic.

When two or more people combine for inflicting unlawful injury upon another person and cause damage to him, they commit *conspiracy*. Originally the law regarding conspiracy had a narrow meaning: that of combination to abuse legal procedure. Its notion, however, has expanded, bifurcating into civil and criminal type conspiracy, with legal consequences for both of them.

There may also be actions by a single party, or in unison, which involve negligence and entail a legal aftermath. *Negligence* is the omission to do something which is part of one's duties. This is often linked to a reasonable man's behaviour, which is an abstract concept but has real impact when associated with a person's behaviour in the execution of his or her duties. For instance in:

- Governance of an enterprise,

- Fiduciary responsibilities, or

- The control of risk.

"Knowledge of risks attributable to a given business allow losses to be controlled or avoided... [but] in order for a bank to account fully for the exposures it assumes all risk dimensions must be considered,"[171]

---

[171] Erik Banks, *Complex Derivatives*, Probus, Chicago and Cambridge, 1994.

says Eric Banks, who further suggests that the legal, regulatory compliance and documentation departments would be responsible for aspects of legal risk.

As every legal counsel will advise, critical in connection to litigation is the role of *motive*. There are several torts with a motive in which liability is an integral part. The word *tort* stands for any private or civil wrong, by act or omission, for which a civil suit can be brought[172] – a definition which is all inclusive, except breach of contract. Experts believe that in the 21st century an increasing number of cases will have tort in their background.

Though in the general case the laws, jurisprudence and ways to define legal risk are quite different from one country to the next, such differences are much greater with tort than breach of contract, including procedural issues differentiating one jurisdiction from the next. The US and Britain provide an example:

- In the US, legal risk frequently involves class actions; judgment is made by jury; there is unlimited liability; and there exists a high environmental liability as well.

- By contrast, in Britain there are no class actions; the judge (not a jury) decides on compensation; and there is a liability cap. Also environmental liability is much lower than in the US.

In nearly all jurisdictions, however, an important development which impacts on legal risk is the emphasis placed on liability. Products and services which do not perform as expected are subject to liability procedures and demands for damages. Both financial experts and legal counsels look at this development, whose origins were traced in late 1980s/early 1990s, as one of the most critical indicators of change in the notion of customer-supplier relationship. The value of a product or

---

[172] D. N. Chorafas, *Operational Risk Control with Basel II. Basic Principles and Capital Requirements*, Butterworth-Heinemann, London and Boston, 2004.

service is no longer defined exclusively through its material characteristics, but it increasingly also depends how it performs on its after-effects, which in the case of financial instruments revolve around assumed risk and the buyer's ability to comprehend it.

Integral to this is *due diligence*. Legal documentation must not only define the transaction but also be comprehensive and comprehensible, so that the customer can *really* understand the product and its risks. The importance of *understanding* is documented through lots of litigation, including the now famed case (in early 1990s) of Procter & Gamble and other companies against Bankers Trust on derivative products.

3. Shareholder lawsuits at Bank of America

Section 1 brought to the reader's attention that in the background of tort is *motive*; which signifies the reason for conduct. It may be an evil motive, or tort may be done wilfully without cause or excuse. Motive often refers to intention, a term which describes the basic reason for conduct and its desired consequences. Motive influences the actor, but:

- If conduct is unlawful, a good motive will not exonerate the defendant, and

- If, apart from motive, conduct is lawful, the way to bet is that a bad motive will not make him liable.

There are, however, several exceptions to both bullets. Fundamentally, it is the act, not the motive for the act, which is judged. If the act, apart from motive, gives rise to damage or injury, the motive will not relieve the actor of liability – a statement equally valid in the physical and in the virtual economy. An example is *shareholder* lawsuits.

As equity owners began to file lawsuits accusing the embattled chief executive of Bank of America of mismanagement, in late January 2009 pressure built up on Ken Lewis to resign. Filed on 23 January 2009 in New York, suits accused Lewis and John Thain, the former chief executive of Merrill Lynch, of withholding important information from shareholders prior to the deal's closing earlier that month, which saw the merger of Merrill Lynch with Bank of America.

An irony was that, on that very same day, Ken Lewis in fact ousted John Thain in the wake of bigger than expected losses at Merrill for the fourth quarter 2008, as well as his secret fund of $4 billion which he used to give Merrill's investment bankers bonuses (these bonuses have become a fad in Wall Street and the City of London (see also section 3)). Paraphrasing Lord Myners, heads of banks are overpaid but have little sense of governance, and no sense of the bank's social functions.

This $4 billion in bonuses was essentially taxpayers' money. As such, the bonuses displayed not only a sense of inverse entitlement that bore a negative relation to the bankers' performances, but were also the wrong incentives, rewarding laxity in bank governance (as well as supervision) and absent ethical standards.

It would be difficult to find a more flagrant case involving legal risk in the virtual economy, and Andrew M. Cuomo, New York State's Attorney General, pressed Thain to reveal the beneficiaries' names. All this took place as the uproar from Merrill's record $21.5 billion operating losses in the fourth quarter 2008 was still strong and Bank of America was seeking additional taxpayers' funds from the government's TARP to digest its acquisition.

It is most damaging to the standing of the banking industry that incentives were paid for business failures. Cuomo's argument in the week of 23 February 2009, when he pressed Thain to reveal the names of the bonus beneficiaries, was that the bonuses were irrational and illegal. They were illegal because they:

- Were done in secrecy,

- Were not authorised by the board of directors, and

- Were paid with money that came out of the $700 billion authorised by Congress to save the mismanaged big banks from outright bankruptcy.

The way the financial news had it on 25 February 2009, John Thain underwent hours of questioning at the New York Attorney General's office. What the authorities particularly wanted to know were the names of the top five Merrill executives who took the lion's share of the $4 billion. Not only did Cuomo grill Thain, but also a day later Ken Lewis, the CEO, had to appear before the Attorney General to answer questions. (A big question mark in the mind of investors was that allegedly Lewis had single-handedly authorised the Thain handouts).

All this came at a very bad time for Bank of America, as the company was also confronted by the need to replenish its equity capital, which had dropped to between 2.6% and 2.8% of assets, versus a minimum of 3% demanded by regulators and the US Treasury. At 1.5% Citigroup was worst off, while at about 3.6% JP Morgan Chase was above this arbitrary 'minimum limit'.[173]

The case of these unwarranted bonuses to investment bankers was not the only reason motivating the late January 2009 lawsuits by stockholders against Bank of America. Another claim was that Ken Lewis should have told the shareholders about Merrill's deteriorating condition prior to the December 2008 vote on the investment bank's acquisition. Equity owners also claimed that the CEO's decision to approach federal officials for help with the deal on 17 December 2008, which was only revealed a month later, should have been disclosed to shareholders prior to the 1 January 2009 close of the transaction.

Afterwards, persons familiar with the case said that during the second week of December 2008 Ken Lewis considered calling off the deal. The Bank of America CEO had asked his lawyers to look into the possibility of invoking the *material adverse conditions* (MAC) clause to justify

---

[173] Notice that 3% is way below the Basel I capital requirements which stood at 8%, of which half, hence 4%, had to be equity capital.

cancelling the transaction. But lawyers as well as merger and acquisition experts reportedly said that it was very difficult to win a court case based on an MAC clause.

This belated query about legal grounds for revocation of an agreement to take over Merrill Lynch suggests that Bank of America had not done its homework when in December 2008 it decided to proceed with the acquisition. As with the case of Countrywide, the takeover of Merrill Lynch reflected a misalignment of interests between the interest of bank executives massively focusing on short-term gains, and longer-sighted shareholders, who had to foot the bill of senior management's failure until the taxpayer was called in to take over that painful task.

Generally speaking, the choice between the short term and the long term has always been one of top management's decision puzzles. Short-term choices by boards and CEOs see to it that the goals of owners and managers are not well aligned. Both shareholders and professional managers may want to husband capital and lend carefully, but managers are increasingly driven by risk appetite and bonuses – leading to billion-dollar losses, bail-outs and brutal bank sell-offs.

4. The twilight between legal and illegal practices

In 1798 Thomas Malthus, the English economist, published 'An Essay on the Principle of Population'. In this he argued that natural populations grow at an exponential rate, whereas the increase in food supply is linear. The same principle applies in finance, with profits, risks and bonuses increasing exponentially, while 'normal' business (defined as one without excess) expands in a linear way. Within the confines of affordable risk and within an annual time frame, the increase in a bank's profits is never explosive, but greed and the lust for power grow at an exponential rate, hence the drive to over-leverage (Chapter 8) and take inordinate risks.

Phantom profits and the exploitation of other loopholes is a case of tort against shareholders that has not so far attracted the court action that it deserves. One of the major problems that shook investors' confidence in the banking industry in the wake of the major economic crisis and credit crunch was its fake profit figures. During the housing boom, for example, credit institutions aggressively sold risky adjustable rate mortgages (ARMs). Under the terms of those loans borrowers paid less than the total interest owed each month, but lenders reported the full amount of interest as income by adding the shortfall to the borrower's outstanding balance.

By exploiting an accounting loophole, banks recorded massive earnings upfront from mortgage backed securities they created and sold to investors. The trick is known as *gain on sale*. A lender bundles together a group of mortgages valued at, say, $50 million. Over the life of the bond – which can be as long as 30 years – the bank may collect up to $100 million in cash flows from that security.

Coming from interest, servicing rights and other payments, that money is still a virtual gain which turns to a loss if the market moves south – as the 2007-2009 events documented. Banks knew this, but still they counted the virtual future gain as income once the security was sold, even though they were not getting those payments for years to come. This is a controversial practice but, thanks to the loophole, it is taken as not being wholly illegal.

A different trick popular among banks in the housing bubble years (2003-2007) was a category of on-balance sheet mortgages called *loans held for investment*. Exploiting still another loophole, lenders largely put loans they made to homeowners (or bought from other brokers) into that special clause until investment banks bought them to securitise. That practice was sanctioned by tremendous losses when the prevailing conditions deteriorated.

Loopholes, as well as subjective and biased judgments, permitted CEOs to turn themselves (by the phantom profits magic) into multimillionaires. According to SEC, in 2007 at Lehman Brothers, its

CEO, Richard Fuld, received total compensation of $34,382,036. But in the dramatic week of 15 September 2008, Lehman went into bankruptcy.

The money Fuld made was small game compared to the $161 million 2007 compensation of James 'Jimmy' Cayne, Bear Stearns' CEO, up to its collapse in March 2008. As William D. Cohan wrote: "Cayne oversaw the ballooning of Bear's balance sheet to as much as 50 times its equity, and an aggressive push into complex credit products that he never fully understood."[174] Bankruptcy came on the heels of these excesses.

At Fannie Mae, the 2007 compensation of CEO Daniel H. Mudd was $14,231,650. The Fed dismissed him on 7 September 2008, as the Treasury took over the mammoth government-sponsored agency. At Freddie Mac the CEO Richard F. Syron (also dismissed by the Feds on 17 September 2008), had a 2007 compensation of $18,289,575.

For his part, in 2008, Robert Rubin, former US Treasury Secretary and former head of Goldman Sachs, earned some $115 million from Citigroup for taking risks that American taxpayers subsequently paid for. So far no attempt has been made to claw that money back from him – or from the aforementioned CEOs and plenty of others whose names could fill an entire book. Nor has any other bank managed to reclaim some past bonuses from its former executives, traders or investment bankers (with the possible exception of UBS).

UBS, however, had its own story of extravagant bonuses. Losses continued to mount in the third and fourth quarters of 2008, with the result that (in spite of fairly good profits made over the year) the bank posted an annual net loss of $18.2 billion. But bonuses were always on call, even when the financials were dismal.

---

[174] William D. Cohan, *House of Cards. A Tale of Hubris and Wretched Excess on Wall Street*, Doubleday, New York, 2008.

Taxpayers' money was thrown at the problem. During 2008 UBS had benefited from the helping hand of the Swiss National Bank to which it unloaded $52.2 billion (Swiss francs 60 billion) of toxic waste set up as a separate fund. One would have been permitted to believe that these awful financial figures translated into firing and levying sanctions upon a very poorly performing management. Instead, apart from the ousting of Marcel Ospel, everybody else continued warming his or her chair.

And bonuses continued their course (albeit at lower rate). According to the *Neue Zürcher Zeitung*, in 2008 the 17,200 investment bankers of UBS were paid on average a yearly compensation of 284,000 Swiss francs – while investment banking booked a loss of about 34 billion Swiss francs that same year. In other terms, the people who during 2008 nearly destroyed the bank pocketed 2.2 billion Swiss francs ($1.9 billion) in bonuses for the year (and rumour had it that another $1.2 billion was hidden in the accounts to be distributed later).

CEOs always manage to arrange extravagant bonuses for themselves, other senior executives, go-go traders and investment bankers. Year-after-year they all collected a steady stream of options and bonuses – irrespective of whether the bank made profits or losses.

Excuses can be easily found to 'justify' the losses – nervous markets, a systemic crisis and unexpected events are all blamed. Yet, if people and companies do not disgorge previous wrongful compensation, then the incentive is to hide the losses and to continue engaging in trades that explode after a period of steady gains. This policy leaves the profits to insiders while the losses are supported by shareholders and taxpayers – a vicious cycle.

The result is a totally asymmetric approach to risk and return in the twilight of legal and illegal practices. That policy demonstrates that the incentive system put in place by banks and other financial companies has produced the worst possible economic system. 'Incentives' are supposedly given for performance, but bad practices see to it that they have become disincentives for prudent management.

5. Transborder legal risk

Extravagant pay, unwarranted bonuses, unearned pensions for life and backdated options are not the only management risks confronted by shareholders. Bad enough in itself, poor governance and its effects are amplified by operations which involve an inordinate amount of product and service liability.

In the banking industry, to a substantial extent product and service liability has to do with what is expected of the counterparty and of the instrument's value; as well as with how the end user, conditioned by practice to confront problems, reacts to product vows – and is or is not willing to stand by his commitments.

These are issues deep rooted in the service economy. We increasingly buy and consume *performances* rather than just material products. However, if quality and performance become the basic criteria, then there should be measurement units and methods that make it possible to estimate exposure associated with them in an objective manner.

Any measurement of exposure associated to performance will be half-baked if it does not account for transborder legal risk; and there is not just one but several factors lying behind transborder legal liability. One of the most obvious is differences in the law of the land, as every jurisdiction has its own. But also quite frequent are cases of a corrupt judiciary, the influence of hidden interests, and economic nationalism.

As an example of legal differences among jurisdictions, Crédit Suisse paid a heavy penalty because its operators in India shorted stocks. This was a practice perfectly legal (at the time) in America, Britain, Switzerland and other Western countries – but the laws of India forbade it.

There also exist cases which give the judiciary an excuse to apply the law in such a way that is favourable to local interests. For instance, banks have entered into contracts involving instruments their counterparties understood, but they produced losses their customers did not wish to pay, and found recourse in the excuse that their vendor provided no information on how large the losses could be to the client.[175]

After the South Korean meltdown in late 1997, the Morgan Bank was faced with an unexpected $480 million in a derivatives claim. Morgan had carried the day in that deal, but its counterparty, SK Securities, refused to perform due to its allegedly precarious situation. The virtual bankruptcy of South Korea and its conglomerates stemmed from market risk which rekindled counterparty risk in its wake, and it translated into legal risk.

Since then it has more or less become a policy that court rulings in South Korea allow local companies to escape from disastrously bad trades in currency contracts and in derivatives. Critics say that the Korean courts set legal precedents that harm not only the counterparties, but also the country's financial stability as a whole in the longer term. But the fact remains that American and European banks continue to play ball with the Koreans, using complex financial instruments.

A popular derivatives game seems to be the knock in/knock out currency options contracts. Theoretically, this provides a way for local exporters to offset the risks of having the won, the Korean currency, rise in value against the dollar or the euro. Korean companies buy call options, allowing them to buy the won cheaply, but to reduce the option's cost to them, they accept a floor, giving up the right to buy won if it falls too far.

To further reduce their costs up front, making the derivatives deal cheaper, South Korean export companies often sell twice as many put options as they buy call options. That makes the derivatives deal much more risky in the longer run.

---

[175] Something similar had happened in the US jurisdiction when Gibson Greetings and Procter & Gamble brought Bankers Trust to court for having sold them derivatives that would save them some money if interest rates stayed level, but the cost to the client rose exponentially when rates soared.

Back in 2006 and 2007 when these contracts were popular and selling well, the dollar was steadily falling against most Asian currencies, including the won. But in 2008 and early 2009, the won collapsed by nearly 35%. With this, companies found themselves confronted with losses (their own fault) and lawsuits began to fly.

Legal risk came on the heels of market risk. As of March 2009, South Korea's courts have blocked enforcement of nine derivatives contracts, using as grounds the Procter & Gamble vs. Bankers Trust case. As will be recalled, the US court questioned:

- Whether the contract was a suitable investment for the companies, and

- Whether the risks were fully disclosed to the companies' management by the bank.

In the case of the South Korean export companies, the local courts followed the same line. Their judgment also referred to changed circumstances, with the judges concluding that the export firms had expected the exchange rate to remain stable, which evidently could not be true because if it were so there would have been no reason for the derivatives contract. The South Korean judges also allegedly added that the change in circumstances had been unforeseeable and the losses would be too great for the Korean companies to bear.

Critics have been quick to point out that Korean courts allow parties that get their investment strategies wrong to pay nothing in the transaction, and even to sue for damages. But the managers of firms benefiting from the banks' legal risk answer that the latter lure companies into buying derivatives contracts without fully explaining the risks. That's the case where credit risk, market risk and legal risk tend to merge.

6. Creative accounting distorts risk pricing

Fraud in accounting and financial reporting is reckless and dishonest. But it is no recent happening, being practised since accounts have existed (often in conjunction with corruption). Examples of fraud abound throughout history, while it is more difficult to find impressive references to its suppression, partly because of embedded interest and partly for the reason that fraudsters are inventive.

Ken Lay, Enron's CEO, was indicted in Houston on 8 July 2004, on eleven counts including conspiracy and multiple cases of fraud. This indictment came on top of that of Jeffrey Skilling, Enron's former president and Lay's protégé, as well as that of the company's former chief accounting officer Richard Causey. Prior to Lay's chairmanship, Enron was a relatively small company that owned a gas pipeline, but he transformed it into a huge hedge fund with a pipeline at the side. He exploited loopholes in deregulated markets by means of energy derivatives speculation.

Enron's rise was largely assisted through junk bond-financed merger and acquisition activity. It was Michael Milken of the (now bankrupt) Drexel Burnham Lambert investment bank[176] who, in 1985, provided the money for Lay to engineer the takeover of Houston Natural Gas by Omaha-based InterNorth, as well as a tandem of acquisitions in a sweep nicknamed the *financialisation of energy*. The tools were:

- Super-leveraging through junk debt, and

- *Creative accounting* practices, a different way of saying 'cooking the books'.

Until its bluff is called and those practising it are brought to justice, creative accounting can be instrumental in giving the impression of an exceptional performance – which is not due to managerial ability or the rising tide of markets, but due to tricks. These tricks distort the pricing of risk and misguide management in its decisions.

---

[176] Other banks which helped in this transformation were Chase Manhattan, Citibank, Lazard Frères, First Boston, Salomon Brothers.

Enron did not discover creative accounting, but used it to its fullest extent. They used it, for instance, to maintain a high stock price, which is a key to corporate success in Wall Street. The Sarbanes-Oxley Act (SOX) was enacted in 2002 by the US Congress to stop wide-ranging manipulation of financial statements.[177] The Bush Administration, however, did not bother to apply it.

This distorted risk pricing in the American capital market. Intended to stamp out fraudulent financial reporting, the Sarbanes-Oxley Act was a milestone in legislation because it put responsibility and accountability exactly where it belongs: with the chief executive and chief financial officer.

It was the misfortune of the American people, and of the country's economy, that a supposedly pro-business Administration dropped Sarbanes-Oxley by the wayside. None of the US regulatory agencies bothered to apply it the way the legislators projected. Neither the Department of Justice nor the Securities and Exchange Commission, Federal Reserve, Treasury (Controller of the Currency), FDIC or any other regulatory agency applied it properly. If they had done, the creative accounting scams with subprimes would not have happened and the American economy (indeed, the global economy) would not have descended into crisis.

Creative accounting is not the only way to hide the facts. Much is contributed by political patronage, which bends the application of the law. According to expert opinion, through its lobbyists and politicians, Enron played a major role in every change in US regulatory policy, from lobbying the Commodity Futures Trading Commission (CFTC) to decree regulatory exemptions for over-the-counter (OTC) derivatives, to pressuring the President's Working Group on Financial Markets to

---

[177] Chorafas, *IT Auditing.*

prevent moves toward the regulation of derivatives. This became particularly important after the collapse of Long-Term Capital Management (LTCM) in September 1998.[178]

As long as things kept going Lay's way – based on high leveraging, an unsustainable level of debt and exploitation of the system – Enron grew to become the seventh largest company in America. Super-gearing, however, may work in the short term, but eventually problems emerge because risk is being awfully mispriced. When Enron collapsed, in early December 2001, plenty of people got hurt.

- Stockholders and bondholders lost practically all of their savings.

- Investment bankers who recommended Enron as a sound investment until a short time prior to its collapse were left looking incompetent.

- Worst of all fared Enron's own employees, who lost their jobs, pensions and their investments in the company they were working for.

This is what happens when risk is mispriced. After the collapse, the skeletons hidden in the defunct company's closet started to come out. One of them was the energy scandal in California.[179] In the summer of 2000, California's energy prices increased rapidly. Enron and its allies in that energy bubble initially blamed the state, even as their traders were pushing up prices through various kinds of practices with telling names such as 'Death Star', 'Fat Boy', and 'Get Shorty'. The goal was to:

- Pull and push the markets,

- Deceive investors, and

---

[178] D. N. Chorafas, *Managing Risk in the New Economy*, New York Institute of Finance, New York, 2001.

[179] Another is the so-called pre-pays to which participated the best known US big banks and insurance companies. The scam was engineered in the Jersey Islands; a tax haven.

- Make a fast megabuck; something dear to the company and its stakeholders.

Then energy prices collapsed and some energy companies faced bankruptcy. There is indeed a parallel between this California energy bubble of 2000 and the global energy bubbles of 2004 and 2007-2008, engineered by hedge funds. Therefore, lessons learned from California's experience – when the electricity price disconnected from demand and supply, at the beginning of the 21st century – can help to make sense of what happened with oil prices four and seven years later.

During the California power crisis of 2000 and 2001, the state was hit with rolling blackouts, soaring rates, and the bankruptcy of Pacific Gas and Electric (PG&E), a major utility company. Timothy Belden, a subsequently jailed Enron operative and chief of the company's West Coast trading division, boasted on one of the recorded tapes that one trader "steals money from California to the tune of about a million" dollars a day.

The damage this unwarranted looting of energy resources did to California went so far as to plunge it into bankruptcy. More than $70 billion was taken away from the state by speculators, leading to a budget deficit of $38 billion to be paid by the citizen.[180] The state senate's president said at the time that sooner or later they had to inform "these buccaneers" that legislators were not going to tolerate that sort of business. But nothing really happened in terms of bringing those responsible to justice.

Not unexpectedly, the scams continued – including pre-pays and other creative accounting gimmicks, which distorted risk pricing. Legal action took a long time to get going. When it did, it hit a bunch of individuals beyond the top brass. On 21 September 2004, nearly three years after

---

[180] Who in conjunction with the presidential election of November 2008 voted in a referendum that the Golden State can no longer increase taxes to cover its deficits.

Enron's bankruptcy, six former Enron and Merrill Lynch executives were accused by a US prosecutor of disguising a $7 million loan to "help Enron out of a jam" as a sale of energy-producing barges.[181]

That transaction is an example of financial manipulations used to hide debt and artificially inflate profit at Enron and elsewhere, ultimately leading to the company's collapse. The trial allowed the US government to test evidence it subsequently used against more senior Enron officials, including former chief executives Kenneth Lay and Jeffrey Skilling – who were charged with directing the fraud that forced Enron into the second largest (up to that time) bankruptcy in US history. Lay escaped the rule of law because he died before he could serve his sentence, but at the time of witing Skilling is serving a hefty prison term.

7. Legal risk, political risk and fraudulent conveyance

Charles Ponzi of Boston, the inventor of the investment scam named after him, was a truly exceptional swindler, but stories from his time also say that he was a likeable, convincing individual able to gain other people's confidence. That helped him persuade American investors in the 1920s that he could deliver returns of 50% in just 45 days, by exploiting a loophole in the pricing of international postal coupons. That loophole seems to have existed but could not be practically exploited; hence, Ponzi exploited his customers instead. He did deliver high returns, but this was done by taking money from new investors to give it to his early customers, until no new customers were forthcoming.

By bringing innovation to financial mischief, Ponzi achieved unenviable immortality. Fraudulent moneymaking operations are generally known as *Ponzi schemes*, even if his wheeling and dealing

---

[181] This statement was made by John Hemann, an assistant US attorney, in federal court in Houston as he accused two former Enron executives and four former Merrill executives of inflating Enron's finances by $12 million with the sham sale of energy-producing Nigerian barges to Merrill.

was preceded by such masters of mischief as John Law[182], the pioneer of paper money in early 18th century France.[183] There were also other well-known fraudulent bankers like Luigi Zarossi, Michele Sindona, and syndicate organiser William '520%' Miller.

All these cases involve a great amount of political risk and legal risk in the sense of responsibility on behalf of regulators who should always be alert to mischief. Governments and legislators are also responsible, particularly so when the laws of the land fail to account for the occurrence of pricing risk associated with extra-curricular (read: political) activities, and for the fact that many looters are very smart and often have insider help in exploiting the vulnerability of the law.

Bernard Madoff, for example, perfected Ponzi's pyramiding art and in 2008 was revealed as the dean of financial scams. He knew very well that he could pay neither top interest nor principal from cash flows his investments generated, but relied on his reputation as former chairman of Nasdaq and the connections he established with other bankers, as well as on rising asset prices, to keep going until his spectacular 2008 crash of $65 billion.[184]

Bernard 'Bernie' Leon Madoff was no novice to the securities trade, nor was he known to be a mega speculator. He was 70 years old when his $65 billion fund crashed in December 2008. As the news hit the wires, lots of people found out to their dismay that they had entrusted him with their entire net worth.

Denounced by his victims as a "financial serial killer", Madoff probably took pride from the fact that defrauding for so long not just one but a crowd of top bankers, movie moguls, hedge-fund founders

---

[182] Law's wealth from the printing press eventually collapsed, but he did have the insight that the creation of credit might increase trade, as well as general welfare, up to the point leverage turns on its head.

[183] Paper money was a Chinese invention.

[184] For which he got a 150-year prison sentence.

and people in charge of well-known charities was an event akin to a black swan (Chapter 1), to use financial jargon. His Ponzi game lasted for well over a decade and was of unprecedented boldness.

What surprises the most in this affair is that regulators looked the other way, even after being informed of irregularities by whistle-blowers. Yet, Madoff's pattern of make-believe was not unprecedented. His victims believed he could achieve stable high returns and no losses, through a blend of a novel stock-and-option-trading strategy (of his own make) that could stand the test of time – really a fact enough, by itself, to arouse suspicion.

Several big banks, some of which had fared badly during the financial meltdown of 2007-2009, were also on the list of those caught out. UBS, Crédit Suisse, HSBC, Santander, BNP Paribas and more had to bear a share of losses that added up to $33 billion, according to a Bloomberg tally.

Asset managers and private bankers who were taken to the cleaners by Madoff have been particularly criticised because they charge huge fees, up to 1.5% of assets, on the basis of their 'ability' to pick out clever people to manage their clients' money. Yet they did not exercise due diligence, missed red flags over Madoff's business (such as the way he kept custody over his clients' accounts and handled the trades himself), and ignored warnings from the market. For instance, trading the big way leaves a footprint and the sums Madoff managed were vast: but in spite of this he rarely caused a ripple in trades and prices, as one might have expected.

Lawsuits have been filed in New York and Luxembourg against HSBC and UBS, and more are being prepared, according to lawyers. The liability of custodians and asset managers is now questioned, in spite of the fact that traditionally custodians and sub-custodians are rarely sued in offshore fund frauds because it is hard to hold them responsible under widely different contracts. The wave of legal risk has an impact on jurisprudence because although the responsibility of custodians is complex, with law interpreted differently in different jurisdictions, watchdogs in Ireland and Luxembourg insist that custodians retain responsibility for what sub-custodians do.

Serial regulatory failures, too, were on display when in early January 2009 the US Congress held a hearing to probe why the fraud went undetected – raising suspicion that there was political meddling in a cover-up. Experts suggested that regulatory oversight was most awkward because SEC examiners seemed to be looking in the right places, yet they still did not uncover what was going wrong. According to one account, investigators were led astray by a well-architectured scheme of deception, but according to other opinions SEC lacked the expertise to keep up with the fraudsters.

Neither is Madoff's case a lonely example of *fraudulent conveyance* risk. Another Ponzi game came to the public eye on 17 February 2009 when the Securities and Exchange Commission charged billionaire 'Sir' Allen Stanford with an $8 billion fraud. This case centred on Stanford International Bank (SIB), which he operated from St. John's, Antigua. Here we have two examples of possible *political risk*: one in the world's superpower, the other in a tiny dot on the map of the Caribbean.

Stanford allegedly sold these $8 billion in certificates of deposits by promising improbable and unsubstantiated high interest rates. While some investors who have lost money in what American securities regulators characterised as a "massive, ongoing fraud" resided in the US, the majority came from Latin America. The SEC accused the Stanford International Bank (SIB) of falsely claiming that customers' deposits were safe, and that it had invested client funds primarily in liquid financial instruments.

Allen Stanford probably chose Antigua as his base not only because of its lax control over the banks, but also because he knew that as his business grew it would dominate the little Caribbean country of just 85,000 people. The SEC's focus was turned on SIB doing something abnormal by an analyst's note, which was highly critical of the bank's apparent ability to deliver consistently and significantly market-beating returns on its depositors' enormous assets.

According to the SEC, SIB's portfolio was not, as claimed, monitored by a team of more than 20 analysts, but by the sole shareholder himself and his chief financial officer, a former college classmate. Among those on the investment committee were Stanford's father and a neighbour with cattle-ranching experience. Other warning signs included:

- A tiny auditing firm, just like Madoff's,

- A stunning lack of transparency,

- The fact that Antigua's financial regulator had reputation for lousy control, and

- Stanford's local clout due to *political connections*,[185] which should always be accounted for when pricing risk, but evidently they were not.

Globalisation proved to an improvement over the original Ponzi model. Like Madoff Securities, this allegedly fraudulent financial empire launched offshoots all over the Americas and investors flocked to it. After the FBI's arrest of the allegedly fraudulent banker, investors tried, mostly in vain, to get their money back. Many rich people in Latin America and the Caribbean had poured their savings into the Stanford International Bank without due diligence. In Venezuela alone investors are said to have lost over $2 billion 'safeguarded' by Stanford-linked firms.

Simplicity, Leonardo da Vinci said, is "the ultimate sophistication". Ponzi, Madoff, Stanford and plenty of other alleged crooks engaged their clients in a game which was sophisticated but simple. To the contrary, the regulators who should police the system and catch the thieves got lost in the complex web of political leadership. Regulatory risk also has a price, which has to be added to that of other risks (more on this in Chapter 8).

---

[185] *The Economist*, 28 February 2009.

In their synergy, political and regulatory exposures hide:

- Legal risks,
- Market risks, and
- Counterparty risks.

Investors will also be well advised to learn a lesson from J. K. Galbraith, who pointed to three traits which, he believed, put the financial community at risk of fraud:

1. Confusing good manners and good tailoring with integrity and intelligence;

2. Failing to appreciate the disastrous interdependence between the honest man and the crook;

3. Subscribing to the dangerous cliché that in the financial world everything depends on confidence.

Chapter 7: Overleveraging Risk

1. Leverage defined

Investors commonly refer to debt as *leverage* (in the US), and as *gearing* (in Britain). Both terms identify a straightforward metaphor for what is going on with debt – amassed when living beyond one's means. The key measure of leverage is the debt-to-capital ratio, one of its metrics being liabilities over assets (L/A). A company's leverage ratio is equal to:

> The market value of its debt, divided by the market value of its assets.

In Chapter 4 we saw the inverse algorithm A/L, where market capitalisation was taken as proxy for the assets, while L stood for balance sheet liabilities. Schools don't always teach the very interesting notion in mathematical analysis that different ways of writing a certain ratio or equation may well suggest different things. Concepts embedded in the two sides of an equation are logically equivalent, but they are not necessarily the same. L/A speaks volumes about a management's propensity to leverage the firm under its watch.

Corporate gearing in the United States increased over the decades that followed World War II, but not all industrial sectors have followed the same gearing policies. An interesting statistic is that outside the financial industry the largest listed firms have little debt compared with smaller listed firms and the large number of private firms.

Non-financial firms in the S&P 500 index account for about a third of national corporate net debt, while contributing a majority of profits. According to the European Central Bank in Europe listed firms have cut their debt since 2000 – cleaning up their balance sheets.

Excluding General Electric (because of GE Capital) and the 'big three' carmakers in Detroit (because of their customer financing affiliates), the debt to equity ratio of the ten biggest listed firms in the US hovers around 12%, but rises slightly for the top 30 and hits 30% for the top 100 companies. This debt ratio increases to over 40% for all listed firms in the US.

Given that appropriate debt levels vary by industry, there are no firm rules for assessing leverage on the basis of the aforementioned statistics; these however can serve as a frame of reference. Utilities, which tend to have a steady income, have fared well historically with 40 to 60% debt to capital, while most other industrial companies do best with debt of 35% or less. In principle, with all other things equal, the lower a company's leverage is the better tends to be its financial staying power. As the recent economic crisis and credit crunch has shown, this principle holds true even if 'other things' are not necessarily equal.

For instance, there exist country and cultural differences. In Europe and America leverage tends to be lower than in newer countries. An average US leverage figure (including non-manufacturing firms) is 62%, but in Australia it is 80%. Some of the difference is due to accounting rules; but another part is pure higher gearing.

Looked at as a statistic, a higher (but not too high) debt figure is not always a big negative, provided that the company has the cash flow to meet payments of interest and principal – and it does not depend on borrowed money in order to survive during a credit crunch. Where leverage strikes back with a vengeance is when companies miscalculate their ability to serve their debt, which is a very frequent case.

A leveraged company (as well as a leveraged sovereign or individual) is loaded with loans which become difficult to service and repay when the economy declines and/or the entity's cash flow (section 6) is destabilised. The fact that in Australia there is a tendency to over-leverage sees to it that 20% of Australian companies have negative net worth, while this figure stands at 8% in the United States.[186]

---

[186] Moody's Investors' Service 'Rating Methodology', New York, December 2000.

The reader should also appreciate that leveraging policies and statistics change radically when the subject of discussion is no more the manufacturing sector of the economy but the banking industry. Super-leveraging tends to be the rule in the financial industry partly, but only partly, because money is both raw material and financial staying power.

Even the 8% capital adequacy ratio of Basel I implies a 12.5% leveraging factor condoned by regulators. But this 12.5% is peanuts compared to leveraging factors of 30, 40, 50 and more featured by commercial and investment banks in the 2003 to 2007 time frame.

This leads to the management principle that while leverage should be approached with care, *overleveraging* must be avoided. As the dramatic events of 2007-2009 demonstrated, the aggressive pursuit of high leverage, and of balance sheet growth at all cost, was the undoing of the big banks. When the crash came, they fell on their swords and nothing could stop the blades from driving home. Their management was 'good' in good times and very bad in bad times.

Turbulence distracted them from doing the job for which they were paid. One of Fred Goodwin's former colleges summed up the career of the CEO who ruined the Royal Bank of Scotland (RBS) in these terms: "He was trying to do everyone else's job, but he was not doing his own."[187] Goodwin's most important duty as chief executive was to safeguard the equity and assets under his watch – rather than balloon the bank's balance sheet through 6500% leverage.

The lesson which should be retained from the many cases of mischief connected to super-leveraging can best be expressed through a developing consensus among financial experts. Though the badly wounded big American and European banks may survive, the estimated $5 to $6 trillion (or more) aggregate hole in the financial industry's

---

[187] *Financial Times*, 25 February 2009.

balance sheet (roughly two-thirds in America, one-third in Europe) is way beyond the ability of the private sector to fill.

The 20-years experience of Japanese banks, whose misfortunes started in 1990-1991, suggests that the bare survival of big banks following the US Treasury's 'stress tests' (Chapter 8) may well mark less the revival of big financial institutions than the beginning of capitalism without capital in America (as well as in Europe, particularly in Britain).

2. The aftermath of gearing is entropy

Like legal risk (Chapter 6), overleveraging kills. This is true of all excesses, not only those connected to a high level of gearing. Too much of anything is a prescription for disorder; with *entropy* becoming the measure of the degree of disorganisation. The second law of thermodynamics, to which reference was made in the Prologue, dictates that as time passes the amount of disorder increases, while the energy required to create order dissipates (see also the Appendix to this Chapter). With disorganisation comes randomness and a lack of patterning.

Neither is overleveraging the only reason for disorder. Mergers and acquisitions (M&As) provide another example. When, in March 2008, JP Morgan Chase bought Bear Stearns (under the patronage of the Fed, to save it from plain bankruptcy), and in January 2009 Bank of America bought Merrill Lynch (for the same reason) these moves were seen as ingenious in avoiding bankruptcy at any cost – though they created more disordered states than ordered ones. The second law of thermodynamics states that when two distinct systems are joined, the entropy of the aggregate is greater than the arithmetic sum of the entropies of the individual components. As an aggregate tends to increase in entropy over time, the information it provides decreases. (Making the job of bank regulation in the aforementioned M&A cases so much more difficult, uncertain and complex.)

In addition, according to the same law applied in information and communication systems, the degree of disorder cannot be decreased without decreasing the entropy in the aggregate. High leveraging and mammoth size are part of the same pattern of pushing up the entropy quotient; they are not independent piecemeal facts.

Good governance and sound finances contrast starkly with a sprawling uncontrollable organisational structure and overleveraging. The two are mutually inconsistent states arising from their own singularity points. The crisis of 2007-2009 provided hard evidence of how wrong the latter management strategy can get.

"The second law of thermodynamics is based on the fact that there are many more disordered states than ordered states," said Stephen Hawking with reference to systems in physics. The same concept prevails in finance and in organisational life at large. (Also the first law of thermodynamics is important to an organisation's survival. In the 1840s the English brewer and scientist James Joule led the experiments that created the foundations for the first law, also known as *the conservation of energy*.)

The control of organisational entropy necessarily involves careful evaluation and rethinking of a company's business strategy, including definition of its risk quotient. Apart from loading RBS with bought money, Goodwin engaged in global expansion, leveraged buyouts and takeovers of other institutions in which the purchase was financed by a large amount of more leverage. The worst example is the takeover of ABN Amro, the Dutch bank, which proved to be RBS' undoing.

Indeed the wild sort of takeovers have seen to it that the term 'leverage' has also taken on a broader meaning: that of the use of a small amount of funds to gain control of an entity whose worth is many times the capital one is putting up – which might itself be borrowed money. The result is that the layers of leverage multiply.

In finance, four kinds of leverage support and feed upon one another:

1. Buying money from banks and other institutions,

2. Tapping the capital market through debt instruments,

3. Selling common stocks and preferred stocks, and

4. Engineering inflated stock prices, while investors fail to understand that the company is already highly leveraged.

One of the risks of this so-called 'multiply-connected' leverage is that failure of any one of the four gearing channels speeds up the destabilisation of the others, with the after-effect spreading fast across the market and hitting the company like a hammer. *Deleveraging*, the opposite of leveraging, is promoted by the need to clean up and downsize the firm's balance sheet when there is still time to do so, which means before approaching bankruptcy (more on deleveraging in section 8).

All this has been known for a long time. It is therefore quite surprising that during the early go-go years of the 21st century most big banks fell into the trap of super-leveraging. As should have been expected, subsequently they found it difficult to enact an orderly deleveraging, which had disastrous effects on their financial condition. Their financial staying power was further destabilised by the switch of emphasis from getting money through longer-term deposits to buying money from other banks and the capital market, where the short-term dominates.

With individual investors, too, leveraging involves borrowing in short-term markets, and buying some longer-term assets, like securities. Sometimes a steep yield curve makes this appear attractive, because one can finance high yielding long-term positions with lower cost short-term money. But by borrowing to purchase securities the investor (or banker) in effect takes on the risk of repayment of loans, as well as assuming an interest rate exposure to longer maturities.

It is indeed curious that bankers don't think of these risks prior to leveraging themselves and their institutions. Disaster hits in a big way with the advent of an economic crisis. High leveraging saw to it that the descent of the economy (since July-August 2007) lead to a compressed deflationary cycle with the result that financial markets and the real economy disconnected. Share prices became too volatile and no longer reflected fair values.

This destabilised management teams that were accustomed to following ratios. Up to a point, but only up to a point, as Figure 7.1 shows, return on equity improves with leveraging. But risk increases too. And when adversity hits, the firm's financial position deteriorates and the cost for redressing the balances becomes exorbitant.

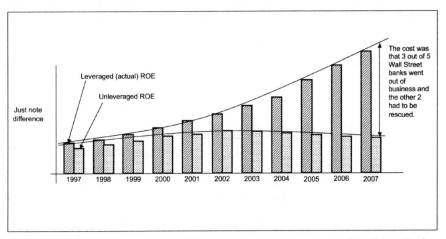

Figure 7.1: Leveraging makes a difference in return on equity (ROE) but it also magnifies risk.

One of the factors promoting leverage is that tax treatment favours debt over equity. Practically, however, there are many limitations in trying to profit from debt over equity. Management contemplating an increase in liabilities should not lose sight of the fact that, to the contrary, the cost of financial distress favours the use of equity over debt. The board may stop the payment of dividends, but it must continue paying interest to bonds and bank loans unless the company declares bankruptcy.

3. Leveraging with financial instruments

The Basel Committee defines leverage as *a low ratio of capital to total assets*[188], and it warns that when banks operate with very high leverage they increase their vulnerability to adverse economic events and boost the risk of failure. In the background of this warning lies the fact that while all banks are leveraged, some are much more leveraged than others – and therefore more vulnerable.

The deep economic and banking crisis of 2007-2009 demonstrated that the Basel Committee was right to be preoccupied with leverage. Both the commercial and investment banks which did not pay attention to this warning were wrong in their strategic decision. According to Dominion Bond Rating Service, all (then) five Wall Street firms Goldman Sachs, Morgan Stanley, Merrill Lynch, Lehman Brothers and Bear Stearns had almost doubled their assets between 2001 and 2006.[189]

With hindsight, it can be said that the results from this overleveraging have been largely negative. In March 2008 Bear Stearns was saved at the 11th hour by a forced merger into JP Morgan Chase, with a $29 billion dowry by the Fed. In September 2008, Lehman Brothers went bust. In December 2008/January 2009 Merrill Lynch just managed to be acquired by Bank of America; and both Goldman and Morgan Stanley got a financial lifeline from the US Treasury.

Figure 7.2 dramatises this ballooning of assets and of derivatives exposure, taking as an example a hypothetical Omega Bank, but it is based on real life statistics. Its core capital is $25 billion but the assets in its balance sheet have ballooned to $1 trillion. That's a leverage of

---

[188] Basel Committee on Banking Supervision 'The Relationship Between Banking Supervisors and Banks' External Auditors', BIS, Basel, January 2002.

[189] *The Economist*, 19 May 2007.

4000%. When it fell by the wayside and was forced into a merger with JP Morgan Chase, Bear Stearns had a leverage of 5000%.

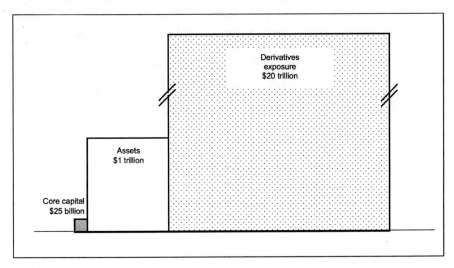

Figure 7.2: Omega Bank; a member of the club of super-leveraged financial institutions.

There is another interesting statistic to bring to the reader's attention. Bear Stearns was rumoured to have warehoused over $10 trillion in credit default swaps, about one-sixth of those outstanding in early 2008. The majority of these bilateral agreements were said to be with Morgan Chase. If so, the merger made sense from the latter's viewpoint: not only did it get an investment bank on the cheap and benefited from a Fed guaranty, but it also cleared a large amount of toxic waste off of its balance sheet.

A characteristic failure in bank supervision is that regulators don't do their duty in stopping institutions from overleveraging. Very few regulators pay due attention to the need for *financial leverage limits*. One of those who did so, albeit post-mortem, was the Swiss Banking Commission. In early December 2008 it released details for its new capital regime aimed at restraining rapid growth in assets when times are good. The two big Swiss banks, UBS and Credit Suisse, will be subject to higher risk weighted capital requirements and a new leverage ratio which caps the amount of total assets that a bank can hold, regardless of the risk they entail.

Leveraging is a two-edged knife. Novel financial instruments promote gearing and their undisciplined use is the single most important reason for deep crises in a company's treasury. Because of easy leveraging, many traders lose money in the futures and in the options market.

Warren Buffett's Berkshire Hathaway provides an example. In mid-March 2009 it was announced that in 2008 it made $4.8 billion in premiums from writing put options for nearly $30 billion. But $4.8 billion was small fry compared to money lost with derivatives, which hit overall 2008 earnings hard. Year on year in 2008 Berkshire's profits were reduced by 96%.

The futures market offers opportunities for a great deal of leverage, because of the way in which it works. Initial good faith deposits, known as *margin* (not to be confused with margin for stocks), are usually at the 5% to 10% of contractual value. This makes leveraging of 20 times feasible – and much more than that if one works on borrowed capital.

In fact, the futures market functions as a money supplier of last resort. It provides virtual capital to players who cannot get cash elsewhere, but market players don't always appreciate that options, futures and forwards make a business prone to missteps. The high risk of leveraged deals is largely a consequence of being careless about future losses and failing to exercise control over one's business activities.

An interesting hindsight of the new regulation is that the two banks' domestic lending activities are excluded from the leverage limit. This makes sense from a Swiss perspective. Putting the brakes on lending to local customers is the last thing the regulator would like to do, particularly in a time of crisis. Waiving the leverage ratio in this connection orients the thinking of global banks towards business at home rather than assuming much higher risk at the international market.

One of the ironies with run-away leverage is that people, companies and governments don't understand how risky their position is until it is too late. Neither do they appreciate that there is no way to avoid the fact that high leverage leads to bubbles (Chapter 8). The Japanese authorities in the late 1980s, as well as the American regulators a decade later and in the early part of this century, allowed a speculative bubble to grow, defying the lessons taught by economic history.

At no time in the past have asset bubbles of major magnitude been deflated in an orderly way. The readjustment is always painful, as evidenced by the crash of the French Royal Bank, the Mississippi bubble, the South Seas bubble, the Nikkei Index/real estate bubble, the Nasdaq bubble and the Big Banks bubble in 2007.

Augmented by creative accounting (Chapter 6), which inflates the earnings figures and hides the losses through derivatives, excesses in asset valuations lead to major collapses, with high rising equities going down 80% or more. In the case of Nikkei and Nasdaq bubbles, for instance, nobody wrote bearish reports in Tokyo or on Wall Street, when it was still time to punch the ballooning prices and leave the hot air out.

Neither, as it is shown in retrospect, had the regulators learned anything from adversity. With high stakes going higher and higher through super-leveraging, busting is an experience which teaches that downturns can have terrible consequences. Lack of rigorous risk control makes matters worse, because there are a lot of people who do not understand what is going on, neither do they appreciate the wisdom of applying the brakes.

4. The fate of leveraged persons, companies and states

"We never wanted to leverage up," said Warren Buffett in 1998, in his heyday. "That's not our game. So we've never wanted to borrow a lot of money. We've got all of our money in Berkshire, along with virtually all our friends' and our relatives' money. Therefore, we never felt that we wanted to leverage up this company."[190]

---

[190] 'Outstanding Investor Digest', New York, NY, 24 September 1998.

Ten years later, however, the tune has changed. Not only did Berkshire lose money with derivatives, but also credit default swaps have revealed something that a few years earlier would have been unthinkable. According to CDS spreads:

- The conglomerate run by Buffett is more likely to default on its debt than Vietnam, and

- GE Capital, fully-owned subsidiary of General Electric, a company which has been part of the Dow Jones Index for nearly 100 years, is a worse credit risk than Russia.[191]

This is revealing because Russia is famous for its default in August 1998 and for its 2008 financial earthquake which flattened the country's oligarchs. Apart from the German investor who lost a fortune in the Volkswagen stock gamble and committed suicide, the people worst hit through overleveraging have been six of the richest Russians who (between themselves) lost around $111 billion.

The oligarchs had taken big loans from banks – largely west European banks – to buy stocks, rival firms and assets all over the world. Just one fortune, that of Oleg Deripaska who carried the title of the richest Russian and reportedly paid euro 485 million to buy a villa in France, fell from $28 billion to $7.2 billion, according to Izvestia. The better known Roman Abramovich had to make do with $3.3 billion, while he used to have wealth of $23.5 billion in mid-2008. Other oligarchs, too, shed billions.

The Russian billionaires had financed their growth by borrowing money, with most of their fortune estimated through the overvalued shares in companies that they owned. The fall of the global markets, the deep drop in the price of raw materials and hardships in paying off debt then naturally wrought havoc upon their fortunes and reputations.

---

[191] *The Economist*, 14 March 2009.

But other very rich investors, too, lost plenty of feathers. Heading the list in the Middle East is the Saudi prince Alwaleed bin Talal, who once laid claim to the 19th largest fortune in the world. Reportedly he lost $4 billion out of $17 billion[192] – which means bleeding 'only' 23.5% of his wealth, much better than Deripaska at a loss of 74.3% and Abramovich at 86%.

Among overleveraged companies, Belgium's Fortis, America's AIG and plenty of other big financial institutions reported massive losses connected to their financial wheeling and dealing. They were particularly hit by credit default swaps and other guarantees, as well as their highly geared banking activities. The fact that a lot of big banks in the United States, Britain, France, Belgium, Holland and Switzerland had to be saved through government intervention is well known. It is indeed surprising that regulators did nothing to stop the super-leveraging and remained simple spectators while there was still time to exercise prudent control.

In the case of AIG, management's ability to service debts and cover losses incurred by its other business units (particularly the one that provided financial guarantees) depended heavily on the soundness and continued operation of its insurance branch, which itself was leveraged. Only after the company's descent did the huge amount of gearing of each AIG division become evident, and this finding created great concern among supervisory authorities about the ramifications of an AIG bankruptcy.

Complex corporate-wide exposure which is interdivisional and spans a global scale, is not caught through current risk management systems. Therefore, this test proposes a meta layer to QED-engineered risk control to be established at a comprehensive level through quantum chromodynamics.

---

[192] *Le Figaro*, 15 December 2008.

This should target counterparty linkages including the after-effects of the likely failure of a guarantor because of its overleveraged balance sheet. In the case of the American International Group, many financial institutions had bought credit default swaps from AIG, but no one knew how many *in-credit* default swaps had been written on AIG itself. This is a stark example of how activities occurring at the vertex of a holding company, particularly linked to its non-insurance units, could detrimentally affect the entire conglomerate and the global financial system.

Banks paid insurers such as AIG to take on the risk that their assets would default, which in itself was an exploitation of a capital adequacy loophole, because it saved them from having to put regulatory capital aside. To make matters worse, in a collusion with rating agencies credit risk was vastly upgraded by converting lower-rated securities into AAA ones – except that AIG went bust and the taxpayer had to put up trillions of dollars to keep the company alive.

After the events, several experts admitted that they would not have imagined that such a massive company with total assets of about $1 trillion would run into such severe problems and would have to be practically nationalised. Experts have also pointed out that one of the key things one can learn from AIG's failure comes by looking at the origins of its problems, which did not stem from the regulated parts of its insurance business but from the largely unregulated financial products operations. AIG engaged in trading of credit risks and in securities lending, and the holding company was too much of a geared structure, with many different supervisory authorities expected to look into deals they could not understand.

In the end no supervisory authority was responsible for the monitoring of AIG's steadily growing exposure. The overall view of the company was simply missing and therefore it was extremely difficult to see where problems arose, how severe these were, whether top management was aware of them and what interrelationships existed between the company's different domains of exposure – while leveraging continued its course unattended. Quantum chromodynamics should help in providing this necessary comprehensive risk pattern.

Countries, too, fall into the same trap of leveraging without limits and without a damage control policy. Four years after Japan's descent, the September 1995 issue of *World Investment Strategy Highlights* (by Goldman Sachs) had this to say about the country's leverage: "The most important change in corporate performance has been the *degearing* of Japan because of equity issuance as the warrant issues matured." Degearing cost Japan two decades.[193]

What the Japanese government should have appreciated in the country's golden 1980s, when it rose to the status of global financial power, is that a large and growing leverage factor is something that the economy cannot sustain for long. When the peak is reached and confidence drops, as it did in Japan, what comes after is rapid degearing with ominous results. The stock market crash which followed wiped out more than half the capitalisation in the Tokyo Stock Exchange, and led to a wave of bankruptcies by Japanese banks, leaving the government helpless as it did not know what to do to turn the country around.

Hit by the effects of super-leveraging, Japan struggled with a recession throughout the 1990s and the first decade of this century. By 2009 things got worse rather than better. Constrained by a weak government, an enormous pile of debt, and big budget deficits which run at 170% of GDP and are still increasing, the country's future is bleaker than it has been at any other time since the end of WWII.

Having learned nothing from Japan's experience, in 2008 Ireland rushed to guarantee all deposits to its banks – overleveraging its economy – a move the country could hardly afford. Rating agencies lowered Ireland's rating, but credit default swaps tell a bleaker story.

---

[193] More detail on deleveraging can be found in section 5.

Their implied probability of the Irish Republic defaulting, over five years, stands at 31.70%. That is just a notch lower than 32.42% which represents the five-year probability of default with CCC credit rating.[194]

Using overleveraging to combat leveraging is also the worst policy ever adopted in American history. The Obama Administration's budget deficit in 2009 is expected to hit 12% of GDP, including the stimulus to the economy, salvage of big banks, medical care for everyone and other projects. This is super-leveraging without limits, and by the end of 2009 the US national debt may exceed 200% of GDP.

5. Exercising due diligence in leverage

Financial leverage should not be confused with *operational leverage*, a term also widely used to mean the extent to which fixed costs impact on operations. Break-even analysis reflects the degree to which operational leverage is employed in connection to business activity. For instance, in manufacturing, operational leverage identifies the pattern of fixed costs, thereby providing the basis for estimating the change in profits, and making it possible to study the behaviour of profit and loss (P&L).

Nevertheless, though financial and operational leverage are different concepts, they do share a downside. Operational leverage is optimised by keeping variable costs low – a policy requiring an increase in fixed costs, usually through capital expenditure (capex). This works fine when production volumes are high, but turns on its head when production volumes are low, because it is easier to cut down variable costs than to get rid of fixed costs, which represent the depreciation of installed equipment and other capital expenditures.[195]

---

[194] Crédit Suisse, Research Monthly, Fixed Income, 10 March 2008.

[195] Up to a point, but only up to a point, fixed costs and variable costs are interchangeable. The choice between them is one of the tough decisions management must make. All other things being equal, capital expenditures (for instance for automation) reduce variable costs but increase fixed costs. Another way of reducing variable costs is through outsourcing and wider procurement of services, which also have their inconveniences.

Investments always have to be depreciated whether the equipment is used or not, therefore depreciation schedules are independent of whether or not capital investments are productive.

In a similar manner, financial leverage can be the gateway to significant profits as long as it allows substantial gains to be realised. But leverage becomes a heavy burden when economic activity slows; therefore it is wrong to count without the risks associated to it, as it exposes the investor, banker or treasurer to market volatility, and market and/or instrument illiquidity.

As we saw in section 2, because a relatively modest cash down payment is posted for each futures contract traded, even a small adverse move in the price of the commodity can wipe out an investor or trader's initial margin deposit. Once a margin call is issued by a broker, the owner of the position must post additional margin immediately or face the prospect of having his futures asset liquidated at significant loss. The higher the leverage is, the greater this loss is going to be if the market moves against the guess the investor has made. Therefore, nothing can be left to chance in facing uncertainties, contradictions, or investments that went sour.

Being ready to confront exposure requires not only being ready to do so but also having the required liquidity and capital reserves. To get an appreciation of a company's financial staying power and the way this may be affected through leverage, alert analysts measure the risks of debt by income statement ratios with liabilities taken at book value, while the proxy for value of assets is capitalisation. Among the more popular are:

- *Total liabilities to total assets.* This is a solvency ratio measuring a company's obligations to creditors accounting for all the funds that have been provided. Liabilities include all debt (short, medium and longer term) in the form of bank loans, bonds, mortgages, notes and debentures, as well as money due to suppliers and labour. The lower the ratio, the greater the cushion against adversity.

- *Current liabilities to net worth.* This measures the amount of equity capital (funds supplied by owners, core capital) against the amount raised by current debt. If equity is insufficient, the company will be forced to resort to stopgap short-term financing which (as already discussed) carries significant risk.

- *Cash flow to current liabilities.* Current liabilities represent financial commitments which cannot be deferred without renegotiation, which damages a company's reputation, or may lead to outright bankruptcy. These commitments will be met through the company's cash flow, which should be stress tested under worst conditions (section 6).

- *Times interest earned.* This ratio is computed by dividing earnings before interest and taxes (but not necessarily EBITDA) by interest charges. Debt, all kinds of debt, has a carrying cost. The times interest earned ratio helps to measure the extent to which earnings could decline without a resultant financial embarrassment to the company, because of inability to meet interest costs.

- Other important ratios include *short-term liabilities over assets* and *long-term liabilities over assets*, respectively known as *short-term and long-term solvency ratios*. An important liquidity ratio is *cash flow plus liquid assets over short-term liabilities*.

The amount of leverage assumed by the company can be expressed in book value terms as the ratio of:

$$\text{Book Value Leverage} = \frac{\text{Debt}}{\text{Equity}}$$

In contrast to good governance, the preference of which for low leverage ratios is well known, CEOs with huge risk appetite use high leverage to magnify egos and earnings. This may work up to a point, but if the debt ratio is too high there is a danger of encouraging irresponsibility on the part of traders, loans officers and the CEOs themselves. Eventually more and more toxic waste will be warehoused, and assumed exposure will go through the roof, turning the company's balance sheet on its head.

Risk measurements are complicated by the fact that derivatives exposure is carried in contracts in notional principal amounts and (with few exceptions) this is not the final cost of assumed risk. Some years ago I developed a model for a major financial institution which demodulated (reduced to real money) the money most likely to be lost in a derivatives contract, as a function of:

- The instrument's type

- Its historical volatility (Chapter 1), and

- A scenario's prognostication of future volatility and economic conditions.

This approach can be strengthened by the use of arrows employed by quantum electrodynamics, discussed in Chapter 6. But, while necessary, the yardsticks for exposure are not sufficient. Once the amount of exposure has been estimated, the bank should allocate economic capital by desk and position. Limits must also be set for each type of exposure decided by the board of directors.

Simulation helps in forecasting trends, and expert systems assist in real-time evaluation of distance from limits. Financial reporting through a *virtual balance sheet*[196] offers an *ad hoc,* fully updated response to queries regarding current gearing, provided that leverage is tracked by the instrument, desk and trader who made the commitment and transaction.

---

[196] A *virtual balance sheet* is accurate at about 4%, which in engineering is an acceptable level. The virtual balance sheet is intended to inform management, and not for financial reporting reasons. Its advantage lies in the fact that with high technology it can be produced in a few minutes. D. N. Chorafas, *The Real-time Enterprise*, Auerbach, New York, 2005.

Quantum chromodynamics may permit the integration of quantitative risk factors tracked through QED with those qualitative factors discussed in this and the preceding sections. The holistic approach being suggested has been followed by financial institutions which are leaders in risk management and technology. Risk integration makes it possible to experiment in real-time testing with different what-if scenarios. An approach based on interactive computational finance is vital because changes in the financial markets take place every split second.

6. Leverage, solvency, liquidity and transparency

A company is *solvent* if the fair value of its assets is greater than the money it owes to its employees, suppliers, bankers, investors, depositors and creditors. Because of market psychology, however, even a solvent bank can be broken by a bank run. Since no bank can redeem at any given time more than a fraction of its deposits, a depositors' run assures that some of them will leave the teller empty-handed. Sometimes insolvency can be masked if confidence of depositors and lenders is maintained, but banks must appreciate that confidence is a dear commodity and it eventually runs out.

A bank may be solvent but illiquid. *Liquidity* is the ease with which the company can meet its financial commitments when due. A liquidity crisis can be met if the company is able to realise its readiest assets to cover its commitment, or if another party, for instance the central bank, provides the urgently needed liquid funds.

Theoretically, liquidity and solvency are two different concepts. Practically, this is not always the case. An example is provided by the stock market crash of October 1987, a time when the Federal Reserve confronted the likelihood of systemic risk. Was some big bank in trouble? Was it maybe insolvent?

"In the short run," Gerald Corrigan, then president of the New York Fed argued, "there was no way to tell the difference between just short-term liquidity problems and outright insolvency."[197] Tail events which damage the bank's liquidity may also affects its solvency. Therefore, a financial institution must watch most carefully for:

- Liquidity, both its own and the market's as a whole (Chapter 2), and

- Its solvency, including the possibility of fast realisation of assets under conditions other than fire sale.

Leverage constitutes an important vulnerability in terms of solvency and for liquidity reasons. In one of its incarnations, leverage becomes the source of funding liquidity risk associated with short-term financing. Though still solvent, an overleveraged firm may not have sufficient financial resources available to it to enable it to meet its obligations as they come due; or, can secure them only at excessive cost, which destabilises it in terms of operational leverage (section 4).

Nobody really knows when adversity will hit. Therefore, good business sense requires being ready for it and remembering that high leverage boosts exposure and risk, making an entity dependent not only on its cash flow (section 6) but also on the stability of its funding, which might be impaired. A leveraged fund manager, for instance, becomes vulnerable to:

- Margin calls for trading positions,

- Inability to roll over margin loans,

- Redemption requirements, and

- Losses on the investment portfolio that may look affordable in percentage terms but are high in absolute value.

Either and all of these factors prompt forced sales and degearing (deleveraging) under unfavourable terms, hence they have potentially

---

[197] Bob Woodward, *Maestro, Greenspan's Fed and the American Boom*, Simon & Schuster, New York, 2000.

adverse implications not only for the entity itself but also for the market. It needs no explanation that deleveraging under unfavourable conditions distresses prices, thereby having a destabilising influence in a nervous market.

Deleveraging aside, one of the fundamental problems with the solvency of credit institutions is that they make promises they do not expect to have to keep. Many of these come in the form of *contingent liabilities* which require banks to come to the support of their clients elsewhere under a variety of specified conditions, which have not been analysed under a worst case scenario. In a downturn a lot of these bills come due at once.

For instance as the July-August 2007 crisis gained momentum, experts estimated that between $380 and $400 billion of loans and bonds linked to pending leveraged buyouts needed to be shifted. The speed of the market deterioration surprised many, but did not alter the fact that banks faced bridging loans to private equity buyers, with a typical one to two month holding period. When in early 2007 the markets were buzzing, banks assumed nothing could go wrong in such a short time. But as market confidence evaporated they faced the prospect of having to keep large amounts of debt on their own books, indefinitely, and at a loss.

Experts suggest that one way to measure the loss is to rely on the discounted price at which leveraged loans are trading in the secondary market, where investors seem unwilling to pay more than 85 to 90% of par value under best conditions, and often much less than that. Buyout issues are not the only non-traditional risks faced by banks.

The crisis associated with subprime mortgages revealed solvency and liquidity risks due to the horde of conduits, structured investment vehicles (SIVs) and other off balance sheet 'assets'. Investors who bought that paper suddenly decided it was not worth the risk. In the aftermath, many banks found funding to be either impossible, or achievable only at exorbitant levels of interest.

Bank policies regarding off balance sheet vehicles raised a great deal of questions about their solvency, and their treatment of off balance sheet exposure diminished market confidence in their governance. Market conditions and reputational risks led several institutions to provide liquidity support and other credit enhancements to their off balance sheet vehicles, while existing accounting standards do not provide clear guidance for:

- Consolidation,

- De-recognition, and

- Re-consolidation of off balance sheet vehicles.

This led to inconsistent financial reporting and to a confusion of market players. It also raised auditing challenges, the effects of which were compounded by a growing lack of transparency.

Everybody knows that banks are overleveraged, but investors would like to see by how much prior to committing their capital. A persistent lack of transparent and reliable financial information from banks and across the system was a major factor in the 2007-2009 crisis. Investor confidence was particularly undermined by the lack of transparency in:

- The banks' valuation methodologies, and

- Exposures in credit, market and liquidity risks, particularly those related to structured products and off balance sheet vehicles.

To their credit, accounting standards bodies in the US (FASB) and internationally (IASB) have played an important role in encouraging consistent and meaningful disclosures about valuation processes and the extent of on-balance sheet and off balance sheet risks faced by banks. But as the economic crisis developed, in many jurisdictions:

- Disclosure standards were twisted,

- The planned integration of balance sheet and off balance sheet items has been delayed, and

- Fair value was taken off the radar screen by cancelling the marking to market rules.

Rather than being a historic meeting, the second G-20 summit, which took place in London on 2 April 2009, was distinguished by two negative issues: lack of sincerity and more debt. The G-20 decided to strengthen bank regulation but what happened that same day in the United States was a disaster for bank regulation, and for the accounting discipline at large. No matter what the G-20 'decided', under pressure by politicians and the big banks on 2 April 2009, the American accounting standards' setters:

- Abandoned the principle of marking-to-market the banks' toxic waste, and

- Replaced it by marking-to-myth, leaving it up to the bank management to say what the value of their 'assets' was.

Reportedly, this was demanded by members of Congress and by trade groups with the connivance of the Obama Administration, but it was bitterly denounced by investors and by two former chairman of the Securities and Exchange Commission.[198] There is no better example of Newspeak than deciding on stronger regulatory rules and enacting precisely the opposite in one and the same day.

Such officialisation of Newspeak has to be integrated into a wholesome risk control system, and quantum chromodynamics may be the best approach for doing so. The market prizes transparency and when politicians and failed bankers conspire to hide the fatal vulnerability of financial institutions and of the economy, they do a great disservice to the economy at large and to themselves.

---

[198] *International Herald Tribune*, 3 April 2009.

7. Cash flow management[199]

A financial instrument is a claim on a stream of future cash flows. These are the sum of a company's earnings and its bookkeeping charges which do not involve cash outlays. Bookkeeping charges can come from amortisation, depreciation, depletion allowances and some other sources varying by jurisdiction, which may reduce net income without taking cash out of the treasury.

The business opportunity with cash flow analysis comes from two sources, of which the more recent is the need to provide a buffer to leveraging: cash flows help in paying interest and principal of debt. The more classical reason is that some companies have rich cash flows – because depreciation and/or depletion may be at impressive levels – and this cash flow can be used for acquisitions and for new ventures. Firms falling into this class are known as 'cash cows'.

Both reasons have been instrumental in changing the way analysts, and a company's own management, are looking at cash flows. Starting in the mid-1980s American financial analysts revamped their approach to valuing equities by junking the more traditional financial measures and concentrating instead on a firm's cash flows. They analysed them as a corporate finance director would and they considered that a company's worth was determined by the flow of cash it generates.

Working along this track, equity analysts and fund managers combed a firm's financial statements to assess its future cash-generating potential. This contrasted with classical investment analysis, which relies heavily on performance measures that often have little to do with the cash flow.

---

[199] Cash flow is not an alien term to the reader. It has been discussed in Chapter 3 in the realm of discounted cash flow, but it was left to this section to elaborate on cash flow in connection to leveraging.

For instance, one of the better-known traditional measures is the price/earnings (P/E) ratio, which compares a firm's share price to its annual earnings per share. It indicates the number of years that it would take a company to earn an amount equal to its market value – based on current earnings.

The problem is that because a company's earnings are affected by many and different factors, which see to it that earnings are not stable over the years, this approach can be misleading. The same is true for focusing on the company's total assets and shareholders' equity. Since these tend to be valued at their historical cost, rather than at their current market value, they can distort the pattern of a company's financial state of health. On the other hand, however, different types of portfolios can generate identical or nearly identical cash flows. Examples are:

- A forward contract versus a leveraged position in the spot asset,

- A bond denominated in one currency vs. a bond denominated in another currency,

- A cross-currency forward contract vs. a leveraged coupon bond position.

The upside in cash flow matching is that it stands a good chance of being sustained, even if portfolios tend to differ for a number of reasons, or being subject to different valuation rules. Differences also exist across markets, such as supply and demand imbalances. In spite of these reasons, which tend to bend the certainty one would like to obtain from cash flow analysis, a careful examination of cash flow is a must. Its results provide the basis for calculating a firm or project's *intrinsic value* (Chapter 3), and its management enables the firm to confront some of the effects of leveraging without having to seek financial assistance from banks or the government.

Smart financiers, merchants and industrialists have been keen to discount cash flows because they appreciate that discounting reflects the company's capability for being in charge of projects which involve time, skill and financial resources to develop and support. What is new in terms of evaluation practices, is:

- The use of cash flow projections for prudent judgment of the level of affordable leveraging, and
- The use of intrinsic value in connection to analysis made on the price of equity.

What the older and the newer approaches have in common is that for any entity *cash flow* means financial staying power. In the longer term, it is a function of its products and services, their market appeal, ingenuity of its salesmen and innovation coming out of its research laboratories. Cash flow is an important criterion both in the very short and in the longer term:

- In the very short term (90-180 days), it makes the difference between a company's liquidity and illiquidity, and
- In the longer term it contributes to its financial freedom from loans and indebtedness, acting proactively in solvency terms.

Few people realise that projecting, measuring and controlling cash flows is a challenging task. It requires aggregating financial resources, adding up all the pluses and minuses that can happen during each time period, and placing particular emphasis on the evolution of financial means as time goes on. The crucial test is one of taking all business parameters into account, in order to develop factual and documented cash flow scenarios.

An able management will use the results of stress-testing cash flow projections in judging whether the company requires deleveraging, or if it needs to assure more financial resources than presently available. They can also decide whether the capital structure of the company should be changed. Typically, the capital structure will include different financing schemes:

- Ordinary shares,
- Preferred shares,

- Reserves,

- Bonds, and

- Long-term borrowing in the form of debentures.

Preferred stock, bonds, debentures as well as short-term borrowing like bank overdrafts and other credit are parts of leverage, which together with commercial paper and bankers' acceptances, constitute financial obligations to be served by the cash flows. Franco Modigliani and Merton Miller may have made a name for themselves by promoting the merits of leveraging, but it should not be forgotten that leverage increases financial risk, and leads shareholders to demand higher returns to cover that risk.

There are many simplifications behind a theory that promotes leverage irrespective of cash flows. Such a theory obstructs the fact that many of its hypotheses don't stand up in the real world. Example of light-weight suppositions used to justify high leverage are:

- The capital markets operate perfectly,

- There are no transaction costs,

- Investors are rational in their behaviour,

- Information is free and readily available,

- All firms in the same sector have the same degree of business risk, and

- The probability distribution of expected earnings is the same as present operating earnings.

These assumptions are rarely if ever satisfied. Therefore, there is every reason to not rely upon them. By contrast, there is scope for optimisation in capital mix. The task becomes more demanding when the model includes, as should be the case, credit risk, interest rate risk, and currency exchange risk, as well as exposure due to leveraging and to derivative financial instruments which are leveraged by definition.

8. Deleveraging

Deleveraging means shedding debt. Also known as degearing or reverse leverage, it signals that people, companies and governments will borrow less, spend less and rebuild their balance sheets. Keynes called it "the paradox of thrift", because while this is good for each person or firm individually, in the cumulative it destroys jobs roughly in proportion to the amount of leverage which preceded it.

In late 2007, as deleveraging in the housing market got into full swing and house prices moved south while those of commodities soared, several CEOs of real estate firms suggested that housing deflation counterbalances the inflation of oil and other commodities. Therefore, its moderating influence should be reflected in the inflation index.

This would make sense only *if* leveraging, deleveraging and associated inflationary or deflationary pressures are part of the risk management model. Precisely for this purpose this text suggests the use of quantum chromodynamics as the meta layer which can reflect the difference between classical risk factors (taken over by QED) and leveraging, as well as its after-effect.[200]

Statistics can be instructive. Without past evidence nobody can really say where the new floor for debt will lie in deleveraging, but using the rule that gearing and inverse leveraging correlate in direct proportion, here is how fast the share of household/consumer debt went up in the US. The gearing was:

- 100% of GDP in 1980, and

- 173% at the end of 2008, or 2.6% per year on average; but after 2000 this average figure nearly doubled.

---

[200] Legal risk (Chapter 6) and risk of defective supervision (Chapter 8) should also be included in this meta layer.

On 29 January 2009 the CEO of JP Morgan Chase was quoted as having said that with unlimited credit banks have given consumers "weapons of mass destruction" (WMDs).

During the period of 2000 to 2008 the average household leverage was 5% in the US, 6% in France, 7% in Britain and a whopping 12% in Holland. On the hypothesis that for the next eight years there will be no leveraging, the above figures show how much consumption might be reduced.

If households want to restructure their balance sheets and save 3% per year, as currently tends to be the case in America, then this 3% must be added to the aforementioned figures of leveraging and deleveraging, in order to return to 1980 ratios.

According to several experts, the wounds created by super-leveraging, which led to the economic and banking crisis of 2007-2009, are so deep that there is going to be an appreciable and material drop in gearing over the next years. The debt model seems to be broken.

For people and companies, high gearing has been part of a bad culture which maintained that non-leveraged balance sheets are inefficient because debt is a cheaper alternative to equity, with little or no attention paid to the fact that debt increases balance sheet uncertainty. Measured by net debt to shareholders' funds (equity), in the 2003 to 2007 time frame:

- Overleveraging ran at an average of about 100% or more, with peak levels reaching beyond that,

- A relatively high leveraging ratio was between 40% and 90% of equity, but

- Better-managed companies kept their leveraging around the level of 30% of equity.

Predictions regarding deleveraging see this 30% coming down to about 20% and staying there, in what is expected to be a relatively longer-term phenomenon. In terms of deleveraging, however, not everything is due to management virtue. For a typical industrial company, banks are likely to tighten covenants and pay much more attention to creditworthiness; which bends the leveraging curve.

The reverse leverage in Asia during 1997-1998 was a rather recent precedence in deleveraging and its after-effects. While highly leveraged nations like Japan and the east Asian 'tigers' made great strides through high leverage, the destruction of their economy was just as fast when the financial edifice began to unravel.

In addition, the meltdown of highly leveraged hedge funds like Long-Term Capital Management (LTCM), in 1998, and Tiger Management in 1999, gave a vivid example of the results of reverse leverage at company level. LTCM went virtually bankrupt, saved through a twelfth-hour action brokeraged by the New York Fed – while in the case of Tiger Management a similar example of moral hazard was demonstrated.

Unravelling can happen at lightning speed because, when deleveraging strikes, bankers and regulators find themselves without a properly prepared action plan. In stock trading, for example, broker margin loans are called in and speculators have to dump equities to meet margin calls, creating a vicious cycle. As this goes on, the options, futures and forwards markets collapse, with the result that imprudent, highly leveraged investors are wiped out.

In the global economy *deleveraging* in one market, or even in one major market sector, causes deleveraging in other markets, triggering a snowball effect. Because financial markets are interconnected, this can happen – swiftly resulting in what financial analysts now call an *all-out blow-up* effect.

Keynesian economists might suggest that the slack created by reverse leveraging should be taken up by government spending. Even if one leaves aside the fact that the government is highly leveraged too, to the tune of 66% in France and Germany, over 104% in Italy, 170% in Japan and probably 200% in the US (by the end of 2009), higher government spending might save the world economy from depression but it cannot prevent a long hangover.

Fear of default and need to reduce leverage correlate. The deleveraging of big banks like Citigroup creates problems for borrowers, obliging them to fight for a shrinking supply of new credit. To get it companies must pay far more, even if the Fed's discount rate is practically zero. Otherwise they lay-off employees, save cash and cancel investments.

Morgan Stanley provides an example. Prior to the severe banking and credit crisis it boasted a leverage of 33 (meaning $33 of assets for each dollar of capital). By end of October 2008, however, the leverage ratio was below 16 (according to the bank). To get it there it had to raise new capital[201] and shrink its balance-sheet to less than $800 billion by the end of October 2008, from more than $1 trillion in May of that same year.

If Morgan Stanley found a way to replenish at least part of its capital reserve, other banks did not have the same experience in the prevailing environment of inverse leveraging. The meltdown of 2007-2009 caused a freeze and credit refused to grow. This resembles the years following the Great Depression when credit and trading in financial markets barely increased.

The message is that both leveraging and deleveraging are bound to have deep and lasting effects. Therefore, they should be integral parts of a comprehensive risk management model. The implementation of the concept of entropy linked to overleveraging and organisational disorder can help in creating a universal pattern of quantitative risk control.

---

[201] Including from the federal government and from Mitsubishi.

Appendix: the basic notion of entropy

Sadi Carnot's *second law of thermodynamics* states that heat will not spontaneously flow from cold objects to hot ones. This simple fact places severe limits on engineering processes (for instance, how efficient a steam engine can be) and also has other quite important repercussions.

It was known for a considerable time that heat flows from a higher to a lower temperature, but never in the reverse direction except through the action of an agent external to the system. What Sadi Carnot essentially did was to consider this phenomenon in deeper terms and deduce that heat would not be converted to work without the existence of a temperature difference.

Entropy was defined in the Prologue as the transformation function underpinning the second law of thermodynamics. Expressed in terms of the heat and temperature, its notion underlines that in any closed system disorder always increases with time – which is one of the laws of science. Stephen Hawking suggests that the laws of science do not distinguish between forward and backward directions of time. Three arrows of time, however, tend to point forward:[202]

- A thermodynamic describes the time direction in which disorder increases,

- A psychological arrow sees to it that not only do we remember the past but also try to predict the future,

- A cosmological time arrow indicates the direction of the universe's expansion.[203]

---

[202] Hawking, *A Brief History of Time.*

[203] That the universe expands rather than contracts is only the prevailing hypothesis.

Four decades after the law by Carnot, Rudolf Clausius used the word entropy to mean *transformation*, but the concept underpinning this term evolved to include *uncertainty*. Information is the negative of uncertainty. It is not accidental that the word *form* appears in the middle of *information* since its able exploitation leads to patterning (see also Chapter 6). But, as Claude Shannon pointed out, meaningful information decreases as entropy progresses.

Shannon's work was preceded by J. W. Gibbs who, about a century ago, formulated the law of *degradation of energy*; this added muscle to the second law of thermodynamics. The basic concept was that thermodynamic degradation is irrevocable over time; for instance, a burned log cannot be unburned, even though there is an equivalence between a certain amount of work and a certain amount of heat.

When a system is restored to its original state, there can never be a net conversion of heat into work, though the reverse is possible. All these are fundamental concepts in understanding the background of scientific thought as well as the contribution it can make to the financial industry, as the latter aims to use scientific concepts. Progress is made step-by-step, not through a big leap forward.

Just as we cannot convert an amount of heat into its equivalent amount of work without other changes taking place in the system, we cannot move from chaos to organisation without the contribution of a number of factors. Expressed statistically, *changes* constitute a passing of the system under study from ordered arrangement into a more chaotic one, with random distribution of risk. It then moves back again from chaotic to more orderly conditions and structures, which will eventually be demolished by entropy.

Taking a case from the real world, while financial integration and novelty in financial instruments are normally associated with better market performance, experience of the 2007-2009 economic and banking crisis shows that distorted incentives can have the effect that several financial innovations are implemented in ways that increase information asymmetries, encourage excessive leverage, lead to inordinate risk taking and boost the entropy and disorganisation of the financial system.

The reader should always keep in mind that entropy is the antithesis of *form* and *organisation*. Herbert Spencer, a contemporary of Darwin, looked at evolution as self-organisation. While entropy worked against order, evolution reconstructed an orderly system at higher and more complex levels through self-organisation.

"The same phenomenon of self-organisation would later intrigue those who noticed it in cellular automata, bird flocking, and insect social behaviour," said Steven Levy.[204] Stephen Hawking looked at it in a different way: "Just throw some matter with a lot of entropy, such as a box of gas, down the black hole. The total entropy of matter outside the black hole will go down."

It is a matter of common experience that disorder will tend to increase if things are left to themselves. In any structure – project, company, the government or personal life – disorder will increase if matters are left to their own devices without the proper planning, staffing, organising, directing and controlling. To create order out of disorder requires expenditure of effort or energy, thus decreasing the amount of available energy in the system.

To better track this concept of order and disorder, scientists have tried to visualise a measure of *entropy per unit time*. They have done so by means of a geometric representation of pictures or surfaces, stretching and folding them in phase space. The notion underpinning this approach lies in drawing an arbitrarily small box around some set of initial conditions and calculating the effect of various expansions, contradictions or twists on the box.

---

[204] Steven Levy, *Artificial Life. The Quest for a New Creation*, Penguin Books, London, 1992.

The geometric figures, for example, might stretch in one direction, while remaining narrow in the other. Area changes corresponded to an introduction of *uncertainty* about the system's past, translated through a gain or loss of information; or, alternatively, a switch from unpredictability toward some sort of predictability.

These are relatively recent approaches to entropy relating, in large measure, to information technology. At the same time, however, they can be seen as an extension of the meaning of the word *entropy* both in thermodynamics and in the financial industry. One of the reasons why entropy is so important to the theory of complexity is that it is itself a dynamic entity.

Thermodynamics problems involve time, hence dynamic considerations. By contrast, *thermostatics* is concerned with equilibrium processes that do not depend upon time as an explicit variable.[205] Paraphrasing Confucius, study thermodynamics if you would define the future behaviour of finance.[206]

---

[205] Myron Tribus, *Thermostatistics and Thermodynamics*, D. Van Nostrand, Princeton, 1961.

[206] Confucius said: "Study the past, if you would define the future."

Chapter 8: Risk of Poor Supervision

1. The hypotheses regulators have to make

When Pierre-Simon de Laplace, the physicist, mathematician and astronomer, presented to Napoleon his *Mécanique Céleste*[207], the emperor asked him why in his study he made no reference to God. Laplace's answer was that he did not need *that* hypothesis.[208]

Depending on the work we are doing, there exist hypotheses which we need to make and others which we don't. One of the most useful hypotheses for regulators is that the banks under their watch are, in the majority, not so well managed. Some years ago a study by Goldman Sachs on the quality of governance of British companies classified them into three buckets. In one of them, the smaller, were well run firms; the rating of another group's CEOs was just average; and those in the third group, the larger, were quite poorly run.

This relatively low distribution of skills has a great impact on company balance sheets, most particularly for banks. It suggests that something will go wrong not accidentally but, rather, because there is the possibility that it can go wrong. Because many things can go wrong, regulatory authorities must have in place a system whose action emulates the principles of quantum mechanics. A particle (and, in this book's subject matter, a risk factor) might be observed at different places with different probabilities. It is difficult to predict which bank burns its assets faster than its peers and contributes the most to systemic risk, but quantum theory provides a good method of prognostication, because it is based on probabilities not certainties.

---

[207] Which he published in five volumes between 1799 and 1825.

[208] As the reader will remember, a hypothesis is a tentative statement; an aid to the investigation or study we do – and which has to be proven.

In addition, a comprehensive system of mathematical representation, which has passed the tough test of the physical sciences, acts as an eye-opener. When asked how he discovered new laws of nature Paul Dirac, the physicist, responded: "I play with equations." And on another occasion he stated: "I feel I understand an equation when I can anticipate its solutions without actually solving it."[209] In these two short sentences Dirac encapsulated the whole sense of:

- *Modelling* (the process), and

- *Models*, the artefacts we build and employ.

While every effort has been made to keep the mathematical formulae included in this book to a minimum, because it is not written for mathematicians, there has been no shortage of references to the power of analysis (therefore to models and modelling). Chapter 1 focused on the effects of volatility and on the fact that the area Enrico Fermi, the physicist, labelled "Here be dragons" is found in the long leg of the risk distribution, not in the bell-shaped body.

Chapter 2 brought to the reader's attention the interest in implementing statistical quality control charts in the banking industry – and of depending on them to show the drift in the process as well as whether tolerances and limits are observed. Chapter 3 addressed risk pricing mainly from the viewpoint of market exposure, but it also brought to the reader's attention the fact that with modern financial instruments market risk and credit risk are adjuncts to each other and often indistinguishable.

Coming closer to the implementation of quantum electrodynamics in the financial industry, for better control over exposure, Chapter 4 concentrated on stress tests and scenarios. Chapter 5 introduced to the reader two of the pillars of quantum electrodynamics: Feynman's

---

[209] Wilczek, *Lightness of Being.*

diagrams and the space-time graph. I do hope that their usage will significantly increase the dependability of information at the service of bankers and supervisors.

Having explained why legal risk is disruptive, Chapter 6 pressed the point that some types of exposure require controls enriched with a much higher level of sophistication, and significantly better flexibility than others. Legal risk and Ponzi risk fall precisely in that class. Chapter 7 documented that overleveraging is like entropy. It leads to excesses and disorganisation, therefore in the medium to longer term it works against the bank because it makes it more fragile – while supervisors wake up to the downside when it is too late.

The present chapter brings this latter argument a step forward by suggesting that there also exists a wrong-way risk whose frequency and amplitude are increasing. In an interview on 10 May 2009 on Bloomberg news Richard Bernstein, the investment strategist, explained that the government was on the wrong track because it was trying to keep the excess capacity of the financial system alive.

Overcapacity in the banking industry is a hypothesis governments (and the G-20) should have explored; as yet they have not. Bernstein is right. The entropy associated with overcapacity is one of the key reasons which brought down the former 'big three' of Detroit. In a similar manner, there are simply too many banks in the global economy, and the problem of overcapacity has recently engulfed Wall Street.

Three of the top five investment banks in New York have disappeared. In a way resembling the glut of a global manufacturing capacity of motor vehicles which (along with aloofness and mismanagement have brought Detroit into real difficulties), there are too many financial companies at both levels:

- International investment banking, trading and wealth management,
- National, regional and local credit entities, from commercial to savings and popular banks.

According to the IMF, the United States and Germany have more than twice as many banks relative to their population as Britain, Canada and Japan, with France and Italy falling in-between.[210] The intense competition for customers means that they are far less profitable than they might have been and, over and above that, they are weakening their financial staying power by warehousing worthless paper in a vain effort to improve their income.

Many economists wonder why the American, British, German and other governments bend over backwards to protect overcapacity in banking, when the major economic and financial crisis we went through would have been an opportunity to reduce it. In any industry, overcapacity's entropy bodes badly for the future. Its alter ego is overleveraging (Chapter 7).

Instead of making the right hypotheses, governments specialise in the wrong ones. For instance, that some banks are 'too big to fail' – while in reality they are 'too big to be pulled up from under'. There were, for example, two problems with the so-called capital adequacy 'stress tests' to which the 19 largest US banks were subjected in February to May 2009 (section 5).

Both the Treasury and the Federal Reserve wanted them to pass these tests. Estimates of the value of these banks' assets ended by being totally subjective, and therefore revealed no truths.

Niels Bohr, the physicist, distinguished two kinds of truths:

1. *Ordinary*, which refers to a statement whose opposite is something false,

---

[210] *The Economist*, 9 May 2009.

2.   *Profound* whose opposite is also a profound truth. The only profound truth associated with the 'tests' in reference is that, when it comes to big banks, capital inadequacy is condoned by regulators.

2. Capital inadequacy is condoned by regulators

In early May 2009, as the stock markets in America and Europe were erasing their losses from earlier that year, projections started being made that nothing was learned from the crisis, and post-recovery the number of risk takers would multiply. The hypothesis was that vulture funds, hedge funds and asset managers would compete to take over the business that used to be done by Wall Street – but which new government regulations would no more condone – and that the Administration would give free reign to the newcomers and even look favourably upon their wheeling and dealing. This is unsettling because both in the US and in Britain a lot of trouble has come from the hand-in-hand relationship between big banks and regulators. Whether for reasons of omission, commission or plain bad politics, the failure to watch after capital adequacy, liquidity, volatility and risk led to the collapse of the whole financial system.

The hand-in-hand relationship between Royal Bank of Scotland, HBOS, Lloyd's TSB, Barclays, Northern Rock and other British banks with the Financial Services Authority (FSA) was a disaster for the British economy and the banks themselves; and it was also a loss of face for the FSA. One in two of the most important British banks under its watch went bankrupt.

The situation was in no way better in the United States. Deregulation was followed by a free reign, hands-off attitude by regulators towards all American big banks, with the consequence that Citigroup, Bank of America, Wachovia (bankrupt), Bear Stearns (bankrupt), Lehman Brothers (still another big bankruptcy), Merrill Lynch and others all committed financial suicide.

The parties responsible are:

- Securities and Exchange Commission (SEC),
- Office of the Comptroller of the Currency (OCC),
- Federal Deposit Insurance Corporation (FDIC),
- Federal Reserve, and
- The Bush Administration as a whole.

"There is nothing so vulnerable as entrenched success," said Henry J. Kaiser, the American industrialist.[211] The aforementioned government institutions and regulators did everything in their power so that commercial and investment banks of mammoth size ran out of control and hit the wall, at great cost to the American economy and the taxpayer.

If the result of this crash was not dramatic and its consequences were not very serious, it would have been a comedy of morals. But it is not so. Therefore it is not possible, let alone advisable, to talk about risk management – QED's domain – without integrating into a holistic picture the policies and actions of regulators. In a global financial environment, the themes discussed in Part Three – legal risk and Ponzi risk, overleveraging of the balance sheet, and risks of poor supervision – are not just integral but also the most basic components of the exposure assumed by banks, and of the systemic risk confronting the broader economy.

No better documentation exists on the recognition of this fact than the institution created under the Bank for International Settlements (BIS) of the Financial Stability Forum (FSF, subsequently renamed the

---

[211] David Haberstam, *The Reckoning*, William Morrow, New York, 1986.

Financial Stability Board), which brought together central banks, financial regulators and treasuries from the big Western economies.[212]

The 2007-2009 crisis has seen to it that public confidence in the capital adequacy and other rules of Basel II[213] is at rock bottom. Already, since its predecessor Basel I, banks felt absolutely free to massage their balance sheets (a practice that leading investors in financial firms characterised as "window dressing and truth dodging"). They have been doing so with tacit collusion by some regulators.

The 2007-2009 crisis started as one of illiquidity, but in reality insolvency was the main problem. Capital inadequacy for counterparty risk provides a good example on the inability and unwillingness of big banks to honour their transnational accords. As financial intermediaries, banks take deposits and give loans, keeping a relatively small amount of capital in reserve. With Basel I, the 1988 original capital adequacy accord by the Group of Ten, this was 4% for banks of local and national charter and 8% for international banks operating in many jurisdictions.

In terms of capital adequacy, Basel II has offered commercial banks three options in calculating capital requirements. The more sophisticated is the Advanced Internal Ratings Based (A-IRB) method, followed by a so-called Fundamental approach (F-IRB) and by the more elementary Credit Risk Standard (CRS). As of 2009 in the European Union, implementation-wise the share of each has varied by jurisdiction within the following ranges:

- 30% to 36% for A-IRB,

- 25% to 39% for F-IRB, and

- 35% to 40% for CRS.

---

[212] And has been pencilled out by the G-20 'summit' of 2 April 2009 in London – just at the moment it started delivering results.

[213] D. N. Chorafas, *Economic Capital Allocation with Basel II. Cost and Benefit Analysis*, Butterworth-Heinemann, London and Boston, 2004.

Counterparty ratings are at the core of the two IRB versions. At the positive end, their introduction into the banking system brought along a certain amount of cultural change. For instance, a result of preparatory work for IRB's implementation was that many banks strengthened their method in calculating probability of default (PD), particularly in regard to discriminatory power.

At the negative end, one of the drawbacks was the existence of relatively short data histories (or none at all), in each bank's database. This inhibited dependable calculation of PD, as well as of loss given default (LGD) and exposure at default (EAD), which are Basel II's pillars. In many cases, the pool of historical information hardly went beyond the required minimum history. This provided a poor basis for calculating exposure through past events.

Another problem which has come up in a big way is the conflict of interest involved in to credit rating by independent rating companies. This became evident with the AAA ratings of securitised subprime mortgages, found at the origin of the severe economic and banking crisis of 2007-2009. Practically in one stroke, the biases in credit rating killed the development of a nearly universal counterparty rating system.

Still another drawback is the absence of integrated bank supervision in the global economic and financial landscape. This is equally true of the European Union and of the more closely knit euro zone. The absence of a global sheriff[214] has most severe implications – involving the supervision of how Basel II rules and the IFRS accounting standards are upheld.

One of the larger global banks provides an example on aforementioned reporting standards. The way an article in *The Economist* had it, HSBC's definition of capital excluded marking to market losses on asset-backed securities (ABS), as well as marking to

---

[214] Chorafas, *Financial Boom and Gloom.*

market losses on its loan book (see Chapter 3 for definition of marking to market). HSBC carries these at book value and is impaired as customers default.[215]

When the marked to market losses are excluded from financial reporting, capital adequacy increases, fulfilling Basel II standards. When, however, these market value losses are included, the core tier-1 ratio (which should be higher than 4% (half the 8% or better)) would drop to just 2%.[216]

Not only have the rules governing how exposure is calculated become very elastic, varying from jurisdiction to jurisdiction and often from bank to bank, but also hybrids in other items included in tier-1 capital have harmed the banks' solvency.

When on 7 May 2009 the results of 'stress tests' of 19 bigger American banks were released (section 5) the message was that Bank of America needed $34 billion of core capital; Wells Fargo $15 billion; Citigroup nearly $6 billion; and so on. These capital needs were computed compared to what standard?

Rumour on Wall Street had it that the Treasury and Fed accepted a 3% capital adequacy (more exactly capital inadequacy). Counter-rumours suggested that the targeted capital level was not 3% but 4%. Curiously, nobody spoke of the fact that Basel capital adequacy is 8% and while tier-1, or core, capital must be half of this 8% or more, there is also the other 4% to account for.

Reference to this 'other 4%' disappeared from the screen. Whether the end results were massaged or not massaged the Treasury silently admitted that the big American banks were undercapitalised. The IMF

---

[215] *The Economist*, 7 March 2009.

[216] That's a good example of the difference accounting for exposure in their loan books makes in balance sheet terms. Some banks will still be well capitalised, while other banks would be insolvent.

noted that in the mid-1990s prior to the overleveraging of the financial industry, the equity ratio was 6%.

3. Basel II should undergo a major overhaul

The Basel II capital adequacy framework took five years to negotiate, but the sense of capital reserves to assure solvency and their importance to the health of the banking industry got lost in these protracted negotiations. What's more, as section 2 brought to the reader's attention, bank supervision proved to be rather dysfunctional and ineffectual.

The whole process of Basel II implementation started badly with interminable negotiations between regulators and commercial bankers. In addition, when the new framework was finally settled, Roger Ferguson, then vice chairman of the Federal Reserve, publicly stated that only the top ten US banks would apply it, that the option they use had to be A-IRB, and that the other 8000 or so US banks would stay with Basel I (rechristened Basel IA).

This was curious for two reasons:

1. It was the American regulators and commercial bankers who had pushed hard for model-based calculation of capital requirements (originally known as pre-commitments) and for inclusion of credit ratings by independent credit agencies (mainly S&P and Moody's).

2. More importantly, the twelfth-hour Fed decision arbitrarily divided US banks into black and white. The top ten profiting from the use of models (at least, the way it was thought at the time); while thousands of other banks were being left behind in terms of banking technology.

In retrospect, coupled with very loose supervision, that decision proved to be awfully wrong. Capital adequacy waned (and not only in the United States), while risk appetite – with loans and derivative financial instruments – increased.

The proof is provided by the fact that not all of the losses that wrecked the banking system were found in the trading book alone. Big banks also failed in proactively estimating their capital requirements in regard to age-old classical loan losses. Responsible for this were regulators, credit rating agencies, the clauses of the Basel II capital adequacy framework, its manipulated models and evidently the top brass of the big banks themselves.

There were also some gaping loopholes in regulatory capital, particularly for 'non-bank banks' (for instance GE Capital), which resemble the big commercial banks like twin sisters, except that they don't have a banking charter. An example from the non-bank bank industry is AIG: its capital base was a heavy burden and the US Treasury had to use over $200 billion of taxpayers' money to keep it from failing completely.

The structure of supervisory responsibilities in the US also has something to do with the system's malfunctioning. The way an article in *The Economist* had it, the state-by-state smoothed assessments of capital by American regulators have been dwarfed by losses. Rob Haines, an analyst at CreditSights, reckoned that at end of 2008 the big six US life insurance firms had regulatory capital of $43 billion, but that this calculation excluded $80 billion of unrecognised marked to market losses mainly on corporate bonds.[217]

Loopholes aside, confidence in the integrity of banking supervision particularly in the US and Britain (section 2), and the ability of Basel II to serve as capital adequacy standard, is by now so low that many investors are not thrilled by the measures governments take to confront the solvency and liquidity failures. Moreover, it is widely discussed that some banks and regulators have abandoned Basel II as their main test of capital.

---

[217] *The Economist*, 14 March 2009.

Confidence was further weakened by the mounting campaign from bankers who, with full conflict of interest, succeeded in ceasing marking to market (Chapter 3). Both accounting standards bodies and accountants now worry that their standards are being fiddled with needlessly, having been established to provide accurate information to investors.

To escape political pressures, lobbyists and hidden interests, the implementation of a meta layer of quantum electrodynamics should be based on market discipline. It should also incorporate the principle that accounting must not be twisted around to serve the interest of the moment. Therefore, independent bodies like FASB and IASB should be endowed with the authority to make objective judgments on accounting rules which have universal applicability.

Beyond this, because novelty in financial instruments has become a constant, the rules of bank supervision must be kept dynamic. As an after-effect of lessons learned from the financial crisis of 2007-2009, the Basel Committee is raising the risk weights for resecuritisations – which means securitisation transactions based on other securitisations, which have used pools of loans and asset-backed commercial paper.

For its part, the European Union is planning changes to the securitisation rules as part of a forthcoming directive amendment. Conversion factors for liquidity facilities will be amended, and institutions will be allowed to assume securitisation risks only if originators confirm that they will retain a percentage of the exposure. To provide regulators with better oversight current quantitative criteria will be supplemented by qualitative criteria – which I suggest doing through QED. Also, penalties will be imposed if the qualitative requirements are not met in accordance with the EU directive.

In implementing QED, special attention should be paid to resecuritisations because they have a large quotient of leveraging (Chapter 7), along with an increasing uncertainty about risk pricing. Because these instruments often have a complex structure, institutions must pay much greater attention to analysing potential exposure over the longer term. There are a number of risk factors often neglected under a regime of simple securitisations.

The interpretation of semi-global regulations also poses interesting problems. Evidence from the last few years suggests that local regulators interpreted the Basel II capital rules differently; and in several cases, against all good sense, they have failed to fully enforce them. In addition,

- No attention has been paid to the financial players' need for liquidity,

- Regulatory procedures differ across countries, depending on their history and preferences, and

- Trade-offs have been made along many lines of reference, making it impossible to establish a balance between financial stability and innovation.

If this was not enough, from Bear Stearns to AIG and Citigroup, each successive rescue has affected different parts of the capital structures, while compromises and manipulations ended up in a mess. In conclusion: supervisory authorities allowed plenty of regulatory arbitrage in connection to Basel I, so far that it encouraged risky short-term borrowing. In addition, Basel II's reliance on credit ratings and the banks' own risk models to generate weights for capital requirements proved clearly inappropriate, as documented by the debacle.

4. Stress tests of default risks

IRB's risk sensitivity rests on the notion that capital requirements react cyclically, rising in line with credit risk. Therefore, an essential condition for IRB implementation is that banks can demonstrate how well they are prepared for this interrelationship. In turn, the ability to do so requires that they regularly conduct *stress tests* (Chapter 4),[218] Under Pillar 2 of Basel II.

---

[218] Chorafas, *Stress-testing.*

Such tests are designed to prove that a credit institution can meet its regulatory capital needs even in a volatile business environment. The tests' major contribution to solvency lies in their ability to forecast and address the effects inherent in the markets that the bank addresses itself to (and its risk control framework).

The particular measures under which the impact of stress tests is evaluated depends on the purpose which they serve. Often, a range of measures is needed if the test is expected to convey a factual and documented pattern of financial staying power or exposure. For instance, the stress test may involve:

- asset values;
- accounting and economic profit and loss;
- economic capital;
- regulatory capital;
- risk weighted assets;
- market liquidity;
- funding liquidity (Chapter 2);
- funding gaps and other factors.

Developing and administering coherent stress-testing is no easy task as risk factors for different portfolios (and financial institutions) differ widely and horizons vary. To effectively challenge financial conditions, or a business model, stress tests have to assess the nature of risks correlated across portfolios and across time, including liquidity conditions.

The Basel Committee has made no specific commitment that the conditions qualifying stress tests should be adjusted to reflect the evolution of exposure in the financial industry and/or prevailing economic conditions. But the severe 2007-2009 crisis has documented the need for such adaptation, shifting from so-to-speak normal stress-testing to 'stressed' stress-testing (see also section 5).

In addition, not all salvage programmes launched in the middle of the crisis by governments and central banks have made use of stress-testing; and even when they did so, the stress conditions were too mild. Interviewed on 9 May 2009 by Bloomberg News, Alan Blinder, of Princeton University and former Fed vice chairman, said that three months earlier (in February) the adopted criteria represented an adverse scenario. However, in the elapsed months the American economy deteriorated and the test conditions looked subdued because they were closer to the May environment.

Between these two dates, February and May, March 2009 provided an example of lack of synchronism between stress tests and analysts' expectations. Many experts were surprised that the US government's announcement of the Public-Private Investment Program (PPIP, Chapter 3) made no mention of the stress tests that banks with over $100 billion in assets had to undergo.

Whether this was a lapse or it was intended, it created a question mark in the mind of economists and of investors in regard to the coordination of the government's different plans and funds. It also led market participants to believe that there is a bit of a silo effect in the execution of governmentmandated programmes, raising some interesting questions:

- Are the different government programmes in the banking industry disconnected from one-another?

- Will the PPIP clearing prices impact the assumptions made by the mandated stress tests?

- Will the government rely upon PPIP-dictated clearing prices when determining capital adequacy for the banks undergoing stress tests?

- *What if* the market clearing price set by PPIP is more onerous to the banks than the valuation suggested by the stress test assumptions?

The message the reader should retain from these references is that the results of real life tests often hold surprises because they unveil not only hidden strengths and weaknesses but also gaps. Analytical developments, too, impact upon the nature of stress tests. For instance, a procedure which became popular with Moody's KMV model, and could be seen as 'a fair value stress test', is that of judging credit risk through quoted equity prices.[219] Several central banks, as well as many investment banks and rating agencies, use signals from the stock market as a guide to the riskiness of a company's debt.

Debt underpins default risk, which is in turn influenced by *credit events*. Several happenings can have adverse effects on the solvency of a borrower, or security issuer, thereby damaging his credibility. Often, though not always, a credit event impacts the credit rating of the entity which it affects, as well as the characteristics of securities associated with the name of that entity. For instance, credit default swaps.

- A simple credit event can be arrears in paying due bills.

- Complex credit events reveal hidden sides of debtors, and can have a lasting impact on financing.

The nature and magnitude of a credit event's impact may be triggered through covenants attached to a transaction altering its credit terms. Or, it may be an effect of the economic nature of a financial institution's product(s), its guarantees and other commitments, as well as its cash flow (Chapter 7) and liquid assets position. With securitised instruments, the ratio of sub to senior spreads is often viewed as a reflection of the relative losses at different seniorities following a given credit event.

When they are based on the current state of the art models, and performed in an orderly manner, stress tests bring attention to outliers at the legs of the risk distribution. Or, alternatively, at the peaks of a time series. With these references in the background, the idea of stress-testing the US big banks was based on the need to reassure the market

---

[219] Chorafas, *Economic Capital Allocation*.

rather than just measure the size of further capital injection with taxpayers' money.

That idea was introduced by Timothy Geithner, the Treasury Secretary of the Obama Administration, in his first public conference on 11 February 2009, and it was rather well received by the market. But some critical issues connected to these tests remained open, and soon after that conference many analysts raised questions about:

- How uniform the stress test would be?
- How dependable the results they provide would be?
- What would happen to those banks that don't pass the stress test?
- Once the procedure is established, would the Treasury repeat the tests annually, semi-annually or quarterly?

Economists suggested that failure to pass the stress test should be followed by nationalisation. This, however, was not what Ben Bernanke the chairman of Federal Reserve had in mind. Stress tests of big US banks were not likely to lead to seizures by regulators, he told Congress on 24 February 2009. According to some experts that was not the plan fleshed out by the Treasury either. Instead, what Tim Geithner was thought to have implied was stress tests able to bring much-needed light to banks' murky balance sheets and return a reasonable amount of predictability to the market.

Uncertainty also came from the fact that Geithner kept close to his chest what he would do to banks facing severe solvency problems, but considered 'too big to fail'. If a bank is taken over by the Federal Deposit Insurance Corporation (FDIC), will bondholders suffer along with shareholders? Or will bondholders come out unscathed?

Answers to these queries were conditioned by whether or not the stress tests in reference were intended solely to indicate how much additional capital (read: taxpayers' money) a bank might need to continue lending through a deeper-than-expected recession. Or they were only the tip of the iceberg of a still secret master plan by the Treasury.

Critics pointed out that if the tests were made to find out which balance sheets were suffering losses, then they represented an uneven approach, which would definitely be the wrong policy. This approach would reduce regulators to evaluators of likely losses on bank loan books without providing the option to close down those banks that failed the stress test. This, the critics added, would only add up to the amputation of the stress test concept, and the downgrading of its after-effects.

5. The 2009 stress tests mandated by the US Treasury

Let me start with the way an article in *The Economist* put it: the stress tests were lax, one of the reasons being that the way core capital was defined ('Tier-1 common') allowed banks to take advantage of the recent relaxation of accounting rules (see Chapter 3, section 6). Quoting from that financial weekly's commentary: "The stress tests state that the 19 banks' core capital be at least 4% of risk-weighted assets (this equates to 2.7% of their assets)."[220]

This miserable 2.7% in core capital amounts to a self-admitted defeat. In fact Alan Greenspan warned on 21 May 2009 (two weeks after the results of the pseudo stress tests were made public) that "US banks have large unfunded capital requirements"[221] – no matter what Tim Geithner at the Treasury and Ben Bernanke, his successor at the Fed, may say. Compared to other expert opinion, the aforementioned 2.7% is:

- Just over half the 5% in risk-weighted assets at end of 2008,

- Less than 40% of the prevailing European bank core capital of 7% (in May 2009),

- A small fraction of IMF's suggested range of 6% to 9%,

---

[220] *The Economist*, 16 May 2009.

[221] Bloomberg News, 21 May 2009.

- Just one-third of the 8% (or more) in core capital featured by the stronger global banks.[222]

According to expert opinions, there are significant differences between what the Treasury claims to have found through 'stress tests' and what has been estimated by independent persons like Nouriel Roubini, professor of economics at New York University. True enough, Roubini's study (and a similar analysis by IMF) looked at the whole US banking industry. By contrast, the Treasury examined only the 19 biggest American banks. But on the other hand, according to Pareto's Law, these 19 big banks feature the vast majority of losses; and they were specifically tested for that reason:

- The Treasury says that projected losses in 2009 and 2010 are $535 billion; Roubini's number is $811 billion.

- The Treasury's estimate of bank earnings over that period is $363 billion, Roubini's projection is $210 billion.

- The Treasury's corresponding reduction in capital is $111 billion; Roubini's calculations show a gap of $601 billion, over 540% bigger than the Treasury's.[223]

This large discrepancy speaks volumes about the longer-term danger – that in a couple of years the banks will again reach a crisis point, precipitating a new and bigger economic crisis. The foundations of this new financial earthquake are being laid today through leniency and cover-ups. The more the weakness of the US banking system unfolds, the more it will become evident that current policies are distorted and counterproductive. But it will be too late.

* * *

---

[222] At the beginning of the 20th century the banks core capital stood at the level of 18%.

[223] *Financial Times*, 13 May 2009.

With this warning in mind, here is (in brief) the complete story. In the week of 23 February 2009 the US Treasury released details about the *stress tests* to be applied under the new Capital Assistance Program (CAP). Officially, the Administration's objective was to gauge the big banks' capacity to weather a downturn under an adverse scenario in which:

- The US economy shrinks by 3.3% in 2009,

- Unemployment rises to 8.9% in 2009, and 10% in 2010, and

- House prices fall by 18% over the aforementioned two years.[224]

Also officially, these 'stress tests' have been expected to indicate whether financial companies will have to raise more funds from the market and, if this is not possible, from the government. Critics said that with taxpayers' money thrown at the problem, the US government would end up owning majority stakes in several private banks; and for a number of reasons it was better that they were outright nationalised.

In reality, however, the motivation officially given for the tests was the second, not the first, in the pecking order. The primary objective was to show that the banks were fairly well capitalised, which would give some confidence to the market. Critics answered that this would not be true because these 'stress tests' lacked spine. Contrary to the hypotheses being made:

- The US economy downsized by 6.2% in fourth quarter 2008, and a stress test should have taken this as the likely scenario for 2009, rather than 3.3%.[225]

---

[224] More precisely, by 14% in 2009 and by 4% in 2010, as a baseline case.

[225] In fact, a stress test should have considered 4%, 6% and 8% – the latter as a nearly worst case scenario. The economy of Latvia was expected to cave in by 12% in 2009.

- American house prices might continue to tumble well beyond 18% over the 2009-2010 time frame, and

- US unemployment may well hit 12% in 2009 – rather than 10%.[226]

The rise in unemployment and drop in housing prices could be more dramatic than the worst-case expectations of the government, commented Barry Eichengreen, professor of economics and political science at the University of California, Berkeley, adding: "My hope had been that when they did a stress test it would be the equivalent of turning up the treadmill beyond a trot."

"Given the surge in unemployment, the government is not testing for an absolutely worst-case scenario," said Michael Feroli, an economist at JP Morgan Chase, who used to work at the Federal Reserve.[227] As James Baker, the former Treasury Secretary and Secretary of State, suggested in an article in the *Financial Times*, any analysis which is worth its salt should include worst-case scenarios.

Examples of what this means have been provided by Goldman Sachs. One of the fixed income stress tests the investment bank is doing is a replay of the 1998 LTCM and bond-market meltdown. For its part, the bank's equity division has used a supercrash test that assumes an instantaneous fall in the price of equities of 50%. A combined worst case experiment aggregated the worst that has happened in both fixed-income and equity markets over the past 30 years.

Goldman also assessed combined credit and liquidity risk. The credit risk test was based on whether a counterparty might default on a loan or fail to honour a derivative contract. The liquidity risk considered

---

[226] According to some estimates, everything considered (including those not registering for unemployment benefits), unemployment in the US had already reached 11% at end of March 2009 – while unemployment and underemployment, added together, accounted for about 16%.

[227] Bloomberg News, 25 February 2009.

instrument and market worst conditions (Chapter 2). Most of these tests are based on simulations.[228]

The Treasury's tests were biased by the fact that (against all evidence) US regulators insisted that big banks were, by and large, well capitalised, and some regional banks were thriving, especially those that avoided subprime mortgages and loans to property developers. But analysts contested this mild version, and some said that although the 8000 community US banks were in generally good health until the end of third quarter 2008, this has since deteriorated. The number of banks on the Federal Deposit Insurance Corporation's problem list rose sharply to 256 in 2009.

Another weakness of the Treasury's stress test concerns the projected 0.5% growth of the US economy in 2010. This is in no way assured, as the figure might be negative or zero. In other words, the test's criteria are *not* pessimistic enough to evaluate the effect of outliers hitting the financial staying power of the banks.

Experts have also been concerned that rather than checking the ability of banks to withstand losses in case of stress, the Treasury's tests were primarily designed to convince investors that the big banks didn't need to be nationalised. As an alternative to nationalisation, the US government planned to take preferred stock, paying a 9% dividend that converts into common equity, if needed. This was criticised as being near-sighted, at a time when the markets wanted boldness.

Taking an option on equity 'as needed' avoids the appearance of nationalisation, but this is adding to the complexity of banks' capital structure, and does not reveal what constitutes capital adequacy.

---

[228] See D. N. Chorafas, *Financial Models and Simulation*, Macmillan, London, 1995.

The banks' solvency was a particularly sore point since in the go-go years of this century regulators looked the other way as institutions diluted equity capital by using the so-called *hybrids*. On 25 February 2009 a panel of Bloomberg Financial Services said that the Treasury and Fed wanted big banks to have at least 3% equity capital (which is simply insufficient), but not all of them met even this low standard.

- Citigroup had just 1.5%.

- Bank of America between 2.6% and 2.8%.

- JP Morgan Chase between 3.6% and 3.8%.

Indeed JP Morgan Chase proved to be the better capitalised of the 19 banks subjected to the 'stress test', though the exact level of its capital adequacy has not been revealed. Critics said that policymakers have not been as tough on Wall Street as they should have been. The big banks were even given the chance to challenge the test's results – akin to a professor asking his students if the grades he gave them pleased them.

Simon Johnson, former IMF chief economist, was one of the stress test's most important critics.[229] One of the negative opinions heard in the US was that the Obama Administration's toxic waste plan for the financial industry was not free from bias. In Europe a critical opinion was that because we live in a globalised economy it was better if the Treasury's stress tests were conducted in collaboration with the Basel Committee on Banking Supervision and the Financial Stability Forum. This would have made it possible to develop a uniform method for rating the financial staying power of banks, and learn specific lessons from the credit crisis which could be valuable to the global financial markets.

---

[229] *The Economist*, 9 May 2009.

Aware that solutions based on throwing money at the problem have short legs, and also destabilise the financial market, failed bankers who brought their institutions into difficulty wanted the government to take an even bolder approach. The underlying concept of the so-called *bad bank* has been tried in Sweden and in China (among other countries), as we will see in section 6.

6. Bad banks, bad assets and the experience of China's AMCs

Josef Stiglitz criticised the *bad bank* idea as swapping "cash for trash". In these three words, he accurately described a concept which first came up in 1988 when the Mellon Bank spun off its energy and property loans, which had turned sour, into Grant Street National Bank. The 'Grant' was financed with junk bonds and private equity. A couple of years later, the Swedes created Securum and Retriva, which took over the worst assets (respectively) of Nordbanken and Gota Bank, two nationalised institutions. The notion of creating a bad bank is that of creating a separate entity which:

- Takes ownership of non-performing assets,

- Manages them to maximise their recovery value, and

- Sells them as the crisis subsides and market prices of its inventoried assets start edging up.

As far as value recovery is concerned, it depends a great deal on two factors: the nature of these wounded assets and the quality of management. Professionalism is a plus. The Swedish government put people in charge of Securum who were capable of restructuring bad loans, but also in the early 1990s Securum's loans and investments were much simpler than modern securitised assets and other complex derivatives. Securum took over real assets from Nordbanken, and their intrinsic value was quite different to today's useless toxic waste.

By contrast, the idea underpinning the US Treasury's concept of a bad bank, euphemistically called *aggregator bank*, is that it can both manage and dispose the toxic and other damaged virtual assets *it buys* from US big banks.

The pros say that the advantage of the bad bank approach is that its management can focus on the job: fair-value the assets and sell them. At the same time, taking toxic assets off the balance sheet of wounded banks leaves behind a cleaner credit institution, which should find it easier to raise capital or even find a buyer. At best, this statement is superficial. Finding a 'buyer' is a pipe dream, as the example of China's AMCs documents.

"Bad assets in a bank are like a rotten spot in an apple," says Tian Guoli, chief executive of China's Cinda, "you must cut it out if you want to eat the apple, and if you don't get rid of it the rotten part will spoil the rest."[230] Following the near-collapse of big Chinese banks, during the Asian financial crisis of late 1990s, the Chinese government decided to clean out the bad assets of giant state-controlled lenders like Industrial and Commercial Bank of China and China Construction Bank. Ten years later, as of March 2009, the two became the first and second largest banks in the world by market capitalisation, and are also among the most profitable.

The Chinese-style solution was that of requiring the country's four biggest banks, which were insolvent or nearly so, to establish their own separate bad banks. Known as *asset management corporations* (AMCs) these were modelled on the American Resolution Trust Corp (RTC), set up after the savings and loans crisis of late 1980s and 1990s. The AMC process, however, never received general approval. Some analysts say that, while China's decision to establish the AMCs was effective in revitalising the four big banks, the problems were just shifted elsewhere, and issues connected to their bad assets have never been fully dealt with.

---

[230] *Financial Times*, 18 February 2009.

The liabilities are still in the AMC balance sheets, which became the rotten apples. They are not the banks' problems any more, but they are the Chinese government's problem as they have been for over a decade, and that experience is set to continue. Is this really what the American and German governments want?

From the late 1990s until early 2009, China's AMCs have received a total yuan 2.4 trillion ($351 billion) in non-performing assets from the banks. Reportedly, in 2008 China's state auditor raised concerns that the AMCs were unable to repay the interest, let alone principal, on bonds issued to the large banks in return for their bad assets. Subsequently as returns on those 'assets' have dwindled, the future of the AMCs has become much less certain. This obliged their management to lobby strenuously for government approval to transform themselves into investment banks.

It is of course highly doubtful that providing a range of financial services would ease the bad banks' problems. Rather the fact that after more than a decade they still linger on is a good reminder of troubles ahead for both the American and the German governments. The experience of Sweden's Securum was quite positive, but this was a different case altogether.

The AMCs case suggests that both American and German banks which are pushing their respective governments to create a bad bank to which they unload all their toxic waste, are acting with a conflict of interest. Germany's banks have tabled proposals for creating state-backed vehicles to buy their toxic assets, and they have used as chief lobbyist BdB, the commercial banks' federation.

The Chinese, American, British and German examples of dealing with self-wounded banks are different from one another in terms of immediate aims and of the solution being adopted, even if their rationale is similar. Germany's approach rests on the Financial Market Stabilisation Act, of October 2008, which established a Financial Market Stabilisation Fund (SoFFin). On 13 May 2009, that piece of legislation was complemented by the Act to Develop Financial Market Stability. This Act:

- Treated the 'bad banks', to be established, as special purpose vehicles (SVPs), and

- Assigned their oversight to the Financial Market Stabilisation Agency (FMSA).

The government's Financial Market Stabilisation Agency was assigned the power to decide on the validity of applications by credit institutions and other financial entities, for participation in this program financed by public money. The top criteria for approval are:

- Systemic relevance,

- Urgency of each bank's condition, and

- The principle of most economical and effective use of available resources.

The characteristics of applicants have been defined to include credit institutions established in Germany as of 31 December 2008. Provided the application is approved by FMSA, wounded assets can be transferred to the SPV at reduced book value compared to the one stated at the entity's latest audited annual financial statement.

The flat rate haircut on book value is subject to the provision that the transferring bank retains a core capital ratio of at least 7%.[231] Structured securities can be transferred to the SVP, but not plain vanilla loans. Moreover, the SVP may only take over impaired assets the financial entity acquired prior to 31 December 2008. SoFFin's guarantee will not run beyond the contractual maturity of longest-dated structured security.

---

[231] Deutsche Bundesbank, Monthly Report, May 2009.

Debt instruments issued and sold by the SVP are guaranteed by SoFFin in exchange for remuneration at market rate. Over a period of 20 years, repayment of the difference between reduced book value and market value is capped at amount of income paid as dividend to the institution's stockholders. Everything counted, this seems to be a more balanced process than the handouts made to wounded banks, because of their toxic assets, in other jurisdictions.

7. Assessment of toxic after-effects in central banks' vaults

One of the two major unconventional measures taken by central banks in connection to the severe economic and banking crisis was their early 2008 decision to inject liquidity into the market by accepting any security as collateral. More precisely, they accepted the toxic waste warehoused by commercial and investment banks. The other unconventional measure was quantitative easing, which will be covered in more detail later.

This was a *de facto bad bank* created within the monetary institution, and without parliamentary approval. It is appropriate to notice that no monetary institution's status specifies, let alone requires, that it can act as repository of last resort. In addition, the risks associated with this policy are significant, uppermost among them being that:

- It promotes disintermediation in commercial banking, and

- Creates an overhang of very low value financial instruments, discounted at a much higher price than they are worth.

In connection to the first bullet, a few months after the European Central Bank, Federal Reserve and Bank of England started to make an inventory of the commercial banks' wounded assets, the latter no longer placed freshly created asset-backed securities (ABS) with investors, but placed them with central banks. The risks have been shifted from private banks to the public purse.

Closely connected to this switch is the fact that monetary institutions accepted a wide range of financial paper[232] as collateral in their refinancing operations – including ABS for which there is temporarily little or no trading. The only provision is that the tranche is the most senior and graded A- or above by one rating agency. This is easily met, given that the rating agencies have an interest in being generous. According to published reports, this led the more astute commercial banks to design ABS tranches purely for central bank consumption. These were backed mostly by mortgages, and designed by the same people who created the financial products of the July-August 2007 debacle.

The statistics are startling. According to JP Morgan Chase, as of mid-June 2008, of €208 billion (then $320 billion) of 'eligible securities' created for the above-mentioned purpose, less than €6 billion was placed with investors. In December 2007, for example, Rabo Bank, Holland's huge agricultural bank, issued €30 billion (then $44 billion) of mortgage-backed securities, 90% of which were designed exclusively for refinancing with the European Central Bank.[233]

Moral hazard aside, the risk taken by the main Western central banks is proportional to the fact that they have too few tools, skills and procedures to cope with the requirements posed by toxic assets transactions, and they may well overpay for what they collect. In spite of this, central banks widened the range of collateral they accepted. The Bank of England did so with its special liquidity scheme of April 2008 (the restriction being that the illiquid financial products it accepted were held in the commercial banks' balance sheets before the end of 2007 – which means five whole months after the crisis started).

---

[232] A more common term is commercial paper, but in most cases this is a misnomer. Dr Carlo Pesenti who chaired a group of five Italian banks used the term 'commercial paper' only when there was a commercial transaction in the background. Everything else was 'financial paper'. Securitised and structured instruments are not commercial paper.

[233] *The Economist*, 14 June 2008.

For its part the Federal Reserve threw open its emergency lending facilities to investment banks, and it has generally accepted a much broader range of collateral than it used to in its open market operations. An example is complex credit derivatives, which it welcomed in its liquidity drive, even if this practice had many critics who pointed out the huge risks associated with central banks acting as repositories of toxic assets and buyers of last resort.

One of the arguments critics make is that if credit institutions and investment banks start to default, then the central banks, and ultimately the taxpayer, will be badly hurt. Moreover, lack of coordination and the existence of different standards among Western central banks sees to it that commercial and investment banks do not stop manipulating the system.

As an example, the supply of European Central Bank cash to Spanish and Irish banks more than doubled year on year to August 2008, both in size and as a share of the euro zone's total, while creditworthiness took a dive. In May 2008 Fitch, the independent rating agency, said that standards for newly structured Spanish mortgage-backed securities had slipped since the credit crunch started in July-August 2007.

A growing number of experts have also expressed concern that affiliates of non-euro zone based banks employ the ECB as a source of funds for lending around the globe. Macquarie, an Australian investment bank, was able to secure an ECB loan through a euro zone subsidiary against a security backed by Australian car loans. (In March 2009, Macquarie said that it would buy back its bonds at 50% of face value, which speaks volumes about the worth of its financial paper).

It therefore comes as no surprise that, at the end of August 2008 the ECB announced that it would tighten its rules for collateral to assure that what it offers to banks is strictly liquidity support. A particular worry was that in countries where housing bubble bursts have made investors wary of mortgage-backed assets, like Spain and Ireland, banks continued to create 'securities' for the express purpose of gaining central bank funding. This exposed central banks to too much credit risk and stalled market recovery for mortgage-backed assets.

Critics also say that not only should the ECB shield its constituent central banks from the risk of loss if one of the banks depositing collateral defaults, but also ensure that banks are not shifting their credit risk onto the monetary institution's vaults on favourable terms. This would amount to an unwanted subsidy to private commercial banks.

One way to make this liquidity-injection process more orderly is to increase haircuts, which presently vary from less than 1% (a triviality) for the safest and most liquid government bonds, to 18% for some long dated asset-backed securities. But with the euro zone featuring 16 different members and jurisdictions, there is no general agreement as to how much the haircut should be increased by to really obtain extra protection.[234]

Critics of the policies adopted in late 2007 and subsequent years also point out that neither governments nor central banks have summoned the courage to pass legislation able to stop gambling with derivatives, which serves no commercial purpose and has only fictitious 'profits' and real bonuses as an aim. Closely related to this issue is the fact that cleaning the toxic waste is not the same goal as boosting economic growth, though both have much to do with reforming financial regulation, which re-launches, and keeps a close watch over, the mechanism of credit.

Governments and central banks must, however, be careful with their policy of trying to solve problems by throwing money at them. That is what happens with so-called *quantitative easing*. The creation of money

---

[234] In addition, central banks should require that collateral is backed by income streams in local currency, which would curb some commercial banks' policies of using central bank money to finance loans made around the world.

to ease credit flows by buying up assets is an unorthodox policy which has plenty of unexpected consequences. This policy started in America and Japan, and by March 2009 migrated to Britain, though it is wisely still avoided by the euro zone.

As a British expert interviewed by CNBC on 11 March 2009 succinctly said: "Quantitative easing is a nuts policy." Most of the opinions I have heard in the course of my research converge on the conclusion that the printing press is merely a 'solution' fit to produce future troubles.[235]

8. Thinking out of the box, when confronted with insolvent banks

The policy of throwing good money after bad money to the big banks, month after month, risks perpetuating what Paul Krugman calls *lemon socialism*. The term stands for private banks reaping the gains and taxpayers eating the losses. In an article in the *Financial Times* James Baker said that handouts without proper workouts led to Japan's two lost decades.

Another point James Baker aptly made is that nationalisation is not an unthinkable alternative for the deeply wounded banks. In his opinion, right after being nationalised, they should be emptied not only of their toxic waste but also of their toxic management.[236] Then a new set of more capable managers could take over and turn the institution around.

It is indeed difficult to understand how two consecutive administrations in the US (Bush and Obama) have accepted giving

---

[235] Indeed, it is worth consulting *The Economist* of 15 August 2009, with its fascinating article on John Law, who fought a duel, invented quantitative easing, and ruined the French economy; and Ben Bernanke, who recently had doubts about its wisdom in America.

[236] *Financial Times*, 2 March 2009.

hundreds of billions of dollars to the banks and not required that management is removed at every institution where public money has been used to tidy up the balance sheet. So far little sacrifice has been required of the boards, CEOs and CFOs responsible for the financial mess. On the contrary, the mismanagers have been allowed to walk away with unprecedented bonuses, and they have not even been officially castigated for their greed and unprecedented failure.

According to knowledgeable opinions, bringing to justice executives and other professionals who have ruined their institutions – and the economy – will allow the dust to settle by reassuring the markets that wild excesses will not start again tomorrow. This is normal practice in other professions; an engineer who miscalculates a bridge's statics and dynamics, with the result that it collapses, is brought to court. The same is true of a doctor whose patient dies because of medical error. Why should a banker be sacrosanct? It is a tall order to introduce legal responsibilities in mismanagement, but it is necessary. To assist with this approach, lessons should be learned from previous major financial management errors and their consequences.

Plenty of evidence suggests that the first major mistake made by governments, central banks and regulatory authorities after the start of a crisis is to choose the easy way out as if nothing serious has happened. This is a widespread managerial error. Not only financial companies but also nations fall into the trap of 'hope rather than facts'.

Following its financial industry's collapse, in 1990-1991, Japan took what was considered to be the easier approach out of the tunnel and paid for it with nearly 20 years of economic instability. In-between deep recessions, small recoveries were characterised by feeble economic performance as the country's export industry encountered headwinds.

January 2008-2009, Japan's overall exports fell by 45.7%. With its export industry all but collapsing in the first months of 2009 (because of the global economic crisis), and its automobile industry in bad shape, Japan found itself in a mess worse than in 1990. With 20 years' delay its government started to see that half-measures don't work and that the country desperately required major changes. Economic recovery requires policies which:

- Are radical and painful,

- Involve critical thinking and dissent, and

- Reach all levels of society, including – in Japan's case – the Keiretsu and their banking institutions.

Probably based on this evidence, in his *Financial Times* article James Baker said that America "may be repeating Japan's mistake by viewing our current banking crisis as one of liquidity and not solvency. We risk perpetuating the problems US banks are having and suffering a lost American decade."[237] He added that evidence is provided by:

- Sharp economic recession,

- A mountain of toxic assets,

- Housing market declines,

- Rising unemployment, and

- Increasing taxpayer exposure through guarantees, loans and infusion of capital.

These five bullets share some basic reasons which were clearly expressed on 26 March 2009, in an interview with Bloomberg News by Alan Meltzer, professor of economics at Carnegie Mellon University. His opening statement with reference to America's wounded banks was that: "Nobody should be too big to fail," adding that if it is so, then that somebody is too big.

Meltzer then focused on quantitative easing by the Fed, which he did not like. In his opinion, the Federal Reserve did the wrong thing when it bypassed Congress. Historically, the Fed did not go against its charter,

---

[237] *Financial Times*, 2 March 2009.

Meltzer said. In the 1920s it was asked to help the farmers, and it said "No!" because that was not its business. In the 1930s, it was asked to help the homeowners. Again it answered "Not our business." But now the Fed is doing everything for everybody.

The government and the Federal Reserve should not finance big banks, argued Meltzer. They should tell them to go to the capital market to find half of the money they need. If they are able to do so *then*, and only then, the government could put up the other 50% under draconian conditions. But if they cannot find half the money they need in the market, then this means nobody trusts them, and they should be closed down.

The interviewer asked if there was a need for new laws. "Not so," answered Meltzer. "The laws are there but they are not applied. They only talk of new laws to avoid closing down the banks." Meltzer did not make reference to the failure to implement the Sarbanes-Oxley Act of 2002. However, this might have been in his mind as it is the most important piece of legislation for prosecuting wrongdoers in the banking crisis of 2007-2009, and it has never been properly implemented.

Just as important in better understanding the failures James Baker referred to in his article, is a document published by the Basel Committee on Banking Supervision.[238] *Inter alia*, this brings attention to the fact that financial instruments and banking transactions have become increasingly complex, and there can be a large amount of uncertainty surrounding the model-based values of some complex instruments.

---

[238] Basel Committee 'External Audit Quality and Banking Supervision', BIS, Basel, December 2008.

The associated uncertainty, Basel says, can be exacerbated by:

- Lack of industry consensus on how to model these exotic derivatives and synthetic CDOs with asset-backed underlying,

- Absence of observable input parameters, like correlations in structured credit products and equity derivatives,

- Insufficient data histories on novel products like new issues of ABSs, and

- Non-traded or illiquid products like private equity, distressed debt, some corporate bonds and (it should be added) over the counter deals.

This kind of detail both explains and complements the points Baker made in his article. In the opinion of the former Treasury Secretary, current facts strongly suggest that some American banks face a *solvency problem* and not merely a liquidity one – leading to the need to divide the wounded banks into three groups:

- Healthy,

- Hopeless, and

- Needy.

The needy should be reorganised and recapitalised; hopeless closed, and the healthy ones left alone. Baker does not exclude temporary nationalisation for the needy, and that's where meaningful stress tests (section 3) may be useful, in order to ascertain which banks are insolvent. The government's task should then be to take them over, clean them of toxic assets and sell them over time.

Many economists and Wall Street practitioners have also come to the opinion that this is the best option. Hasty takeovers, such as those of Bear Stearns, Countrywide, Washington Mutual, Merrill Lynch and Wachovia are no real solution. If anything, they have made the situation worse because government intervention did not allow the economy to function the free-market way. The answer to those who say that it is a violation of free market principles to nationalise unmanageable banks, is that the US government and the Fed have already violated many of these principles through:

- Debt guarantees,

- Central-bank facilities,

- Capital infusions, and

- Loss-sharing agreements.

In fact, Paul Krugman suggests that nationalisation is "as American as apple pie". Banks have often been seized by the state in the form of the FDIC's intervention. Moreover, some of them, such as Washington Mutual in 2008, Bank of New England in the 1990s, Continental Illinois and Seattle First in the 1980s have been big. Besides that, today's banks are only a shadow of their past glory. All that is left of them is a deadly weight on the economy.

* * *

The purpose of this chapter, and of the two that preceded it, has not been to accuse anybody but to bring attention to the fact that risk is not only polyvalent. It also morphs into unfamiliar forms, which get well beyond the factors of exposure we have treated.

The uncharted territory of risk management, where quantum chromodynamics may be the best available method, includes a sprawling legal risk; growing possibilities for Ponzi games; unprecedented overleveraging propelled by egos, bonuses and conflicts of interest; handholding between commercial banks, investment banks, and regulatory authorities; warehousing of toxic waste by monetary institutions; and the fact that in the US and Britain central banks have lost their independence, becoming appendages of the government.

These 21st century changes work against the free market economy, and so does the policy by some regulators to look the other way when banks under their watch engage in excesses. Risks beyond those of pure financial nature, affecting the free market economy, should be addressed at the metalevel of control through the best methods and tools – plus a revival of business ethics.

The free market is promoted when transparency is king. Cover-ups have short legs, slowly but surely leading to disaster.

Conclusion

1. The Bank for International Settlements is worried

Capital comes from savings and investments; not from the printing press of the Federal Reserve, the Bank of England or any other monetary institution. Capitalism is promoted through entrepreneurship; and not by the government's generosity. If anything, the economy is only harmed by the State Supermarket, and business activity is subdued.

"A financial crisis bears striking similarities to medical illness," states the 79th Annual Report of the Bank for International Settlements. "In both cases, finding a cure requires identifying and then treating the causes of the disease."[239] The instrument proposed by this book for identifying the cause of the disease – for example the inordinate and unsustainable risks assumed by financial institutions, as it happened in the first decade of the 21st century – is *quantum electrodynamics (QED).*[240]

Since 2000, the global banking industry has persevered with a well-honed new brand of big risks taken with novel instruments, but without one basic ingredient: *real money.* As leveraging reached for the stars, first came the stock market crash of 2000, then the subprimes, credit crunch, illiquidity, insolvency and deep recession of 2007-2009, which saw to it that capitalism was left without capital.[241]

To save themselves from outright bankruptcy, all sorts of financial institutions went to governments for financial aid. The latter were ready to oblige, but through improvisation. The central bank and the

---

[239] BIS, 79th Annual Report, 1 April 2008 to 31 March 2009; Basel, June 2009.

[240] The most sophisticated method presently available in the physical sciences.

[241] Lawrence Summers, former president of Harvard University and Treasury Secretary, currently senior economic advisor to Barack Obama, began a paper on financial markets with the words: "There are idiots. Look around."

Treasury in each jurisdiction acted on their own. A plan on how to handle a global systemic crisis has simply not been put in place.

It is not this book's purpose to lay any accusations, but it is proper to state that the crisis illustrated the big banks' hubris, and it has shown that the financial industry deliberately thumbed its nose at the governments and the regulators. In addition, the regulators did not do their job when there was still time to avert the worst.

Politics was one of the reasons for the disaster, but only one. Another basic reason was the lack of metrics enabling the measurement of exposures assumed by banks and other financial institutions, in a way which is fairly accurate. QED is proposed as the method and tool to correct this major gap which:

- Affects *risk pricing* in a negative way, and

- Dilutes personal responsibility for the *mismanagement* of risk.

Financial innovation and technology have seen to it that the approach of counting credit risk and market risk separately no longer allows the regulators, and the bank's own management, to watch over exposure. Working Paper No. 16 by the Basel Committee on Banking Supervision makes the point that in their rapid development the credit risk transfer markets have blurred distinctions between risk factors and raised questions regarding approaches that treat credit and market risks separately.

The way the Basel Committee puts it: "From a supervisory perspective, these developments raise important questions related to how the two types of risks can be defined and what relationships exist between them, how should they be aggregated and how precisely their joint risk is measured, what role liquidity plays in their interaction and under what conditions securitisation – as one driver of the above developments – can work as a risk management approach."[242]

---

[242] Basel Committee, Working Paper No. 16 'Findings on the Interaction of Market Risk and Credit Risk', BIS, May 2009.

If it is properly adapted to the financial landscape, benefits from experimentation to test its applicability and is correctly implemented, QED can provide the way to answer this challenge. This is particularly true in account of the Basel Committee's viewpoint that the first major obstacle to integrating credit and market risk, starting with their measurement and following up with their management, is that metrics currently used for each of them:

- Are *not* fully comparable, and

- They are *not* easy to integrate.

Another problem closely associated with the debacle that led to the severe 2007-2009 economic and banking crisis is that it is very hard to find enough truly first class minds to staff all of the risk control groups in the proliferating institutions of the global financial industry. Regulatory authorities, too, are confronted with this problem of human resources. Hence the need for a high-level risk measurement model, like QED, which assists in doing a clean job and serves as universal frame of reference.

2. Central banks find themselves in a hard place

Adding to the challenges briefly outlined in section 1, is the recently developed practice of running the banking system not as a vital social service but as a bunch of off balance sheet vehicles. The after-effect has been a radical change to the mission of monetary institutions, as they found themselves obliged to proceed with a massive salvage operation of banks that were 'too big to fail', the invention of quantitative easing and super-leveraging of their own balance sheets.

The result is that off balance sheet gearing spread from the private to the public sector. Mervyn King, governor of the Bank of England, has repeatedly spoken about the central bank's statutory responsibility for financial stability. But financial stability and off balance sheet leveraging are incompatible with one another.

Critics say that banks too big to fail have proven themselves as a liability, not as an asset. In his interview with Bloomberg News on 17 June 2009, Ron Paul, US congressman and 2008 presidential candidate, made reference to a statement by Paul Volcker, the respected former chairman of the Federal Reserve. "If some institutions are too big to fail then they are too big to exist."

The problem, the way cognisant people see it, is that governments and supervisory authorities are not ready to break up the super big banks into pieces of a manageable size. The least they can do, therefore, is to measure their exposure in real-time, in an integrative way – as the Basel Committee stipulates. This should be the goal to be reached through the implementation of *quantum electrodynamics*.

In fact, many central bankers and regulators presently concur that new methods are necessary for risk measurement, management and pricing – as there is also a need for better tools. Mervyn King is quoted as having said: "Experience suggests that attempts to encourage a better life through the power of voice is not enough."[243] And he is right.

Not only does a new powerful model have to be implemented to keep risk under close watch, but also the many basic assumptions that comprise the current risk control culture have to change. For instance, when two different assets are thought to be uncorrelated banks hold the same capital as a cushion against losses on both, because it is believed that they would not turn sour simultaneously. But as the 2007-2009 crisis documented, under conditions of market stress normally uncorrelated assets can become highly correlated and hedges considered to be as stable as the Rock of Gibraltar turn on their head.

---

[243] *The Economist*, 20 June 2009.

Stress tests help, but only as far as the hypotheses underpinning them are sound, and to the extent that they truly focus on the long leg of the risk distribution. This has not been the case with the stress tests that in early 2009 involved the 19 largest US banks. By mid-year, the default ratio on prime mortgages was well above the Treasury's stress test limit set for the banks, while the crisis spread very quickly to smaller institutions in the American banking system.[244]

Even among the bigger banks, which profited handsomely from public money, the credit crisis hitting their balance sheets is far from over. Four months after the Treasury's stress tests took place amidst an unprecedented public relations campaign, American financial institutions had nearly $900 billion in losses from the credit crunch. They also expected another $600 billion from the recession in the corporate and consumer sectors, through 2010.

What the foregoing references suggest is that the fire-brigade practice adopted by some governments and central banks is not a good way to address toxic waste warehoused in the vaults of financial institutions. The example of the failure of the asset removable scheme of the US Treasury, labelled Public-Private Investment Program (PPIP, see Chapter 3), is thought-provoking.

This was supposed to take troubled loans off the banks' books but it stalled, partly because of accounting rule changes (that gave the banks more leeway in valuing their assets), and partly because it was a half-baked concept. Another US Treasury programme intended to address toxic securities finally got going in July 2009, but in substantially scaled-down form.

---

[244] In the first 220 days of 2009, 72 medium to smaller American banks went bankrupt; or one every three days including weekends and holidays.

Volatility has fallen, but worries remain. It is small wonder therefore that David Viniar, CFO of Goldman Sachs, admitted on a call with analysts that "we are way far away from being out of the woods."[245] In an interview he gave on 25 June 2009 on Bloomberg, Warren Buffett pointed out that deleveraging is a slow process; it cannot be done in a short time. He then quoted a friend of his who said that leverage is something that smart people don't need, and dumb people have no business using.

Banks took tremendous risks, both with shareholder assets and with bought money. The European Central Bank's (ECB's) Governing Council is still concerned about "a stronger or more protracted negative feedback loop between the real economy and the turmoil in financial markets."[246] As for the Troubled Assets Relief Program (TARP, Chapter 3), which was the largest of all US government plans aimed to save global institutions from self-destruction, it is too early to have an opinion about the final bill to be footed by taxpayers, and whether the plan itself will succeed or fail beyond the salvage of some big banks (which is of questionable wisdom in any case).

By contrast, the size of accumulated American public deficits seems to be more certain. The cost of the bailout may reach $23.7 trillion said the TARP inspector in late July 2009.[247] That astronomical amount represents 177% of the gross national product of the United States, practically bankrupting its economy.

Other estimates presently made over the policy-relevant horizon put the refinancing of the wounded financial system at $26 trillion in terms

---

[245] *The Economist*, 18 July 2009.

[246] European Central Bank, Monthly Bulletin, July 2009.

[247] Bloomberg News, 20 July 2009.

of total funding by 2011. While some of this money may come from private sources, it is clear that without an implicit state backstop this would be impossible. As a recent mordant observation has it: the profits are *shared* among the big banks top echelons, but the liabilities remain *unshared*, residing wholesale in the public purse.

Also to be counted in the liabilities side is the sharply diminished value of banks' assets sheltered by central banks' asset purchases, and sugar-coated by generous accounting rules. What all this suggests is that America, Britain and continental Europe have a thinly capitalised banking system that is being allowed to earn its way back to health on the back of taxpayers – with ominous effects on the increase of national debts in Western nations,[248] whose interest payments will weigh heavily on future state budgets.

Five weeks prior to the aforementioned estimate of $23.7 trillion as the most likely cost of bank bailout, precisely in the second week of June 2009, the US Treasury had let ten financial companies repay a combined total of $68 billion in loans they had received under TARP. These included JP Morgan Chase, Goldman Sachs, Morgan Stanley and American Express. The repayments looked encouraging, but they were connected to the permission to pay big bonuses rather than to financial health.

Citigroup and Merrill Lynch filled the pockets of their executives and traders with $9 billion in bonuses in 2008, said Andrew Cuomo, New York State's attorney general, on 30 July 2009. This was more than a quarter of $32.6 billion in bonuses paid that same year by American big banks getting government aid. This practice of wounded banks awarding taxpayer's money to their top brass is, as has been argued, inexplicable and rather revolting.

---

[248] Japan is already in the deep hole of a public debt at 170% of GDP, and Italy confronts a figure at about the 110% level.

While there is value to the argument that people who produce exceptional results should be properly compensated, the crisis of 2007-2009 documents that 'exceptional results' have been exclusively in the negative territory. Governments, regulators and central banks are right in their desire to bend the curve of astronomical salaries and bonuses in the banking industry, but they lack a standard to measure the creation and destruction of wealth. As a tool for universal risk measurement and for risk pricing, QED can provide the missing link.

3. Socrates said that virtue is knowledge which cannot be taught

The way a Reuters article by John Kemp had it: "Much of the academic defence of the way prices (for commodities) are set was based on fancy econometrics and some version of the efficient markets hypothesis, both of which have been discredited by the financial crisis. [There is] growing public scepticism about how the financial services industry... can now be reporting massive profits and paying large bonuses."[249]

In Kemp's opinion this combination of excesses and of the economic crisis' after-effects is seeing to it that, as a regulator, the Commodity Futures Trading Commission (CFTC) is becoming proactive and that "the iron triangle of industry, academics and regulators that prevented stricter regulation of commodity markets has been thrown onto the defensive". To perform their duties in an able manner, all regulators should follow that path re-establishing long-held values for:

- Risk pricing,
- Compliance, and
- Virtue in business.

---

[249] Reuters, 5 August 2009.

Virtue is something that during the last two decades waned while rules have been broken; laws (like the Sarbanes-Oxley Act, Chapter 6) were disregarded; risks to the economic outlook ran wild; myth and artifice replaced reality; CEOs and CFOs had no clue about their institutions' exposure; and arrogance had a field day.

The arrogance shown in some quarters is associated with a revisionist theory of the 2007-2009 economic crisis and credit crunch. In a feature article in *The Economist*, one could read: "Jamie Dimon, the boss of JP Morgan, has fantasised about sending an ironic ... thank-you letter to America's treasury secretary, Tim Geithner, saying 'We hope you enjoyed the experience as much as we did.' The boss of Wells Fargo called the solvency tests 'asinine'... Other big banks make similar cases, albeit less vocally."[250]

To say the least, this is a startling lack not only of virtue but also of self-respect. When millions of people lost their jobs; financial gloom fell over America, the European Union and the rest of the world; and trillions of dollars/pounds/euros of taxpayers' money have been spent to save the banking system from its self-made meltdown – it is plain bad taste to add insult to injury.

Neither is the banking industry over the worst of the situation. While self-gratification and public mockery is going on at the big bank's headquarters', experts suggest that more than 2000 American community and regional banks, roughly a quarter of the total, could fail or be forced to merge. This both shows a great disparity in terms of who is favoured by the state as recipient of public money, and creates a situation that would be logistically overwhelming for regulators.[251]

---

[250] *The Economist*, 13 June 2009.

[251] It can also run dry FDIC's deposit insurance scheme.

Whether deliberately or lethargically, drifting is not an option. Evidence provided all the way from lack of virtue among CEOs to rising unemployment and subdued economic activity, documents that it is far better to be proactive in risk measurement and management than rush in with emergency measures when it is too late. Being proactive, however, presupposes a steady watch alongside realistic *risk pricing* – without political interference (Chapter 6).

The use of a powerful method like QED for risk pricing can permit regulators to be craftier than they were when estimating the hits a bank's capital must absorb. Rather than snapshots of the financial institutions' balance-sheets, which are the site of plenty of accounting tricks, the authorities should use a reliable universal method such as *quantum electrodynamics*, with the goal of:

- Capturing losses intraday and over the longer term,

- Paying great attention to the long leg of the risk distribution, and

- Taking full account of off balance sheet activities as well as of each bank's core profits and losses.

One of the major failures with regulation prior to the severe economic and banking crisis of 2007-2009 was that the money-making franchise of big banks was considered to be practically unassailable. If prior to the crisis, or at the latest early into it, the New York Fed's Division of Bank Supervision had performed a routine analysis to see where the banks' profits were coming from, then the US, European and global economy would have not sustained so much damage.

Absenteeism in prudential regulation is wrong and dangerous, and the same is true of being comfortable with lofty visions rather than details. Investigation along the lines of a thorough analysis of facts, with emphasis on the measurement of assumed risks, would have led to the investigation of the unstable nature of structured products and from there to the next inquiries:

- Whether the big banks' huge profits came from cutting corners

- How well each one of them stood in terms of risk control and compliance.

It is nobody's secret that huge profits always have in the background an inordinate exposure that unavoidably ends either in major banking bankruptcies (as in the mid-1980s), or in salvage through the printing press. And in case governments and supervisory authorities say that they do not have the means available to measure the banks' booming risks, QED should be used to provide them with the information needed to take timely corrective action.

4. A call for action

To sum up, it is appropriate that central banks, regulatory authorities and ministries of finance (or treasuries) have a top-level research laboratory employing some of the best analytical brains that can be found worldwide. Its mission should be *risk measurement and risk pricing*, with results brought not only to the boss' attention but also to the public eye, since its budget will be paid by taxpayers' money.

This will tremendously strengthen market discipline, which is Pillar 3 of Basel II[252] but it is presently dormant. Notice that since the late 1980s/early 1990s each big bank employs a large number of 'rocket scientists'. Moreover, the banking industry as a whole sponsors the Washington-based Institute of International Finance (IIF) – which is first class, but at the same time also the banking industry's lobby.

Until and unless regulators, including the Basel Committee itself, have their own analytical engines featuring first class minds (not just models), they will be condemned to run after the facts rather in the manner of a fire brigade. There are good reasons why the Bank for International

---

[252] Chorafas, Economic *Capital Allocation.*

Settlements states in its 79th Annual Report that: "The financial stress which began in the summer of 2007 has revealed a myriad of limitations in microeconomic financial arrangements." According to BIS, these include:

- Flaws in techniques used to measure, price and manage risk,

- Inadequacies in corporate governance structures used to monitor risk,

- Different problems with (the wrong) incentives, and

- Failures of the regulatory system, which can only be corrected through analysis.

Among the negatives which resulted from these severe shortcomings is the fact that they permitted "the entire financial industry to book profits too early, too easily and without proper risk adjustment."[253] *Risk pricing* was cast aside and responsibility for sound governance went with it. The advent of a sophisticated approach like QED will help to right the balances of management accountability and of prudential supervision.

Furthermore, it will help in implementing, at a scale commensurate with the globalisation of finance, the *systemic capital charge* (SCC) currently in discussion among regulatory authorities. Its objective is to create a distribution of capital in the banking and financial system that reflects in a dependable way the systemic risk posed by the failures of individual big banks and other major institutions.[254]

QED can also assist regulators in being creative and in using the aforementioned capital surcharge (over and above the global minimum standard), in an intelligent *risk weighted* way, supported by stress tests

---

[253] BIS, 79th Annual Report, 1 April 2008 to 31 March 2009; Basel June 2009.

[254] As a suggestion, SCC should be based on three main factors: the size of the institution, its global scope, and its risk exposure measured by QED as universal standard.

and other evidence based on research. It needs no explanation that banks that pose a bigger threat to the global financial system and to taxpayers should pay more in SCC terms.[255]

All this is written on the understanding that, even more than liquidity, solvency – and therefore capital – is the really powerful means in the regulatory toolbox. It must be used to protect taxpayers, as well as to persuade banks to reform themselves. But to do so in an able manner, the capital amount should correlate to assumed risk, with the latter being measured in an objective fashion. QED could help in doing so. Sooner rather than later, subjective approaches overturn because they are open to a myriad of political pressures and to a vast amount of manipulation.

---

[255] A flat ratio of capital adequacy is not able to provide assurance for solvency. Neither is there a point in expecting that a limited tool does more than it can intrinsically deliver.

Bibliography

Books

Anders, George, *Merchants of Debt*, Basic Books, New York, 1992,

Antall, J. and Szebelledys, G., *Pictures from the History of Medicine*, The Semmelweiss Medical Historical Museum, Budapest, Corvina Press, 1973.

Banks, Erik, *Complex Derivatives*, Probus, Chicago and Cambridge, 1994.

Boslough, John, *Masters of Time*, J.M. Dent, London, 1992.

Chorafas, D. N. and Steinmann, Heinrich, *Expert Systems in Banking*, Macmillan, London, 1991.

Chorafas, D. N., *Chaos Theory in the Financial Markets*, Probus, Chicago, 1994.

Chorafas, D. N., *Financial Models and Simulation*, Macmillan, London, 1995.

Chorafas, D. N., *Rocket Scientists in Banking*, Lafferty Publications, London and Dublin, 1995.

Chorafas, D. N., *The 1996 Market Risk Amendment. Understanding the Marking-to-Model and Value-at-Risk*, Irwin/McGraw-Hill, Burr Ridge, IL, 1998.

Chorafas, D. N., *Reliable Financial Reporting and Internal Control: A Global Implementation Guide*, John Wiley, New York, 2000.

Chorafas, D. N., *Managing Risk in the New Economy*, New York Institute of Finance, New York, 2001.

Chorafas, D. N., *Modelling the Survival of Financial and Industrial Enterprises. Advantages, Challenges, and Problems with the Internal Rating-Based (IRB) Method*, Palgrave/Macmillan, London, 2002.

Chorafas, D. N., *Economic Capital Allocation with Basle II. Cost and Benefit Analysis*, Butterworth-Heinemann, London and Boston, 2004.

Chorafas, D. N., *Operational Risk Control with Basle II. Basic Principles and Capital Requirements*, Butterworth-Heinemann, London and Boston, 2004.

Chorafas, D. N., *After Basel II. Assuring Compliance and Smoothing the Rough Edges*, Lafferty/VRL Publishing, London, 2005.

Chorafas, D. N., *IFRS, Fair Value and Corporate Governance: Its Impact on Budgets, Balance Sheets and Management Accounts*, Butterworth-Heinemann, London and Boston, 2005.

Chorafas, D. N., *IT Auditing and Sarbanes-Oxley Compliance*, Auerbach/CRC, New York, 2005.

Chorafas, D. N., *The Real-time Enterprise*, Auerbach, New York, 2005.

Chorafas, D. N., *Stress-testing for Risk Control Under Basel II*, Elsevier, Oxford and Boston, 2007.

Chorafas, D. N., *An Introduction to Derivative Financial Instruments*, McGraw-Hill, New York, 2008.

Chorafas, D. N., *Financial Boom and Gloom. The Credit and Banking Crisis of 2007-2009 and Beyond*, Palgrave/Macmillan, London, 2009.

Chorafas, D. N., *Capitalism Without Capital*, Palgrave/Macmillan, London, 2009.

Clausius, Rudolf, *Abhandlungen über Mechanische Wärmetheorie*, Brunnswick, 1864.

Cohan, William D., *House of Cards: A Tale of Hubris and Wretched Excess on Wall Street*, Doubleday, New York, 2008.

Copeland, Thomas E. and Weston, J. Fred, *Financial Theory and Corporate Policy*, Addison-Wesley, Reading, Massachusetts, 1988.

Crawford, Nancy, *How the Laws of Physics Lie*, Oxford University Press, 1983.

Feynman, Richard P., *QED: The Strange Theory of Light and Matter*, Penguin Books, London 1985.

Grove, Andrew S., *Only the Paranoid Survive*, Currency Doubleday, New York, 1996.

Haberstam, David, *The Reckoning*, William Morrow, New York, 1986.

Hawking, Stephen W., *A Brief History of Time*, Bantam Books, New York, 1988.

Krass, Peter, *Carnegie*, Wiley, New York, 2002.

Levy, Steven, *Artificial Life. The Quest for a New Creation*, Penguin Books, London, 1992.

Lowenstein, Roger, *Buffett, the Making of an American Capitalist*, Weidenfeld & Nicolson, London, 1996.

Machiavelli, Niccolò, *Il Principe*, Einaudi Editore, Milano, 1974.

Maestro, Bob Woodward, *Greenspan's Fed and the American Boom*, Simon & Schuster, New York, 2000.

Marsh, David, *The Bundesbank*, William Heinemann, London, 1992.

Samuelson, Paul A., *Economics*, McGraw-Hill, New York, 1951.

Tribus, Myron, *Thermostatistics and Thermodynamics*, D. Van Nostrand, Princeton, 1961,

Tzu, Sun, *L'Art de la Guerre*, Flamarion, Paris, 1972.

Walton, Sam, *Made in America: My Story*, Bantam Books, New York, 1992.

Wilczek, Frank, *The Lightness of Being*, Basic Books, New York, 2008.

Wolf, Martin, *Fixing Global Finance*, Yale University Press, London, 2008.

Articles

Wilczek, Frank, 'Profound Simplicity', The New York Academy of Sciences Magazine, Autumn 2008.

Newspapers

The Economist

Financial Times

International Herald Tribune

Le Figaro

Index

A

AAA tranches, 149

ABN Amro, 255

Abramovich, Roman, 263

acceptable quality level (AQL), 86

adjustable rate mortgages (ARM), 234

AIG, 44, 83, 131, 145, 156, 263-4

A-IRB capital adequacy models, 62

aggregator bank, 310

Amaranth, 60

American Express, 331

Anders, George, 145

asset-backed commercial paper (ABCP), 199

asset-backed securities, 73, 120, 195, 295, 314-5

asset management corporations (AMCs), 310-2

auction-rate securities (ARS), 199

B

bad bank, 310-12, 314

Bailey, Kevin, 132

Bair, Sheila, 143, 151

Baker, James, 307, 318, 320

balance sheet analysis, 135

Bankers Trust, 81, 230, 239

Bank for International Settlements (BIS), 292, 325, 335

Bank of America, 125-6, 135, 230, 232, 254, 291, 295, 309

Bank of England, 48, 314-15, 325

Bank of New York Mellon, 156

Banking System Stability Index (BSI), 77

Banks, Eric, 229

Barclays Bank, 195

Basel Committee on Banking Supervision, 45, 56-7, 62, 139, 141, 151-2, 159, 169, 174, 177, 190, 258, 300, 309, 320, 326, 335

Basel II, 127, 139, 151, 169, 293, 296-7, 299

Bayes theorem, 166

Bear Stearns, 80, 83, 145-6, 209, 235, 291

Bell Laboratories, 39

Berkshire Hathaway, 107

Bernanke, Ben, 49, 303-4

Bernstein, Richard, 289

beta, 31

Black-Scholes algorithm, 197

Blackstone, 58

black swan(s), 54-5

Blinder, Alan, 301

Bloomberg News, 188

BNP Paribas, 246

book value leverage, 268

Bohr, Niels, 290

bosons, 14-15, 224

bridging loans, 272

Buffett, Warren, 95, 107, 116, 168, 260-1, 330

Bush, George W., 211

C

calculus, 213

Capital Adequacy Pricing Model (CAPM), 31

Capital Assistance Program, 306

Carnegie, Andrew, 94-5

Carnegie Mellon University, 113, 320

Carnot, Sadi, 283-4

Cartesian coordinates, 215-16, 218

Cartwright, Nancy, 11

cash flow analysis, 275-7

Cayne, James, 235

chaos theory, 198

Chicago Board Options Exchange (CBOE), 30, 58

China Construction Bank, 311

Chronos, 18, 203, 206

Cinda, 311

Citigroup, 125, 145-6, 209, 232, 235, 291, 295, 309, 331

Class actions, 229

Clausius, Rudolf, 20, 284

Clinton, Bill, 46

Cohan, William D, 235

collateralised debt obligations (CDOs), 46, 72-3, 105-6, 120, 149, 158, 185, 191, 199

collateralised loan obligations (CLOs), 78, 193

Commodity Futures Trading Commission (CFTC), 241, 332

compound events, 195

computational finance, 177

conduits, 70, 73

confidence limits, 84

Continental Illinois, 323

contingent liabilities, 272

Copeland, Thomas E., 103

correlation coefficients, 169-70

correlation risk, 193-4

Corrigan, Gerald, 270

Countrywide, 209, 233

creative accounting, 239-41, 261

credit default swaps (CDSs), 46, 72, 74-6, 79-80, 106-7, 111-12, 120, 185, 259

credit events, 302

credit insurance, 44

credit risk transfer (CRT), 72, 206

CreditSights, 297

Credit spread risk, 112

Credit spreads, 107-09

Crédit Suisse, 237, 246, 259

Cuomo, Andrew M., 231-2, 331

D

data insufficiency, 165

Davies, Brandon, 195

da Vinci, Leonardo, 248

debt deflation, 104

default risk premium, 108-9

deleveraging, 256, 272, 279-80

Delphi method, 164-6, 170, 172, 188

Deripaska, Oleg, 263

derivative financial instruments, 29, 52, 98, 100-1, 106, 119, 278

Dimon, Jamie, 333

Dirac, Paul, 38, 288

discounted cash flow, 113-16

Donaldson, William, 211-12

Dow Jones Industrial Average, 35

Drexel Burnham Lambert, 240

due diligence, 230

E

econometrics, 103

Economist, The, 187, 294

Eichengreen, Barry, 307

Einstein, Albert, 9

electricity, 11

endogenous liquidity, 69

Enron, 244

entropy, 19-21, 254, 282, 284-6, 289

ethical values, 207

European Central Bank (ECB), 48, 77, 108, 171, 251, 314-15, 330

exogenous liquidity, 69

expected risks, 13

expert arbitration, 166

exposure at default, 294

F

fair value, 66, 100, 130, 134, 273

Fannie Mae, 235

fat tails, 186

Federal Deposit Insurance Corporation (FDIC), 123, 126, 143, 150, 241, 292, 303, 308

Federal Reserve, 48-9, 123, 241, 290, 292, 295-6, 303, 307, 314, 320, 325, 328

Feigenbaum, Mitchel, 198

Ferguson, Roger, 296

Fermi, Enrico, 13, 288

Feroli, Michael, 307

Feynman diagrams, 180, 182, 196, 214, 216-17, 219, 288

Feynman, Richard, 177-8, 181, 182, 205

Financial Accounting Standards Board (FASB), 96, 127, 298

financial leverage, 266-7

Financial Market Stabilisation Act, 312

Financial Market Stabilisation Agency (FMSA), 313

Financial Market Stabilisation Fund (SoFFin), 312

Financial Services Authority (FSA), 291

Financial Stability Board, 292

Financial Times, 65, 318

first law of thermodynamics, 255

Fortis, 83, 263

forward rate agreements (FRAs), 98

forwards, 99

Freddie Mac, 235

Friedman, Milton, 147

Fuld, Richard, 209, 235

funding liquidity, 69-71

futures, 99

G

Galbraith, J. K., 249

Geithner, Timothy, 37, 122-6, 303-4, 333

Gell-Mann, Murray, 10, 224

General Electric, 107, 251, 262

General Motors, 42, 148

GE Capital, 47, 91, 107, 251, 262

Gibbs, J.W., 284

Glass-Steagall Act, 46

gluons, 16

Goldman Sachs, 34, 60, 104, 125, 133-4, 187, 235, 258, 265, 287, 307, 330-1

Goodwin, Fred, 253, 255

Gramm, Philip, 46

gravity, 11, 12

Greenspan, Alan, 174, 304

gross domestic product (GDP), 41

G-20, 289

Grove, Andy, 58

Guoli, Tian, 311

H

Haines, Rob, 297

HBOS, 209

Hammurabi, 227

Hawking, Stephen W., 16, 255, 283

hedge funds, 52, 70, 291

Heisenberg, Werner, 10, 13, 38

high frequency/low impact (HF/LI), 36, 179, 196

Holmes, Oliver Wendell, 226

HSBC, 246, 294-5

Hugo, Victor, 67

HypoBank, 83

I

IKB Deutsche Industriebank, 146

imaginary time, 18-19

implied volatility, 30, 32, 62

incremental default risk charge (IRDC), 153

incremental risk charge (IRC), 139-40, 151, 153, 175, 189, 205

Industrial and Commercial Bank of China, 311

Institute of International Finance (IIF), 335

Intel, 58

interest rates swaps, 98

internal ratings based (IRB) method, 152

International Accounting Standards Board (IASB), 97, 127, 298

International Financial Reporting Standards (IFRS), 97, 127, 131

International Monetary Fund (IMF), 296, 304

International Securities Dealers Association (ISDA), 80

intrinsic value, 114, 116, 276

J

JP Morgan Chase, 80, 91, 125, 146, 232, 254, 280, 307, 315, 331

John Deere, 161

Johnson, Simon, 309

joint probabilities of default (JPDs), 76

Joule, James, 255

K

Kairos, 18, 203, 206

Kaiser, Henry J., 292

Kemp, John, 332

Keynes, John Maynard, 43, 279

King, Mervyn, 327-8

known unknowns, 54

Kohlberg, Kravis, Roberts (KKR), 145

Koontz, Harold, 184,

Krugman, Paul, 318, 323

L

Laplace, Pierre-Simon de, 287

Law, John, 245

laws of men, 226

laws of nature, 226

Lay, Ken, 240, 244

legacy assets, 122

Legacy Loans Program (LLP), 126

legacy securities, 122

legal risk, 27, 42, 142-3, 223, 226-7, 254, 292, 323

Lehman Brothers, 32, 83, 145, 192, 209, 234-5, 258, 291

Leibniz, Gottfried Wilhelm von, 19, 214

level of confidence, 140, 184

Levi, Steven, 285

Lewis, Ken, 230-2

linear vector space, 216

liquidity, 270-1

liquidity risk, 67-8

loan CDSs (LCDSs), 121

lognormal distribution, 197

Long Term Capital Management (LTCM), 59, 242, 281

loss given default (LGD), 294

low frequency/high impact (LF/HI), 36, 179, 196

M

Machiavelli, Niccolò, 212

Macquarie Bank, 316

Madoff, Bernard, 245, 247

magnetism, 11

Malthus, Thomas, 233

management intent, 130

management risk, 42

Mandelbrot, Benoit, 35

Manhattan Project, 184

Mao Tse Tung, 93

market illiquidity, 139

market liquidity, 69

market risk amendment, 172

marking to market, 125, 127, 131-2, 134-5, 274

marking to myth, 130, 274

material adverse conditions (MAC), 232

Maxwell, James Clark, 13

Mécanique Céleste, 287

Mellon Bank, 310

Meltzer, Alan, 113, 320-1

Merkel, Angela, 48-9

Merrill Lynch, 41, 145-6, 149, 161, 209, 244, 254, 258, 291, 331

Metcalfe, Bob, 157

Metcalfe's Law, 157

Milken Institute, 122

Milken, Michael, 240

Miller, Merton, 278

MIT, 48

model risk, 35

model validation, 165

Modigliani, Franco, 278

Monte Carlo method, 172-3, 204

monetisation of risk, 198

Moody's KMV model, 302

Morgan Stanley, 125, 258, 331

mortgage-backed securities, 73

Mudd, Daniel H., 235

Munger, Charlie, 93

N

Nasdaq, 261

negative entropy, 21

net present value (NPV), 114

Neue Züricher Zeitung, 236

Neumann, John von, 177

neutrons, 224

Newton, Isaac, 9, 12, 214

New York Chamber of Commerce, 134

New York Fed, 270, 281, 334

New York University, 305

Nikkei, 261

non-bank banks, 297

nonlinear models, 85

Nordbanken, 310

Northern Rock, 209

O

Obama, Barack, 65

objective uncertainty, 54

off balance sheet (OBS), 70, 75, 272-3

Office of the Comptroller of the Currency (OCC), 132, 292

O'Neil, Stan, 209

operating characteristics (OC) curve, 81, 87, 89, 184

operational leverage, 266

options, 98

organisational entropy, 255

Ospel, Marcel, 209, 236

overleveraging, 251, 253-6, 258-9, 266, 280, 289

over the counter (OTC), 100, 128, 206

P

Pacific Gas and Electric (PG&E), 243

paper economy, 50

Pareto diagrams, 91

Pareto's law, 305

Pareto, Vilfredo, 103, 177

partial reflection of light, 181

Paul, Ron, 328

Paulson, Hank, 106, 122, 126

Phelps, Edmund, 63

photons, 16, 181

physical economy, 63

Pillar 2 of Basel II, 299

Pillar 3 of Basel II, 335

Planck, Max, 10, 25, 38

political risk, 247-8

polygons, 218-19

Ponzi, Charles, 244

Ponzi games, 244, 246-7

Ponzi risk, 289, 292

President's Working Group on Financial Markets, 241

price finding auctions, 121

pricing theory, 103

Prince, Chuck, 209

Princeton University, 301

probability amplitudes, 39, 182, 183

probability of adverse events, 179

probability of default (PD), 294

Procter & Gamble, 230, 239

protons, 224

Public-Private Investment Program (PPIP), 122-4, 126, 301

Q

Q ratio, 117

quanta, 10

quantitative easing, 317

quantity theory of money, 103

quantum analysis, 40

quantum chromodynamics (QCD), 16, 27, 42, 47, 55, 67, 81, 141, 223, 274, 279

quantum cryptography, 185, 186

quantum electrodynamics (QED), 14, 26, 42, 47, 54, 67, 77, 81, 106, 112, 141, 176, 178, 184-6, 189-93, 195-6, 199, 203-8, 211, 223, 298, 326-8, 334, 336-7

quantum field theory, 217

quantum logic, 27, 37-8, 40, 42, 71, 130, 193

quantum mechanics, 9, 38-9, 287

quarks, 10, 224

R

Rabo Bank, 315

radioactivity, 13

Rand Corporation, 172

real assets, 28

real economy, 97

realised volatility, 31

Regions Financial, 105

regulatory risk, 248

reliability engineering, 199

Reshef, David, 48

Resolution Trust Corporation (RTC), 311

risk adjusted return on capital (RAROC), 81-2

risk appetite, 50-3, 268

risk aversion, 50-53, 60

risk capital, 105

risk management, 13

risk pricing, 21, 63, 81-3, 225, 239, 326, 335-6

risk-time diagrams, 202

rocket scientists, 33, 141

Roubini, Nouriel, 305

Royal Bank of Scotland (RBS), 83, 253, 255

Rubin, Robert, 133, 235

Rumsfeld, Donald, 55

S

Samuelson, Paul, 103

Sarbanes-Oxley Act, 147, 207, 208, 241, 321, 333

scenarios, 159-65

Schrödinger, Erwin, 38

Schwartzman, Steve, 58

Seattle First, 323

second law of thermodynamics, 19, 20, 254, 284

Securities and Exchange Commission (SEC), 96, 127, 211, 274, 292

Securum, 310, 312

Semmelweiss, Ignaz, 210-11

shadow banking system, 47

Shannon, Claude E., 20-1, 284

Shewhart, Walter, 39

Sindona, Michele, 245

Six Sigma, 91-2

Skilling, Jeffrey, 249, 244

SK Securities, 238

Société Générale, 146

Soros, George, 142

sovereign wealth funds, 147

space-time, 17, 19

space-time diagrams, 198, 200-3

special purpose vehicles (SPVs), 313-14

Spencer, Herbert, 285

Stanford, Allen, 247-8

Stanford International Bank (SIB), 247

Stanford University, 48

Statement of Financial Accounting Standards 133 (SFAS 133), 96

State Street, 105

statistical quality control (SQC), 39, 83, 85, 179

Steinmann, Heinrich, 14, 17

Stiglitz, Josef, 310

strategic inflection point, 28, 64-5

stress testing, 62, 194, 277, 301-2

stress test(s), 57, 134-5, 156-7, 160-1, 295, 299, 300-304

strong force, 11, 12

structured debt instruments, 148

structured finance, 81

structured financial instruments, 84, 105, 148

structured investment vehicles (SIVs), 70, 74, 272

subjective uncertainty, 55

subprimes, 148, 150

Sullivan, Martin, 131

Sun Tzu, 93-4

swaps, 99

Swiss Banking Commission, 259

Swiss National Bank, 236

synthetic securitisation, 72-3

Syron, Richard F., 235

systemic capital charge, 336

systemic risk, 75, 127, 292

systemic risk tolerances, 208-9

T

tail risks, 44

Talal, Al-Waleed bin, 263

Taylor, John, 48-9

Thain, John, 230-2

Thales, 98

thermostatics, 286

Tiger Management, 281

Tobin, James, 49

Tokyo Stock Exchange (TSE), 265

tolerance limits, 84

tort, 229

toxic assets, 122, 132, 311

toxic securities, 124

toxic waste, 132-3, 274, 311, 318

Tribus, Myron, 20

Troubled Assets Relief Program (TARP), 122-3, 231, 330

Type I error, 87, 89

Type II error, 88-9

U

UBS, 145-6, 209, 235-6, 246, 259

UCLA, 184

unexpected risks, 13

universal risk model, 129

University of California, Berkeley, 307

unknown unknowns, 54-6

US GAAP, 128, 131

V

value at risk (VaR), 85, 87-8, 105, 140, 149, 172-6, 190, 205, 211

vectors, 214-15, 219

Veit, Otto, 43

Vinair, David, 330

virtual assets, 28, 66

virtual balance sheet, 269

virtual economy, 63, 77, 98

volatility, 25-6, 28-31

volatility index (VIX), 30-1, 58-62

Volcker, Paul, 328

Vona, Carmine, 81

W

Walrus, Léon, 103, 177

Walton, Sam, 132-3

Warburg, Sigmund, 18, 203

Washington Mutual, 209, 322-3

weak force, 11, 12

Weibull distribution, 34

Wells Fargo, 135, 333

White swans, 55

Wilczek, Frank, 16, 134, 225

Wolf, Martin, 65

World Economic Forum, 58, 142

worst case scenarios, 144, 163

wrong pricing, 26

Ws, 14-15

Z

Zell, Sam, 122-3

Zs, 14-15